Counseling the
Chemically Dependent

Counseling the Chemically Dependent

Theory and Practice

Rickey L. George
University of Missouri-St. Louis

PRENTICE HALL
Englewood Cliffs, New Jersey 07632

Library of Congress Cataloging-in-Publication Data

George, Rickey L.
    Counseling the chemically dependent : theory and practice / Rickey
    L. George.
        p.   cm.
    Includes bibliographical references.
    ISBN 0-13-181330-7
    1. Narcotic addicts--Rehabilitation. 2. Codependents-
-Rehabilitation. 3. Group counseling. I. Title.
RC564.G375   1990
616.86'0651--dc20
                                                        89-48178
                                                        CIP

Cover design: Ben Santora
Manufacturing buyer: Robert Anderson

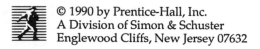 © 1990 by Prentice-Hall, Inc.
A Division of Simon & Schuster
Englewood Cliffs, New Jersey 07632

Printed in the United States of America

10 9 8 7 6 5 4 3 2 1

ISBN 0-13-181330-7

Prentice-Hall International (UK) Limited, London
Prentice-Hall of Australia Pty. Limited, Sydney
Prentice-Hall Canada Inc., Toronto
Prentice-Hall Hispanoamericana, S.A., Mexico
Prentice-Hall of India Private Limited, New Delhi
Prentice-Hall of Japan, Inc., Tokyo
Simon & Schuster Asia Pte. Ltd., Singapore
Editora Prentice-Hall do Brasil, Ltda., Rio de Janeiro

To my best friend and
"The Wind Beneath My Wings,"
my wife, Kathy

Contents

Preface

In the early 1980s I became more and more aware of the increasing frequency with which counselors were faced with clients whose problems were related directly to the abuse of alcohol and other drugs. Students engaged in internship or practica experiences, recent graduates, and experienced counselors with whom I spoke at professional meetings regularly expressed their frustration in not knowing how to help individuals who were experiencing depression and anxiety, marital and family problems, difficulties on the job, and other problems as a result of their drinking and using patterns. At that time, I too believed many of the myths about chemical dependency, particularly that only those whose drinking and using was more or less continuous and who could not "control" this pattern by staying clean and dry for even one week were addicted. The rest just had a problem. However, I still did not know how to help.

I applied for, and was granted, a development leave from the university to study the problem. My leave included working at an in-patient treatment program (the Care Unit Program at DePaul Hospital in St. Louis), where my eyes were opened and I received my first in-depth experience of a twelve-step program. Two people in particular—Mike Nolan and Jack Grady—were especially helpful in my learning about the disease of chemical dependency.

I returned to the university greatly enriched by what I had learned. I began incorporating that learning into my teaching and believe I was able to enlighten at least some of the students as to the destructive nature of alcohol and other drug abuse. Since many of the students worked with young people in schools and other agencies, I began working part-time as the unit psychologist for an adolescent chemical-dependency treatment program at Care Unit Hospital in St. Louis.

Again, the experience was eye-opening. Working with youths from a variety of socioeconomic levels, from rural, suburban, and urban areas, and from a broad range of family types, I learned how chemical abuse and dependency destroys hopes, as well as the future, for many teenagers. I was lucky to associate with such people as Delbert Boone, Kerry Zekert, Oliver James, Melinda Epps, and many other highly dedicated individuals who clearly cared about their patients and were willing to share with me what they knew about adolescent drug use.

The help of the staff at Prentice Hall, among them Wayne Spohr, Susan Willig, Shirley Chlopak, and, especially, Carol Wada, cannot go unnoticed. I owe each of them more than I am able to express adequately, as I do Eileen Lagermann, who used her magical fingers to give my words life.

Through it all I was encouraged and enlightened by my good friend James Hurley, who knows more about adolescents than anyone I have ever met.

This book would not be possible without the help of the counselors and others named above, individuals who have taught me by word and by example. For this I express my deepest gratitude. Much of what is in my work comes from them; however, they are certainly not responsible for any mistakes that I have made.

This book is an attempt to integrate theory and practice and to help bridge the gap between professional, trained counselors and those whose training has been part of their personal experience. Both groups have a valuable contribution to make in counseling the chemically dependent. I hope this book also contributes.

1

Chemical Dependency and Its Impact on Society

INTRODUCTION

During the late 1980s, newspaper and newsmagazine articles repeatedly highlighted the impact of the abuse of various mood-altering chemicals, including alcohol, cocaine, and heroin, on American society. The rapid increase in homicides in major American cities has been blamed on the struggle by various organized-crime factions to gain control of the local cocaine traffic. The recognition of health-related issues linked to the abuse of alcohol has gained increasing attention. The emphasis on the relationship between the use of alcohol and marijuana and accidents of all types, especially automobile accidents, has brought a new interest in controlling drunk driving. All of these media emphases, however, have had little impact on the widespread use, and abuse, of various drugs.

The use of mind-altering chemicals, especially alcohol, has been described in most areas of the world since the beginning of written human history. Kinney and Leaton (1983) report studies of various Stone Age cultures which reveal alcohol consumption as far back as Paleolithic times, where it was often used for medical, religious, and recreational purposes. Noah, in the biblical account of Judeo-Christian beginnings, is perhaps the first recorded inebriate. Egyptian records dating back to 300 B.C. give testimony of beer production.

In today's society, drinking alcohol—the single-most used and abused of all drugs—is a commonly accepted and expected aspect of a wide variety of social events. It is difficult to imagine a celebration of any kind without alcohol, at least for a majority of American families. Thus, alcohol is used as a natural part of living for many people. For most families, the first thing that is said after a visitor removes his or her coat is "May I get you a drink?"

At the very beginning of a book on chemical dependency, then, it is necessary to emphasize that using various drugs is not bad or evil in and of itself. Consuming alcohol, marijuana, or cocaine may be okay (but not legal) for an individual who can use that drug without having a negative effect on his or her life. At some time, most people have had a bit too much to drink and have experienced being drunk and sick and hung over. Those individuals sometimes vow never to drink again. However, the key to examining chemical dependency is not in looking at how many people use various drugs, nor is it in determining how many people have had at least one experience in which they abused drugs; it lies in looking at those persons whose continued use and abuse of drugs has caused problems in their lives.

Counselors in a variety of settings can no longer ignore the problem of chemical dependency. School counselors, vocational-rehabilitation counselors, mental-health counselors, and others increasingly report the importance of recognizing the existence of chemical abuse or dependency and request help in learning how to deal with such problems. This book provides an overview of chemical dependency and suggests some strategies for working with individuals whose use of various drugs has gotten out of control and who need therapeutic intervention.

DEFINITIONS

The once-popular image of the alcoholic or drug addict as a skid-row inhabitant is erroneous; less than 5 percent of all chemical dependents conform to that image. In addition, it is believed that at least half the individuals on skid row are, at worst, moderate drinkers, and many are nondrinkers. Thus, the images that most Americans have regarding the life style and physical appearance of the chemical dependent have little to do with reality. Chemical dependency is a problem for individuals throughout American society, upper class and lower class, highly educated and undereducated, women and men, older adults and adolescents. Chemical dependency is no discriminator of age, sex, geography, socioeconomic status, race, or ethnic culture, even though it may have an unequal impact on specific groups.

Part of the difficulty in dealing with the distorted images of chemical dependency that exist in American society results from a misunderstanding as to how chemical dependency should be defined. Chemical dependency involves the use of any mood-altering chemical which results in problems for individuals, whether that mood-altering chemical be heroin, cocaine, marijuana, or alcohol. Notice the word *alcohol*. From a strictly physiological point of view, alcohol is a drug! And, *a drug is a drug is a drug*. Although alcohol is legal and is therefore often seen as being less dangerous because it has the legal sanction of society, by far the greatest number of problems resulting from chemical dependency stem from the abuse of alcohol. Alcohol as a mood-altering chemical will be discussed later. However, in this book alcoholism and chemical dependency will generally refer to the same physiological and psychological process of addiction.

Alcohol, in many ways, was the first drug to be recognized as creating a major problem for society. Prohibition was one ineffective approach to dealing with the problems of alcohol. However, alcoholism was not considered a disease for many, many years. In fact, as recently as the late 1930s, it was still seen as a moral deviancy, the result of a defect in an individual's character. And it was not until the 1950s that the American Medical Association finally declared alcoholism to be an illness. In looking at definitions of alcoholism, the official AMA statement is a good place to begin. The AMA defines it as:

> An illness characterized by preoccupation with alcohol; by loss of control over its consumption, such as to usually lead to intoxication or drinking done by chronicity; by progression and by tendency to relapse. It is typically associated with physical disability and impaired emotion, occupational and/or social adjustments as a direct consequence of persistent and effective use. (Ohlms, 1988, 3)

Although accurate, this definition is clumsy and difficult to use in a practical sense. For the purposes of this book, then, a person is chemically dependent *who continues to use mood-altering chemicals, despite the problems that their usage causes.* This definition is consistent with the view that chemical dependency is a disorder that is chronic, progressive, and often fatal. Chemical dependency is chronic in that the individual who is a victim of the disorder is *always* subject to relapse, much as the individual with diabetes or heart disease. Chemical dependency is progressive in that the condition results in greater and greater physical and psychological problems unless steps are taken to deal with the disorder. Chemical dependency is incurable in that individuals who have the disorder will always have the disorder, much like the diabetic.

Chemical dependency almost always involves a loss of control. When a chemically dependent individual who has been abstinent, whether overnight or for a number of years, takes a single drink or dose he or she gives up the choice of taking just one drink (or dose) or falling into dangerous, uncontrollable overuse. The social user may choose to get bombed, and occasionally will make a mistake, but learns from that mistake and does not repeat the behavior—he or she *stops.* The chemical dependent makes excuses—"I was unlucky" or "I'll be more careful"—but repeats the behavior in spite of adverse consequences.

An example may help to clarify this issue. Assume for the moment that while you are reading this material you are having a few drinks, and once you have finished reading you have a couple more drinks. Then you get in your automobile and drive somewhere. On the way, a law-enforcement officer stops you and issues a citation for driving while under the influence. The social user is likely to see this situation as one of embarrassment and anger with oneself. He or she is likely to react by saying, "That was a dumb thing for me to do. I knew better. I should not drive after I have had more than a certain number of drinks. In the future, I will be more careful." The chemical dependent, on the other hand, is apt to make excuses or to place the blame on someone else. The thinking process might be, "The police must not have their quota of tickets for this month yet, so they're out to get anybody they can. Well, I'll show them. The next time, I'll drive down side streets where they won't catch me. Besides, they should be out catching real criminals, instead of worrying about a person who's had one or two drinks." The key issue is that the social drinker tends to learn from his or her bad experience, while the chemical dependent tends to avoid any learning by making excuses and by projecting the blame on others.

COSTS OF CHEMICAL DEPENDENCY

Chemical dependency is often a fatal disease. When all drug-related deaths are combined—whether they be drug-related suicides, homicides, automobile accidents, or other types of accidents—they are among the leading causes of death in the United States.

In the nation today, roughly 34.5 out of every 36 people who are chemically dependent are going to die from it, one way or another. Many of these individuals will have never been treated for chemical dependency, although they often have been treated for a variety of problems which resulted from their chemical dependency—hospitalized for treatment of stomach problems, liver problems, problems of the pancreas, problems with the nerves, various psychiatric problems, or problems resulting from physical injuries. Often, such persons never receive treatment for chemical dependency because they are unable or, more likely, unwilling to recognize that the real problem in their lives has to do with their use of mood-altering chemicals.

More specific kinds of statistics may reemphasize this point. Alcohol is a contributing factor in more than 10 percent of all deaths in the United States, according to a former United States Surgeon General, Julius B. Richmond (Fein 1984). Dr. William Mayer, while chief of the Alcohol, Drug Abuse, and Mental Health Administration, noted that "ten thousand young people are killed every year in highway accidents involving alcohol, the leading cause of death in the 16–24 age group." The Office of Alcohol Countermeasures estimates that each day 71 people are killed and 2,000 people are injured in alcohol-related automobile accidents. The National Institute on Alcohol Abuse and Alcoholism reports that up to 68 percent of the people who drowned, 50 percent of those who died in falling accidents, and 50 percent of those adults killed in fires had been drinking. The same report indicates that the rate of suicide among alcoholics is as much as 30 times greater than that of the general population. Fein (1984) goes on to provide a list of various causes of alcohol-related deaths, with numbers indicating the extent of the problem. (See table 1.1.)

Family-Life Costs

In addition to the death and illness costs of chemical dependency to society, there are an even greater number of family-life and other social costs. Families experiencing alcohol problems have a 40 percent divorce rate. There are 5.7 million cases a year of family violence linked to alcohol abuse, and, as will be seen in chapter 3, the overall effect on other members of the family of the chemical dependent is devastating. Spalding (1988) points out that children of alcoholics and other chemical dependents can also be identified as having a variety of health problems themselves. Among these are gastrointestinal disorders, stress-related disorders, allergies, and headaches. Often, such conditions do not manifest themselves until adulthood, even though there were minor difficulties with these problems during childhood. In addition, children often suffer physical, verbal, emotional, and sexual abuse. It has been clearly shown that drug use and family violence go together and that a child in a chemically

Table 1.1   The Number of Alchohol-Related Deaths (per year)

Alcohol Dependence Syndrome	4,350
Alcohol Abuse (nondependent)	889
Cirrhosis—Alcohol Mention	9,166
Alcoholic Cardiomyopathy	650
Alcohol Poisoning	385
Alcoholic Psychosis	454
Alcoholic Gastritis	84
Alcoholic Polyneuropathy	4
Cancer of Liver	3,146
(56 percent of 5,618)	
Cirrhosis of Liver and Chronic	
Liver Disease	9,551
(44.6 percent of 21,417)	
Respiratory Tuberculosis	405
(25 percent of 1,621)	
Acute Pancreatitis	1,008
(35.5 percent of 2,840)	
Homicides	21,121
(87 percent of 24,278)	
Suicides	21,495
(80 percent of 26,869)	
Motor Vehicle Accidents	27,317
(59 percent of 46,300)	
Fire	2,911
(50 percent of 5,822)	
Drownings	4,109
(68 percent of 6,043)	
Falls	6,647
(50 percent of 13,294)	
Other Accidents	13,693
(50 percent of 27,387)	

Source: From *Alchohol in America: The Price We Pay* by Rashi Fein. 1984. Newport Beach, CA: Care Institute.

dependent family has a much greater risk of severe physical abuse. In one Canadian study, more than 90 percent of the cases of child abuse and neglect involved alcohol. It is also officially estimated that drinking is involved in 38 percent of all child-abuse cases, but this number likely represents only the tip of a huge iceberg. Perhaps because alcohol weakens or removes the inhibitors that keep people from acting on violent and sexual impulses, alcoholism has also been a major contributor to the incidence of incest. Few people seem to realize how frequently daughters of male alcoholics are sexually assaulted, not only by their fathers, step-brothers, or brothers, but also by their half-brothers, brothers-in-law, uncles, cousins, adoptive fathers, and grandfathers (Sexias & Youcha 1985). Even more hidden is the incidence of incest between male children and adults, which, again, has an extremely high relationship to the incidence of drug abuse.

Legal Costs

Drug use and abuse is also reflected in the crime statistics. As was noted earlier, drinking is implicated in a large percentage of all homicides, as well as in family violence and assault. Kinney and Leaton (1983) state that in the mid 1970s one-half of all North American police officers killed while on duty were killed in the course of investigating family disputes. Since alcohol is virtually a universal element in family squabbles that escalate to the point that they must be reported to the police, alcohol becomes a major part of the lack of judgment and control that results in such shootings. Approximately one-half of all arrests are related to drug misuse. These may be for public intoxication or for more serious crimes committed while the individual is either under the influence of a mood-altering chemical or is in the process of committing a crime as a means of getting money to purchase drugs. At the same time, there has been an increase in arrests for drunken driving. Kinney and Leaton go on to estimate that the total national bill for alcohol-related crimes during the 1970s was approximately $2.1 billion per year.

Economic and Occupational Costs

A 1977 report for the National Institute on Alcohol Abuse and Alcoholism (Berry, Boland, Smart, & Kanak 1977) estimated that alcoholism and alcohol misuse cost the United States approximately $43 billion in 1975. These costs were calculated (in billions of dollars) in six categories: lost production, 19.64; health and medical care, 12.74; motor-vehicle accidents, 5.14; violent crime, 2.86; social responses, 1.94; and fire, 0.43. These costs (in 1975 dollars) may be underestimated simply because of the difficulty of determining the effects of drug use on the legal, health, and economic systems. In addition, because the abuse of various drugs often makes individuals less functional, society loses part of the economic value that results from normal production. The consequences of drug abuse also include increased expenditures for health care, social services, and police protection, among other items. These extra costs are ultimately borne by the public.

By 1977 (Fein 1984) such costs had risen to $49.374 billion, an increase of more than 14 percent. Of this sum, nearly $36.8 billion consisted of indirect costs—that is, costs associated with earnings lost because of premature mortality, illness, reduced productivity, lost work time, and lost employment.

It is evident that the indirect costs of alcohol and other drug abuse far exceed the direct costs. As a result, the costs that are often reported as resulting from the abuse of mood-altering chemicals are far less than the actual costs involved.

At the same time, the total tax revenue on drugs is limited to that raised by federal and state authorities on the sale of alcohol; it amounts to only a little more than 10 percent of the economic costs of the abuse of drugs in society. All of these costs result from the deterioration which occurs in the life of the chemical dependent, even though the job area seems to be the last part of the person's life which will show the signs of illness. For many people, being able to continue functioning on the job allows them to deny that they have a problem and permits them to make excuses about their drinking or using. However, the economic costs escalate as the individual's illness progresses, resulting in increased absences, tardiness, and inefficiency on the job.

MYTHS ABOUT CHEMICAL DEPENDENCY

Part of the problem of chemical dependency is the modern mythology related to the use of various drugs, particularly alcohol. What we think we know (e.g., "I drive better after a few drinks") can hurt us. The individual who has accepted the myth that it's okay to wash down eight or ten beers every night because "it's only beer" is on the path toward serious problems. The existence of misconceptions about drinking and using have contributed to the wide-spread problems in our society resulting from that drinking and using. The more we know about the effects of alcohol and other drugs, the more likely we are to be able to use those drugs in a safe manner, and to decide whether, where, when, why, how much, and with whom to drink or use. The following myths are representative of those which create problems for our society.

Most skid-row bums are alcoholic. As was previously pointed out, studies have shown that less than half the individuals on skid row have drinking problems.

Most alcoholics are skid-row bums. Only 3 percent to 5 percent of alcoholics live on skid row; most are married, employed, normal people. In fact, anyone can be an alcoholic.

Very few women become alcoholic. Three decades ago it was believed that there were five or six alcoholic men to every alcoholic woman. As we will see in chapter 8, the ratio of men to women who are alcoholic has decreased rapidly and has reached the point where many professionals believe that it is roughly equal.

It's only beer. The idea that beer is somehow different from "hard" liquor has created many alcoholism problems. One 12-ounce can of beer is about equal to one average highball, which is about equal to a glass of wine. The effect may be a little slower, but an individual can get just as drunk on beer or wine as on "hard" liquor.

Alcohol is a stimulant. Alcohol actually depresses the central nervous system. It often results in what appears to be a stimulating effect because it frees the drinker of inhibitions that may have prevented him or her from engaging in certain kinds of behaviors in the past.

Getting drunk is funny. Movies and television have consistently portrayed drunkenness as part of comedy. W. C. Fields in his movies, Dudley Moore in *Arthur,* and a host of other characters have made the American public laugh at their drunken behavior. In reality, however, drunkenness is no funnier than any other illness or incapacity.

You are not an alcoholic unless you drink a pint a day. Being alcoholic has little to do with how much or how often one drinks. Being an alcoholic means that the individual continues to drink, in spite of that drinking bringing about problems in his or her life.

The really serious problem in our society is drug abuse. This myth is really not a myth—it is true that the serious problem in our society is drug abuse. However, the number-one drug problem is alcohol abuse. While Spitz and Rosecan (1987) estimate that twenty to twenty-four million Americans have experimented with cocaine and that four to five million are regular users, these numbers pale in comparison with the number of individuals who have used or are regular users of alcohol. While less than half a million Americans are addicted to heroin, eighteen to twenty million Americans are addicted to alcohol.

Other myths include:

1. A good host never lets a guest's glass get empty.
2. Black coffee will sober you up.
3. Today's kids smoke pot, instead of drinking.
4. It's impolite to tell a friend he or she is drinking too much.
5. Alcoholism is just a state of mind.
6. A couple of drinks can help you unwind and relax.
7. Mixing your drinks causes hangovers.
8. People who drink too much only hurt themselves.
9. Your kids will learn what you tell them about drinking.

TYPES OF MOOD-ALTERING CHEMICALS FREQUENTLY MISUSED

Alcohol

As we have just seen, alcohol is still by far the most highly abused drug in American society. Although legal as long as an individual has reached the drinking age of the state in which he or she lives, alcohol continues to affect the lives of up to twenty million Americans directly, and of as many as eighty million Americans indirectly because of their relationship to an alcoholic.

While alcohol enters the body through the mouth, it rapidly affects every organ in the body from the moment the first drink is taken. Alcohol enters the bloodstream through the stomach and upper intestine, circulating first to the central nervous system and the spinal cord, where it functions as a sedative. Alcohol then acts on the brain, from the outer to the inner layers. Once the outer layer is affected, the drinker feels the "high" of intoxication. However, alcohol can destroy brain cells; over time, permanent brain damage—often called organic brain syndrome—can result.

Even a relatively small amount of alcohol can have an effect on an individual, especially when drunk on an empty stomach. Having food in the stomach slows down the processing of the alcohol, but it does not diminish the effects of the alcohol on the individual. One major concern for social drinkers (i.e., persons who drink on occasion but who have no problems as a consequence) is that of learning how much alcohol they can drink in a particular period without its having more than a minimal influence on them.

Alcohol can have short-term and long-term effects on the heart. By weakening the pumping of the heart muscle, it reduces the blood flow. As a result, alcohol is the most common cause of hypertension in the United States.

Alcohol also has major effects on the gastrointestinal system, including the pancreas, the esophagus, and the stomach. The pancreas, a small organ located at the top of the abdomen, produces insulin and enzymes which aid in digestion. Pancreatitis, the inflammation of the pancreas, often results from the abuse of alcohol, which is poisonous to the pancreas. Approximately 40 percent of all pancreatitis patients are alcoholics, with symptoms of severe abdominal pain, nausea, and vomiting.

The esophagus is the tube through which food passes from the mouth to the stomach. Cirrhosis of the liver (which will be discussed later) leads to increased blood pressure in the veins of the esophagus, which can cause the veins to become varicose. On occasion, the veins may even rupture, with resulting death from internal hemorrhaging. In addition, alcoholics have a greater chance of developing cancer of the esophagus, with a very low recovery rate.

Alcohol is the most common cause of gastritis, an inflammation of the stomach. Gastritis causes nausea, vomiting, headaches, and stomach pain, and can cause hemorrhaging which may result in death. The introduction of alcohol into the stomach results in the secretion of more than normal amounts of acid. This increased acidity often causes ulcers and works to prevent existing ulcers from healing. These ulcers, which are often found in the duodenum, the part of the small intestine which receives food from the stomach, can cause perforations, hemorrhaging, and obstruction of food passage, which can be fatal.

Alcohol also has a major effect on the liver. By affecting the cells of the liver and decreasing its ability to metabolize fat, alcohol use results in fat being accumulated in the liver and cutting off blood to other liver cells. This destruction of liver cells often progresses to cirrhosis unless drinking is discontinued. Cirrhosis, the scarring of the liver, can cause it to either shrink or enlarge, depending on the state of the disease. Symptoms include nausea, vomiting, weakness, weight loss, abdominal pains, swelling of the abdomen, and internal bleeding. Cirrhosis can also lead to liver cancer and is the seventh leading cause of death in America.

In addition, alcoholic hepatitis—the inflammation of the liver—can result from alcohol abuse. With symptoms of fever, jaundice, and swelling of the feet and abdomen, alcoholic hepatitis often develops into cirrhosis.

Most alcoholic beverages also contain various amounts of a cancer-causing contaminant called urethane. Many of these beverages have levels of urethane that are so high as to have been declared illegal in other countries. Studies on rats and mice show that the regular consumption of even moderate amounts of urethane-contaminated liquor (the equivalent of two shots of bourbon a day for a human being) results in a significant increase in cancer risk.

Other potential effects of alcohol abuse include impotency. While alcohol is sometimes viewed as an aphrodisiac, it actually depresses genital reflexes; in some cases, this depressant effect may lead to impotency. In addition, impotency may also be caused by alcohol-related neuritis, liver damage, and malnutrition.

Marijuana

For a long time, the use of marijuana was considered relatively safe. However, in recent years an increasing awareness has developed of its potential dangers. Part of the change has been that, at one time, most marijuana had a low THC (the psychoactive, or mind-altering, chemical) content. However, as opposed to a former content of approximately 1 percent, marijuana now contains 6 percent to 8 percent THC, bringing it closer to the level of hashish (a concentrated form of marijuana with 3 percent to 14 percent THC).

Although marijuana is not always classified as a physically addictive drug, recent studies show that heavy, long-term use may cause mild physical dependencies in some users as they increase their dose to satisfy higher tolerance levels. More important, however, has been psychological addiction from smoking marijuana. In some cases, this has led some users to suffer psychological withdrawal; in others, it has resulted in the use of marijuana to the extent of creating multiple problems in persons' lives.

There is no question that heavy use of marijuana has serious physiological effects. Certainly the increased tar content of a marijuana joint (as compared to an ordinary cigarette) means that marijuana has a much greater potential for doing damage to the body. Thus, individuals who are smoking as few as three joints a day—which would not be an unusual amount for many people—are doing extreme damage to their lungs, damage equivalent to that done by the smoking of three packs of cigarettes a day. This often results in an irritation of the lining of the trachea and the bronchi called bronchitis. In addition, the concentrations of tar and nicotine produced by smoking mari-juana create a definitely increased cancer risk.

Moreover, marijuana's effect on the endocrine, or hormonal, system poses a great risk to the normal physical and emotional development of young people. Research shows that heavy marijuana use can reduce sperm count and sperm mobility in males. Heavy marijuana use has also been shown to cause sexual dysfunction and impotence. While the evidence is less strong with regard to the effects on the hormonal system of females, many scientists are convinced that smoking marijuana interferes with normal ovulation and the entire menstrual cycle. Research indicates a much higher incidence of miscar-riages when women have been smoking marijuana during pregnancy.

In addition, marijuana has an adverse effect on the heart, with studies showing that adults with impaired heart function who exercise after smoking marijuana are much more likely to experience severe chest pain. Thus, the effect of marijuana smoking is similar to the effect of cigarette smoking on the heart, but at a greater intensity.

Likewise, research indicates that marijuana has an effect on brain func-tions. For one thing, marijuana somehow distorts the individual's sense of time. After someone has smoked a joint, time seems to slow down and the individual's overall perception of time is distorted. Furthermore, the person's perceptions in general, such as senses of speed and of distance, are also distorted. People may not only fail to see what is there, they may also see or hear what is not there. Regular marijuana use also seems to decrease the individual's ability to abstract and synthesize or to see appropriate relation-ships when writing. Studies with monkeys have indicated that heavy mari-juana use (one joint a day) produced permanent changes in deep brain areas that affect emotion and behavior. Thus for heavy, long-term users, some neurological impairment is likely to occur and may be irreversible, especially in terms of complex intellectual tasks involving memory and analysis.

Tranquilizers

The so-called minor tranquilizers, which are used in the treatment of anxiety and tension, have become a major source of abuse in American society. ("Major" tranquilizers are used in the treatment of mental illness.) The minor tranquilizers include such well-known trade names as Valium, Librium, Miltown, and Equinel. These tranquilizers are mainly prescribed for treatment of tension, insomnia, behavioral excitement, and anxiety. Some are used in the treatment of convulsive disorders, lower-back pain, withdrawal symptoms of barbiturate- or alcohol-type dependents, and the anxiety and panic that sometimes results from the use of hallucinogenic drugs. While usually taken orally as capsules, tablets, or liquids, tranquil-izers can also be injected for both medical and nonmedical purposes. With the normal therapeutic dose, an individual usually feels a lessening of anxiety, tension, and agitation, and may lose some of his or her inhibitions. (These are like those effects associated with social drinking.) However, as the dosage increases, the individual usually feels more sedated and may experience some depression of nervous and muscular activity, as well as mental confusion and physical unsteadiness. High doses may produce drowsiness, a loss of muscle coordination, disorientation, low blood pressure, personality alterations, and symptoms resembling drunkenness. Death rarely results from the use of tranquilizers alone, but the interaction between tranquilizers and alcohol has been very dangerous to a number of people, particularly because of the synergistic effects. Physical dependence and withdrawal can occur with tranquilizers, but only when therapeutic dosage levels have escalated. Withdrawing from a large habit may involve anxiety states, apprehension, insomnia, fever, loss of appetite, vomiting, and other symptoms.

Recent statistics have shown that the prescribing of tranquilizers is on a downward trend, however, and this trend is expected to continue as more physicians become aware of the danger of tranquilizer addiction.

Cocaine

Cocaine, which stimulates the central nervous system, has become the drug of the late 1980s. Extremely addictive, it can be inhaled through the nose, smoked, or injected directly into the bloodstream. Cocaine is a white crystalline powder, known on the street as "coke," "snow," and "crack," among other names.

The cocaine user ordinarily experiences 15 minutes to 30 minutes of euphoria, tends to talk a lot, and feels energetic and self-confident. This euphoric rush, very similar to those produced by various amphetamines, is seen as a very intense and pleasurable experience. However, the effects are very short-lasting and are usually followed by some degree of psychological depression, nervousness, and irritability. As a result, the regular user often experiences such severe depression and anxiety that he or she frequently repeats the dose. Thus, heavy users will continue to sniff, smoke, or inject cocaine every 20 minutes or so for several hours to avoid the onset of depression. This is particularly true for those who inject or "free base" and for those who smoke "crack." In addition, some users stretch out the euphoria by combining cocaine with a longer-lasting drug such as heroin, a mixture known as "speedballs." A current approach to mellowing the aftereffects of cocaine usage is to mix cocaine and marijuana.

The deaths of several well-known entertainers and athletes have caused many Americans to recognize that the use of cocaine does have some physiological hazards. Large doses may cause shallow breathing, fever, restlessness, anxiety, and confusion. Small doses of cocaine bring about a slowing of the heart rate, but higher doses result in its acceleration. Furthermore, higher doses also affect the motor systems in the brain and spinal cord, resulting in tremors and convulsive movements. Long-term, chronic sniffing of large amounts can destroy tissue in the nose and lead to cancer. Nausea, vomiting, and abdominal pains can occur. Death from cocaine overdose is usually due to convulsions, respiratory arrest, or an overreaction to the cocaine in which the body tends to exceed its own metabolic limits. This often occurs because the user makes an error in determining the effects of the cocaine resulting from a miscalculation of how pure the cocaine is. Since cocaine dealers attempt to increase their profits by multiplying the quantity of the drug by adding a variety of adulterants, the user may not be clear as to the purity of the cocaine. Occasionally, when pure cocaine is used in the same quantity as the adulterated product (without the user being aware that the cocaine is pure), severe ill effects result, often quickly leading to death. Dependence on cocaine has been characterized as an "irresistible compulsion to use the drug at increasing doses and frequency, even in the face of serious physical and/or psychological side effects and the extreme disruption of the user's personal relationships and system of values" (Gold 1984, 15). When a cocaine-addicted person attempts to stop using cocaine, withdrawal occurs, involving profound depression, irritability, sleepiness, loss of energy, and an intense craving for cocaine. The use of cocaine has other dangers. Individuals who are considered seizure-prone are particularly at risk when using cocaine, since cocaine-induced seizures can and have led to death. In addition, cocaine has a serious effect on the heart, since one of its actions is to narrow the blood vessels, affecting both the heart and the circulatory system. As a result, the use of cocaine can increase the heart rate, cause heart palpitations, angina, arrhythmia, and heart attacks. Using cocaine while breast feeding can have a serious effect on the infant. Most important, cocaine affects the individual by becoming an all-consuming drug for which he or she becomes willing to sacrifice everything.

Other Stimulants

For many years, amphetamines have been used as central-nervous-system stimulants for a variety of purposes. Students cramming for exams, long-distance truck drivers, night-shift workers, and individuals seeking general stimulation have, collectively, taken an enormous number of amphetamines to relieve sleepiness and fatigue. In addition, physicians have prescribed amphetamines for such conditions as obesity, depression, some kinds of hyperactive behavior in children, and sleep disorders.

However, in the mid 1960s, the increased number of individuals who began injecting amphetamines directly into the bloodstream created a group of abusers called "speed freaks." As a result, physicians have sharply restricted their use of amphetamines to a limited number of conditions.

Amphetamines are available in a variety of forms, the most common being tablets or capsules. "Speed," or methamphetamine, usually appears as a powder or crystal and is made illicitly. Other common slang terms for the various amphetamines and amphetamine-like drugs include "crystal," "bennies," "uppers," and "pep pills."

At typical therapeutic doses, amphetamines stimulate the central nervous system, increase blood pressure, widen the pupils of the eyes, increase the respiration rate, depress the appetite, relieve sleepiness, and decrease fatigue and boredom. However, in some individuals, even a moderate dose can have adverse effects, among them blurred vision, heart tremors and palpitations, anxiety, confusion, or agitation. At times, the adverse effects can even lead to amphetamine psychosis, a mental disturbance similar to paranoid schizophrenia. With higher doses, such effects are likely to become even more severe.

Although there have been few reports of individuals dying as a direct result of their use of amphetamines, some individuals have died as a result of burst blood vessels in the brain, heart failure, or high fever.

Since amphetamines have a long "half-life," meaning that they tend to stay in the blood system for a long time, the effects of their use often stay with the individual for an extended period also. Thus, people who have not had any amphetamines for a number of days may continue to be agitated, to show increased motor activity, and to exhibit anxiety and confusion. Abruptly stopping amphetamines after chronic heavy use often leads to such symptoms as fatigue, prolonged sleep, voracious appetite, stomach cramps, and severe emotional depression.

Longtime users of amphetamines often suffer from a broad range of illnesses. The chronic user is likely to experience dehydration, weight loss, and vitamin deficiency, reduced resistance to disease may lead to sores and nonhealing ulcers and to chronic chest infections. Such individuals also have higher than normal rates of liver and cardiovascular disease, hypertensive disorders, and psychiatric problems. While the use of amphetamines has fallen with the increased use of cocaine, it is still a major drug problem in the United States.

Sedative-Hypnotic Drugs

The sedative-hypnotic drugs, which are capable of inducing varying degrees of depression, include a disparate number of chemicals. Alcohol, which has already been discussed, is the leading sedative abused in the United States. However, there are other sedative-hypnotic compounds, called barbiturates, which are also widely abused. They comprise a group of drugs that are capable of producing all degrees of behavioral depression, ranging from mild sedation through anesthesia to coma and death. The extent of the effect depends on a variety of factors, including the particular drug, the dose, the route of administration, and the rates of absorption, distribution, metabolism, and excretion. In low doses, the short- or intermediate-acting compounds, such as amobarbital, pentobarbital, secobarbital, and butabarbital, are used in the treatment of anxiety and tension. In higher doses, they are used to induce sleep. Phenobarbital, an ultra-short-acting barbiturate, has been important in the treatment of acute convulsions and in the treatment of asthma, premenstrual tension, motion sickness, nausea and vomiting, peptic ulcers, and high blood pressure and other cardiovascular diseases.

Most barbiturates are white powders, odorless, but with a slightly bitter taste. They are ordinarily packed in capsules and tablets of varying colors, but are also available as liquids. In slang terms, they are often referred to as "blues," "yellow jacks," "reds," and "downers." Barbiturates are usually taken orally and are readily absorbed by the stomach and small intestine. Absorption into the bloodstream can be very rapid, especially on an empty stomach, with the effects occurring within 20 minutes. Barbiturates enter the bloodstream and depress central nervous activity by slowing down many bodily functions, such as breathing and coordination.

The short-term effects of barbiturates are similar to those of alcohol. At low doses, the use of barbiturates tends to result in a feeling of relaxation, a sense of well-being, and drowsiness; it also tends to loosen the individual's inhibitions, making him or her seem more sociable, jovial, and impulsive. As the dose increases, the drug reduces the individual's ability to react quickly and to perform skilled, precise tasks. Often there is a sense of sedation, and the user may alternate between feelings of euphoria on the one hand and hostility and aggressiveness on the other. At still higher doses, the symptoms may be similar to those of drunkenness, with the individual appearing confused and having difficulty communicating. The person may eventually fall into a stupor or sleep.

When barbiturates are used repeatedly over a long period, tolerance of the euphoric effects develops quickly, so that larger and larger amounts of the drug must be taken to achieve the same effect. However, as this tolerance develops, the risk to the user increases—the amount needed to get high may eventually become only a couple of pills away from an overdose. Physical dependence occurs when the barbiturate user is unable to stop taking the drug without suffering withdrawal symptoms, including physical weakness, dizziness, anxiety, hyperactivity, sleeplessness, nausea, and vomiting. A long-term user who has developed a severe addiction faces the possibility of having a grand mal seizure, which can occur up to two weeks after the barbiturates are withdrawn and can be fatal. Thus, barbiturate addicts are almost always withdrawn under a physician's supervision.

Barbiturates are also used frequently in conjunction with stimulants. Amphetamine abusers will often take barbiturates to "come down" after prolonged amphetamine use. Moreover, the combination of the upper and the downer can increase each drug's effects. Individuals who drink alcohol in combination with barbiturates run the risk of accidental overdose. In part, this results from what is called a synergistic effect, in which the combination of drugs has a greater than expected impact on the central nervous system. Thus, instead of adding two drinks to two pills and attaining the effects of four usages, the effects multiply and may be equivalent to six usages.

Narcotics

Narcotics generally refer to opium and other drugs derived from the Oriental poppy, such as morphine, codeine, and heroin. In addition, certain synthetic chemicals that have a morphine-like action are often abused. Narcotics, in general, are used for such medicinal purposes as relief from pain, especially during the later stages of terminal illness.

The most abused of the narcotics is heroin, which is often referred to as "junk," "smack," "horse," or "harry." Although it may be smoked or sniffed when in powdered form, the more common method of injection produces the most rapid and intense effect. Upon absorption, heroin stimulates the higher centers of the brain, then depresses the activity of the central nervous system. A normal dose may exert its action from 2 to 6 hours or more. At first, the user feels a rush, followed by a feeling of contentment and detachment from the world around. With moderately high doses, the body feels warm, the arms and legs feel heavy, and the mouth feels dry. The user nods off and on, alternately drowsing and waking. Often, a dreamlike state occurs, one that is somewhat ecstatic in mood.

The immediate physiological response usually includes a reduction in heart activity, reduced breathing, a warming of the skin, nausea, and sometimes vomiting. As dosages increase, the effects become more acute, with insensibility and unconsciousness often occurring. With very high doses, the user may experience coma, shock, or death. Many of the physiological problems, however, have to do with the impurity of the drug itself, the use of unsterilized shared needles, and the unhygienic living conditions which the heroin addict experiences frequently. Abusers commonly report hepatitis, tetanus, heart and lung abnormalities, scarred veins, and skin infections. In addition, of course, heroin addicts have a high risk of contracting AIDS.

With low doses and intermittent use, withdrawal symptoms may be relatively slight, usually resembling the flu—tears, runny nose, body discomfort. Withdrawal after heavy, chronic use results in severe and painful effects, similar to those associated with alcohol and barbiturate withdrawal. Symptoms usually appear from 6 to 12 hours after the drug was last taken, peak at 26 to 72 hours, and usually take up to a week to cease, although complete recuperation may take 6 months or longer.

Hallucinogens

Although the use of these drugs has decreased over the past decade, the danger of using any of them is still serious. Among the most popular of the hallucinogens are PCP (often called Angel Dust, THC, dust, or super weed) and LSD (known as acid). PCP, a white, crystalline powder, soluble in water, is most commonly smoked, though it occasionally may be injected. Another popular method is to dip cigarettes or joints into liquified PCP and to smoke the resulting combination drug. With a low or moderate dose, PCP produces a state of euphoria lasting 3 to 5 hours when smoked, or 5 to 8 hours when eaten. The effects on the user vary greatly, depending largely on his or her personality and the surrounding circumstances. The expectation of how PCP will affect the individual is the most important feature in determining the sensations that the user reports. When persons believe that they are getting PCP, the most common reactions from low or moderate doses are auditory and visual distortions, time disturbance, and a deadening of the extremities. This loss of feeling often results in cuts, bruises, and torn muscles and ligaments. Drownings (in bathtubs or swimming places) are also reported, which happen when users are so anesthetized that they forget to breathe.

Higher and more consistent doses of PCP have led to incidents of violence. These, however, are rare in proportion to the millions who use the drug. The more common adverse reactions concern the user, rather than those around him or her. These include feelings of paranoia, severe agitation, an intense withdrawn feeling, and bizarre delusions. With prolonged regular use, the effects can linger on after the intoxication itself has worn off, necessitating therapy or rehabilitation. PCP causes increases in the heart rate and blood pressure, sweating, salivation, and flushing of the skin. It also interferes with the action of hormones which relate to normal growth and development in young people. Moreover, PCP has been related to decreased learning capacity, difficulty in concentration, poor grades, and poor social adjustment.

LSD, odorless, colorless, and tasteless, is an extremely potent drug: One ounce contains enough doses for about three hundred thousand adults. While most users take the drug orally, some inject it intravenously. Tolerance develops rapidly. Repeated daily doses become completely ineffective in three to four days. Recovery, however, is equally rapid, so weekly use of the same dose of LSD is possible. LSD use results in changes in external and internal sensory inputs and in the way these inputs are integrated. As a result, LSD users frequently cite the phrase "taking a trip" to describe their experience. In the 1960s, using the drug was viewed as a process of self-discovery, of self-confrontation, of deep self-encounter, leading to self-acceptance, a heightened capacity to love, and spiritual harmony (Wallace 1969).

The effects of LSD can be divided into three general categories. Such somatic symptoms as dizziness, weakness, tremors, nausea, and blurred vision are not emphasized much by the user. Perceptual symptoms, among them altered shapes and colors, visual hallucinations, a mixing of senses (synesthesia), and a distorted sense of time, are those experiences which users seem to seek through LSD. Finally, affective and cognitive symptoms, including mood changes and difficulties in thinking, also result.

An LSD "trip" is difficult to describe, in part because every individual who uses the drug appears to have a different experience. Moreover, most users report that each "trip" is unique. Thus, one of the attractive aspects of LSD use may be its unpredictability. With each new experience come sensations that have not been fully experienced before; they may be seen as magnificent or horrendous, depending on a variety of factors. The feeling of depersonalization, for example, may be viewed as revealing, or simply cause anxiety.

A major problem in the use of LSD is that drugs obtained on the street frequently are not what they are claimed to be—in purity, chemical composition, or quantity. As a result, a variety of adverse reactions may occur, with panic reaction and overt psychosis being the most likely. The panic reaction, an extreme anxiety attack, usually results from a person's response to some particular aspect of the experience. When an overt psychosis develops, the individual ordinarily needs to be hospitalized for prolonged treatment.

Perhaps the most frightening aspect of LSD use is the flashback. More than any other reaction, the recurrence of symptoms weeks or months after an individual has taken LSD suggests the possibility of brain damage and permanent biochemical changes. Flashbacks consist of the repetition of certain aspects of the drug experience after a period of normality and in the absence of any drug use. The frequency and duration of these flashbacks are quite variable and appear to be unpredictable. They are most likely to happen, however, just before going to sleep, while driving, and during periods of psychological stress. They seem to occur primarily in immature individuals and diminish in frequency and intensity when the individual stops using LSD.

Solvents and Inhalants

In the 1960s, there was an epidemic of glue sniffing. While the incidence of the abuse of various solvents and inhalants has decreased, there is still a small, but consistent, use of various solvents, aerosols, and gases across the nation. Inhaling such volatile substances as plastic-model glue, nail-polish remover, aerosol sprays, and gasoline fumes has resulted in problems for a number of individuals.

Many of these solvents and gases have some euphoric and intoxicating properties. The user often places the substance on a rag and then inhales the fumes for the most rapid and effective high. The resultant feeling of well-being, reduction of inhibitions, and elevated mood make the experience a pleasurable one for the individual. Higher doses often produce laughing and giddiness, feelings of floating, and delusions. The effects may last anywhere from 5 minutes to an hour, depending on the substance and the dose.

Acute use of solvents often brings on confusion, slurred speech, a feeling of numbness, headache, and muscular incoordination. Frequently, there is nausea and vomiting. If the dose is high enough, the general sedative anesthetic effects take over, and drowsiness and depression may result. Judgment is often impaired; there is also confusion, irritation, and tension. While a few deaths have been attributed to solvent abuse, these have usually occurred when the user fainted from inhalation and suffocated. A more important adverse effect has to do with the permanent, irreversible damage that can be done to various parts of the body, particularly the brain. However, temporary abnormalities have been found in respect to liver and kidney function, bone-marrow activity, gastritis, hepatitis, jaundice, blood content, and peptic ulcers.

SUMMARY

Problems resulting from chemical abuse and dependency affect all facets of American society: the family, personal health, accidents, the job, crime, the school, and so on. Alcohol—the single-most used and abused of all drugs—is a commonly accepted and expected aspect of many social events. Counselors in a variety of settings can expect the use and impact of alcohol and other drugs to be a major factor in the lives of a large number of the clients with whom they work.

Addiction or dependency does not depend on how frequently or how much a person drinks or uses. Rather, a person is seen as chemically dependent if he or she continues to use mood-altering chemicals in spite of the fact that this usage causes problems in the individual's life. As such, chemical dependency is a disorder that is chronic, progressive, and often fatal.

The costs of chemical abuse and dependence in the United States are staggering. Thousands are killed each year in drug-related accidents, including automobile accidents, drownings, fires, and falling. Suicides and homicides have been shown to be greatly influenced by drug use. Deaths and serious illnesses from the effects of various drugs on the body, particularly the heart, the liver, the pancreas, and the stomach, are widespread. Family violence, as well as the enormous effect of drug abuse on the functioning of family members, are now widely recognized as major problems in our society.

Myths about chemical dependency and its victims are widespread and need to be corrected. These myths often involve the effects of various drugs, and a need exists for counselors to have some understanding of the effects of alcohol, marijuana, tranquilizers, cocaine and other stimulants, sedatives, narcotics, hallucinogens, and solvents and inhalants on physical, mental, and emotional functioning.

2

Etiology of Chemical Dependency

INTRODUCTION

Part of the difficulty in treating chemical dependency results from the lack of a comprehensive model that explains chemical dependency in terms of its causes. Related to this has been a problem with societal attitudes toward the whole area of chemical dependency. From a historical standpoint, society has typically seen the alcoholic or the drug addict as someone to ostracize and to get out of the community. Jails all over the country have had their "drunk tanks," which were used to get the chemically dependent person off the streets. From a medical standpoint, chemical dependency was seen either as a moral problem in and of itself or as a symptom of another underlying problem. Thus, chemical dependency could not be treated directly, but was seen as a symptom of another disease which could be treated—depression, anxiety disorder, or character disorder, for instance. The typical success rate in such cases was only about 5 percent. In the late 1950s, a variety of pressures—mostly political—let the American Medical Association declare alcoholism a specific disease. However, the AMA gave no scientific arguments as to why alcoholism was a disease at all. Rather, it built on the concepts and ideas of Alcoholics Anonymous that had received such positive notices in the community. Almost immediately, there was a rapid increase in the recovery rate, ranging from 60 percent to 80 percent.

Thus alcoholism and chemical dependency have not always been distinguished from drunkenness and being a dope fiend. Rather, chemical dependency has been seen as a sin or a character defect. The argument today tends to dwell not on whether or not chemical dependency is an illness, but rather on the nature of the illness. This includes the predisposing factors for becoming chemically dependent, including genetics and environment. In addition, the argument has an impact on the treatment of chemical dependency, particularly on the need for the recovering chemical dependent to abstain totally from all mood-altering chemicals.

Certainly there is little disagreement that treatment should place some degree of focus on enhancing the client's feelings of self-esteem and personal mastery, especially through the provision of opportunities to plan for and practice appropriate coping behaviors in situations that have previously been dealt with through using. This focus on personal responsibility, however, sometimes is viewed as placing the blame for being chemically dependent on the individual, rather than on recognizing that the responsibility for maintaining sobriety now rests with the individual. That is, individuals can learn to take responsibility for resolving their problems without being forced to shoulder the blame for having the illness itself.

Brickman et al. (1982) help to clarify this issue by categorizing models of helping and coping by the concept of *attribution of responsibility*. They point out that whether or not people are held responsible for causing their problems and for solving those problems is related to four fundamentally different orientations to the world, each somewhat incompatible with the others. They define four models that influence the helping process:

1. The moral model, in which individuals are responsible for both creating and solving their problems.
2. The medical model, in which individuals are responsible neither for their problems nor for the solutions.
3. The enlightenment model, in which individuals are responsible for creating their problems, but not for solving them.
4. The compensatory model, in which individuals are not responsible for creating their problems, but are responsible for solving them.

The moral model attributes full responsibility for the problem to the individual affected. Willpower becomes the solution. This attitude was previously dominant in society and still continues to be the attitude of many people. On the other hand, the medical model suggests that neither the problem nor the solution is under the control of the individual. As a result, the individual should not accept blame for his or her addiction, nor can he or she resolve the problem without treatment. The enlightenment model, which suggests that people bear the responsibility for what they have done in the past and can be helped by surrendering personal power to a stronger force outside themselves, and the compensatory model, which expects individuals to assume the responsibility for solving their problems, despite the fact that the problems were not the result of their own behavior, constitute intermediate models.

While the approach of Alcoholics Anonymous is most similar to the enlightenment model (in that the individual is encouraged to recognize that his or her alcoholism is the result of a disease, and that sobriety rests largely on a person's willingness to recognize and accept the need for a higher power to help maintain that sobriety), some aspects of the AA program are similar to the compensatory model, in that individuals are expected to assume some responsibility for taking the appropriate steps toward abstinence. A number of AA slogans, which will be discussed in chapter 7, point this out by stating, for example, that the individual must take "one day at a time."

Meyer (1989, 268) points out that the current thinking about how alcoholism (and by implication all chemical dependency) develops is still dominated by a kind of "biobehavioral reformulation of the disease concept of alcoholism." However, this reformulation is a medical model that recognizes that nonmedical treatment is still largely influenced by the Alcoholics Anonymous model.

In this chapter, the traditional disease concept of Alcoholics Anonymous will be presented, followed by a review of the literature related to findings concerned with genetic factors in chemical dependency. In addition, a summary of social-learning models for understanding the development of chemical dependency, as well as some family factors, will be presented.

DISEASE CONCEPT

It is clear that viewing alcoholism and other forms of chemical dependency as a disease has distinct advantages. It changes the focus from a moral or legal perspective to one of medical concern and makes available the resources of the health-care system. Scorn and neglect are much less likely to occur, and providing help for the individual and his or her family is emphasized. A second advantage is that chemical dependency becomes the recipient of scientific investigation, with research grants provided for its study (Nace 1987). Of course, other groups have a direct interest in chemical dependency being viewed as a disease, among them health-care providers (including hospitals and professionally trained therapists), recovering alcoholics, and Alcoholics Anonymous itself.

However, just calling chemical dependency a disease does not make it a disease. Instead, for alcoholism and other forms of chemical dependency to be viewed as a disease requires a medical-scientific justification for a disease concept.

Some argue that chemical dependency should be seen as an illness rather than as a disease, since illness is a personal, subjective experience of being sick. The illness does not become a disease until it has been diagnosed as such. Therefore, an illness may occur in the absence of a disease, just as a disease can exist without illness itself. In the field of chemical dependency, both *disease* and *illness* are commonly used (often interchangeably) to refer to drug dependence. While there are studies that demonstrate the likelihood of specific brain-functioning changes, it is still not proven whether these changes are the result of some genetic defect triggered by the use of the mood-altering chemical or whether the changes are secondary to the chemical abuse itself. In addition, the kinds of physiological damage done to the body can be seen as being the result of the abuse of drugs, rather than as being a symptom of the disease of chemical dependency. Thus, it is difficult at present to provide medical-scientific evidence that clearly demonstrates that chemical dependency is a disease.

Another way of examining this dilemma is to look at a disease in terms of its etiology, which will be reviewed later in this section, as well as in terms of its signs and symptoms. Signs are the physical characteristics that a physician can actually see or measure in an individual. These include the fever that accompanies many diseases, the sugar that will be in the urine of a diabetic, or the swelling that accompanies inflamed tonsils. Symptoms are the complaints that the individual brings to the physician. These include feeling fatigued or thirsty or dizzy.

Phases of the Disease

This question becomes particularly important for chemical dependency in that there is a specific set of signs and symptoms that are part of the disease. Jellinek (1960) was probably the first to highlight them with a precise description of the progression of the disease from early to middle to late stages. Jellinek and others had the symptoms down so well that they could ordinarily determine the stage of a person's disease after a single interview.

Based on a survey of more than two thousand members of Alcoholics Anonymous, Jellinek's discussion of the phases of alcoholism was largely descriptive, but it had a statistical foundation. Certainly differences existed between individuals, but there were a great many more similarities. The progression of the disease was described in terms of increasing dysfunction, with the signs and symptoms clustering together. Jellinek developed the idea of four different phases of alcohol addiction: pre-alcoholic, prodromal, crucial, and chronic.

In the early, *pre-alcoholic* stage of drinking, the individual will move between occasional and constant relief drinking, turning from socially motivated drinking to being a drinker who experiences some type of relief as a result of drinking. This usually psychological relief eases the stress and tension affecting the person, and he or she learns to seek out occasions where drinking will occur. It soon becomes the individual's standard means of handling stress, though the drinking behavior will not look different to the outsider. This phase may last for several months or as long as 2 or more years, with a gradually developing increase in tolerance.

In the *prodromal* phase, the individual begins to experience the onset of "blackouts." (Prodromal means "warning or signal of disease," and the warning that usually occurs first is the blackout.) Blackouts do not involve loss of consciousness, but are instead instances where the individual continues to act in a "normal" manner, perhaps appearing slightly inebriated, but has no memory of the experience the next day. This amnesia-like period during drinking does not occur every time the individual drinks too much, but occurs often enough that it usually leads to the person having some trial "abstinence" periods. Sometimes such individuals are able to stop the pattern of drinking for relief and either return to carefully monitored social drinking or become totally abstinent. However, many others move on to intensify their drinking and begin to drink in a different pattern. Sneaking extra drinks before or during social-drinking occasions, gulping the first drink or two, and experiencing guilt about drinking all become part of a preoccupation with alcohol that indicates that it is no longer simply a beverage, but a "need." For this individual, alcohol consumption is likely to be heavy, even though overt intoxification does not occur often. This period ordinarily lasts from about 6 months to 4 or 5 years, depending on the individual's circumstances, and ends with the onset of "loss of control."

This highlights the third, or *crucial*, phase. According to Jellinek, this means that any drinking starts a chain reaction that will soon be felt by the individual as a physical demand for more drinking. Thus, the drinker can no longer control the amount he or she will have once a drink is taken, though the individual can control whether or not he or she will take a drink at all. With loss of control, the drinker drops the cover-up and begins a period of explanation or rationalization about the drinking. Sometimes a period of abstinence occurs through which the drinker attempts to prove to self or to others that drinking is not a problem. At other times, the thinking becomes "if I just _____, then it will be okay for me to drink." Common maneuvers include changing the desired form of alcohol (e.g., switching from whiskey to beer), changing jobs, drinking in different locations, and modifying drinking patterns. However, these maneuvers, which almost always end in failure, lead to guilt, a loss of self-esteem, an increase in aggressive behavior, and a deterioration in family life and friendships. The individual is likely to become by turns resentful, remorseful, and aggressive. Life has become centered around the use of alcohol.

Finally, the drinker enters the *chronic* phase of the process, in which alcohol dominates his or her daily round of activity. While the individual may have been able to maintain a job and social relationships during the crucial phase (even though both were likely to deteriorate), during the chronic phase the person is likely to lose his or her job and to have major conflicts with family and friends. Drinking begins earlier in the day, with cravings appearing at regular, 4-hour intervals. The individual finds that guilt and remorse have become reasons to continue drinking. Thus, a cycle develops in which the person drinks to relieve the bad feelings he or she is experiencing because of the drinking. "Benders," in which the drinker may go on day- or even week-long drinking binges, become more frequent. The individual may begin drinking with persons that he or she previously would have avoided. Tolerance decreases sharply, and the individual is no longer able to hold his or her alcohol, but become stuporous after only a few drinks. Tremors develop. All kinds of alcohol-related illnesses become likely. Even the person's system of rationalization fails as the long-used excuses no longer fit. At this point, if the individual is neither dead nor suffering from organic brain damage, he or she is a prime candidate for treatment, since the bottom has finally been reached.

Types of Drinking Patterns

Jellinek, who is often considered the "father" of the study of alcoholism, also categorized five types of drinking patterns in an attempt to delimit particular kinds of drinking behavior. His studies of alcoholics in other countries, as well as in the United States, demonstrated differences that he believed could not be accounted for simply by the four phases of alcohol addiction. Instead, he theorized that these differences seemed more of kind than of degree, which led him to postulate five categories of drinking.

Alpha alcoholism is a purely psychological dependence on the effect of alcohol to relieve bodily or emotional pain. There are no signs of progressive deterioration, nor does this drinking lead to loss of control or inability to abstain. Rather, the damage from drinking is restricted to relationships or to job performance as a reliance on alcohol develops for coping with any, or all, problems in life. While Jellinek was reluctant to call this type of drinker a "problem drinker," he acknowledged that others would be likely to do so. He also admitted that while progression was not inevitable, many alpha alcoholics might become gamma alcoholics, though many alphas remained at the same level of drinking for as long as 30 or 40 years. On the basis of his own research, which involved drinking patterns of the 1940s, he estimated that 10 percent to 15 percent of the two thousand AA members were alpha drinkers. More recent research suggests that the proportion is likely to be in the 25 percent to 50 percent range. There is some argument about whether or not alpha drinking is truly alcoholism, since there appears to be a minimal loss of control and an absence of physiological addiction to alcohol.

Beta alcoholism appears when the various physical problems resulting from alcohol use develop, including nutritional deficiencies and such physical diseases as cirrhosis of the liver, gastritis, and neurological problems. However, beta drinkers are not psychologically or physiologically dependent on alcohol and do not experience withdrawal symptoms when abstaining. Jellinek believed that this pattern was likely to occur in cultures where there was widespread, heavy drinking that was part of the cultural norm. He also believed that while the beta alcoholic might progress to gamma or delta alcoholism, it was less likely to occur than was the step from alpha alcoholism to gamma alcoholism.

Gamma alcoholism is marked by a change in tolerance, physiological changes leading to withdrawal symptoms, and a loss of control. It also involves an acquired increased tissue tolerance to alcohol, as well as some adaptive cell metabolism. In gamma alcoholism, Jellinek described a definite progression from psychological to physiological dependence, with marked behavioral changes. Jellinek held that gamma alcoholism was the most devastating phase of alcohol addiction in terms of physical health and social disruption, and believed that it was the predominating type of alcoholism in the United States and in the other Anglo-Saxon countries. The pre-alcoholic, prodromal, crucial, and chronic phases of alcoholism previously described are actually phases of gamma alcoholism.

Delta alcoholism, very similar to the gamma category, includes its first three characteristics, but, instead of losing control, the delta drinker is unable to abstain from drinking for even a day or two and thus has measurable alcohol in the bloodstream at all times. On any particular occasion, the delta alcoholic could control his or her intake, but would be unable to go "on the wagon" for even a day without suffering withdrawal. This drinker was described by Jellinek as rarely appearing intoxicated and was the predominant type of alcoholic in countries where wine drinking was highly promoted. Jellinek pointed out that the delta drinker does not live through the social and psychological experiences of the gamma drinker and would rarely experience the need for any kind of treatment, including Alcoholics Anonymous. Because of the absence of intoxication and of loss of control, the extent of the alcoholism is hidden and the individual's drinking is generally socially approved.

Epsilon alcoholism was described by Jellinek as "periodic alcoholism," marked by binge drinking in which the individual would abstain for weeks or months at a time, but then be drawn to a binge that continued with uncontrolled drinking until a state of unconsciousness occurred. The epsilon drinker does not drink on a regular pattern, such as weekend drinking in order to avoid problems on the job, but drinks on an unpredictable schedule. Jellinek believed that the epsilon drinker is often unaware that he or she is moving toward a binge, although the increased agitation in behavior might signal to others that the person was likely to begin the drinking pattern again. Because the individual has no ability to stop after a few drinks, the epsilon alcoholic is usually categorized as a late-stage alcoholic.

Jellinek also suggested that the remaining nineteen letters of the Greek alphabet could be used to describe other kinds of alcoholics, but he did not delineate those types. His descriptions of these five categories are instructive to individuals who wish to work with those who are chemically dependent because his findings help bring some kind of scientific order to a field that had formerly been dominated by intuition and personal experience. In addition, his descriptions offer some insight into the different kinds of drinking patterns of individuals who are chemically dependent. At the same time, reliance on these five categories needs to be limited, since there were flaws in the way that Jellinek gathered his information (his sample was limited to members of AA who, at that time, were predominantly late-stage, male, gamma alcoholics). This in no way, however, suggests that Jellinek's contribution was unimportant.

Thus, Jellinek's research suggests that there are distinct signs and symptoms, as well as a progressive course of development, of the disease of alcoholism. The signs and symptoms, as many as fifty or sixty of them, are characteristics which are clearly descriptive of the individual who is chemically dependent. In the early stages, an individual uses to get relief from something: physical pain, emotional pain, money worries. Drunk driving and memory blackouts often appear during this early stage. In the middle stages of the disease, the classic symptoms—absenteeism from work, poor job performance, financial problems, family problems, changes in moral or ethical behavior—make the disease fairly visible and detectable. Treatment is certainly needed at this point, because this is the beginning of alcoholism's physical problems. While the chemical dependent may be more susceptible to treatment at a later stage, when he or she has hit bottom, the difficulty is that by this time the individual may have organic brain damage, or be dead. Thus, it is important that the chemical dependent be identified and receive treatment during the middle stages.

Unfortunately, the picture that exists in American society of the alcoholic or drug addict involves the chronic-stage person—the semihuman with the body gone rotten, the liver shot, the brain only flickering on occasion, the skid-row bum. Since it ordinarily takes 20 to 25 years of heavy drinking, and a number of years of heavy use of various drugs, to reach the chronic stage, there are not too many people who make it that far.

Even with such a list of signs and symptoms, and a general description of the stages of the disease, such an illness as schizophrenia is still better accepted as a disease than is chemical dependency. Schizophrenic symptoms are alien, bizarre, and unlike our own experiences; the chemically dependent individual is very similar to us. He or she usually drinks the same beverages in the same place and at the same time. Even the overt symptoms of drinking, including slurred speech, uncoordination, and hangovers are familiar to those who have never overindulged. Thus, this comparison of the chemical dependent's behavior to our own experience often leads to the conclusion that the chemical dependent chooses his or her pattern of drug use. In other words, it is a matter of defective will, character, and values, and, as such, is both perplexing and disgusting. Thus, the alcoholic and the drug addict have been readily considered as social misfits, moral degenerates, and objects of pity. Understanding this disease, then, has been obscured by an unrealistic expectation that the individual can simply choose to regulate his or her use of alcohol and other drugs more appropriately (Nace 1987).

Unlike more commonly accepted mental illnesses, recognizing the disease of chemical dependency will not come from an understanding of its etiology, nor from the observation of the external manifestations of use. Instead, acceptance of chemical dependency as a disease emerges as one comprehends the internal experiences of the chemical dependent and the impact of drugs on his or her thinking, motivation, and personality functioning.

Nace (1987) proposes six constructs which make up the essential phenomena of alcoholism, and which can also be applied to the wider field of chemical dependency. These include psychological dependence on a chemical, craving, loss of control, personality regression, denial, and conflicted behavior.

Psychological Dependence

Psychological dependence, which precedes physiological dependence by at least 5 years for alcohol (Mandell 1983) and remains long after a person has been successfully detoxified, often exerts a profound influence on the thinking and behavior of the individual for a number of years during recovery. In many ways, psychological dependence refers to a central organizing, cognitive experience of the individual in which he or she continues to be influenced, controlled, or determined by another event, situation, or substance. This condition brings about profound changes in the thinking of the person, including psychological primacy, self-doubt, sense of loss, and an inability to abstain.

PSYCHOLOGICAL PRIMACY

Psychological primacy is the term used to describe the evolving priority of alcohol in the individual's life. For example, in the early uses of the drug the individual may be concerned with the pleasure that he or she receives. Later, the user makes the drug the most important part of his or her life. Still later, when psychological primacy is established, using the drug may be the only thing that matters to the person, who will allow his or her relationships and job performance to deteriorate because nothing is more important than the drug. As the individual ignores personal health, family, and career, he or she begins to feel guilt and shame about the damage being done to his or her life. So, in order to understand the psychological dependence involved in chemical dependency, one has to respect the strength and tenacity of a process in which the main priority of the individual comes to be to use.

SELF-DOUBT

Self-doubt becomes a major part of psychological dependence when the individual begins to believe that he or she is unable to cope without alcohol or marijuana or cocaine or whatever the drug of preference may be. This conviction that the individual is inadequate in meeting the demands of daily living reflects the damage of chemical dependency to the thinking patterns of the person. Only the effects of the desired chemical restore confidence and allow the individual to again believe that he or she can be successful. This fear, or self-doubt, undermines self-esteem and often results in the individual feeling overwhelmed by a future without drugs.

SENSE OF LOSS

Since many recovering individuals talk about the sense of "losing their lover," the sense of loss related to psychological dependence results from the individual giving up that which has become the most important part of his or her life. The possibility of living without the drug results in the individual feeling a pervasive dread in which life has no meaning, and boredom and loneliness are expected. This sense of loss is similar to a grief reaction in which the individual must grieve for the loss of the major focus of his or her life. The sense of loss is often experienced as a removal of all joy or zest from one's experience and can have a damaging effect on abstinence.

INABILITY TO ABSTAIN

The belief of the individual that he or she cannot stop using is also a result of a psychological dependence, though this conviction is rarely verbalized. Resulting from repeated failures in attempting to reduce or refrain from the use of various drugs, which most chemically dependent individuals have attempted periodically, the fear of not being able to quit is particularly ominous to the person who is chemically dependent. Already feeling a great deal of shame and guilt, as well as a sense of failure from previous efforts to stop using, the individual is particularly afraid that this will be the final straw demonstrating that he or she is a totally inadequate person. Thus, many individuals say something like "I wish I wanted to quit," suggesting that the person believes abstinence could be maintained if he or she really wanted to, and protecting themselves from the anxiety associated with the possibility of failure in abstinence. Thus, the "one day at a time" emphasis provides a more reasonable goal for the individual in terms of success.

Not only does psychological dependence affect the cognitive functioning of the individual, it is also related to the other constructs of craving, loss of control, personality regression, denial, and conflicted behavior which are part of the disease concept.

Craving

Within the context of chemical dependency, craving may be defined as "a subjective experience of desiring, needing, or longing for the euphoric and tension-relieving properties" of various mood-altering chemicals (Nace 1987, 71). Craving for a drug is located in the experience of taking the drug for the relief of withdrawal symptoms. Thus, the repetition of the experience of using drugs to alleviate the discomfort that comes from withdrawal appears to lead rapidly to a changed attitude toward the drug and to the behaviors that constitute addiction. As a result, many individuals do not get hooked on the pleasures of the drug itself, but on the experiences of relief that occur immediately after taking the drug. Thus, addiction is established in the experiences that occur immediately after each use and not in the way the person feels during the remaining time between using. Thus, increased heart rate, tremors, and insomnia, which characterize withdrawal from any drug, may trigger craving when reexperienced for whatever reason.

Wise (1988) proposes that craving can best be understood in terms of the two classes of reinforcement, each of which contributes to the addictive liability of drugs. The first, positive reinforcement, is produced by a stimulus that brings pleasure or euphoria to an individual who is in a normal mood state. The second class, negative reinforcement, is produced by a stimulus that terminates distress or dysphoria, moving the individual toward a normal mood state. In this distinction, craving results from an attempt to escape normality or it may result from an attempt to return to normality.

The positive-reinforcement concept describes craving as resulting from a previous history of positive experiences with a particular drug or class of drugs. This craving is sufficient to explain initial addiction in cases of relapse following prolonged detoxification. In addition, such a perspective helps to explain the long-sought common denominator for a variety of addictions. If a number of addictive substances have positive-reinforcement effects, then one drug may be substituted for another, or another addictive experience—for instance, an eating addiction or a sexual addiction—may be substituted for drugs themselves. These cravings, based on the positive-reinforcing effects of a drug, will generally vary in strength with the memories of past reinforcements, and these memories will often vary with the presence of secondary reinforcing stimuli in the environment. Thus, an individual may desire a drug (craving) when he or she is in the presence of other people who are using, because the individual is then reexposed to cues associated with prior use.

This emphasis on the positive aspects of drug use is important for many users in that it helps to describe the other side of the coin—that for many individuals craving is the result of a desire to enhance their sensory perceptions to a level different from those which they are currently experiencing or from those in their normal lives.

At the same time, the emphasis on negative reinforcement, in which using becomes an attempt to remove unpleasant experiences in one's life, presents the other side of the same coin, in which the individual's using is an attempt to block out or to dull unpleasant events and memories in his or her life. Thus, the need to use can be a means of coping with stress and tension, of blocking out memories of abuse and abandonment, and of forgetting how inadequate the individual feels he or she is.

Reports of craving are regularly given by patients in rehabilitation programs. Isbell (1955) studied sixty alcoholics, 78 percent of whom reported craving. However, when the concept was more carefully explained to them, the number reporting craving rose to 95 percent. Nearly two-thirds of the patients stated that craving increased after one or two drinks, and about half of the patients indicated that their cravings increased when they were around people who were drinking or when they were in places where alcohol was available. Other studies have indicated that the intensity of craving is related to the length of sobriety—the longer the period of abstinence, the less frequent and less severe the craving. One study (Mathew, Claghorn, & Largen 1979) found that alcoholics who reported no craving at all had been abstinent for an average of 19 weeks, as compared to the 3 weeks reported by those who stated that they were experiencing severe craving.

Mello (1972, 261) has criticized the concept of craving, calling it a "logically and empirically inadequate explanatory concept to account for addictive drinking." Arguing that drinking behavior could be explained as part of a multiple-change schedule of reinforcement, Mello found that alcoholics could control their drinking and not drink to complete intoxication each time they took a drink.

However, Denzin (1987) points out three findings that he believed contraindicated Mello's conclusions. First, he suggests that the people in Mello's study regularly consumed large amounts of alcohol. In addition, he pointed out that once these individuals reached a stable level of blood alcohol, they regularized their drinking at a high plateau in order to avoid withdrawal symptoms. And finally, the individuals increased their drinking in anticipation of withdrawal, rather than lowering their intake. He believed that this revealed anticipated craving upon cessation. Thus, Denzin suggests that loss of control, or drinking to excess, occurs when the individual believes his or her supply is about to be ended; when a stable, regular drinking supply is available, the alcoholic stabilizes his or her drinking at a high, alcoholic, addictive level.

Nace (1987) also lists different manifestations of craving. These include:

1. Physical. An individual who, for instance, is an alcoholic, feels as though he or she can taste the alcohol and has sensations of dry mouth, thirst, and a gnawing feeling in the stomach.
2. Compulsive. The individual cannot think of anything else.
3. Cognitive. The individual's thoughts of using are unaccompanied by physical sensations or a compulsive urge. However, the person makes frequent verbal references to using and has a euphoric recall of using experiences. This individual may or may not be aware that thinking about using reflects an impulse to use.
4. Affective. The person experiences a dysphoric mood state characterized by irritability, depression, anxiety, and resentment. At the same time, he or she is usually unaware of the relationship between the feelings being experienced and the frustrated need for drugs.

By helping the chemically dependent individual understand that craving can be either biologically determined, as during the withdrawal phase of detoxification, or lie within the realm of basic conditioning psychology, he or she is encouraged to understand it in familiar human terms. As such, this helps to undermine the fears that the craving will always be present in an intense manner and that the individual is hopeless as a result of the craving. Even more important, the professional counselor must recognize that the individual who experiences craving and demonstrates it by verbal or other means does not have a poor prognosis, but is, instead, simply coping with the struggle of abstinence.

Loss of Control

Loss of control is closely related to craving, which usually precedes it. That is, the individual experiences a need to use, uses, craves more, and a vicious cycle begins. Loss of control does not mean that the individual who uses an initial amount of a drug invariably proceeds to excessive use. The idea that a physiological chain reaction triggered by a small amount of a drug constitutes loss of control is one of the myths that has existed for a long time. This myth is partially based on a recognition that the individual who uses even a small amount generally does lose part of his or her option of stopping before abuse occurs. In one sense, then, the key to loss of control may be the use of the term *unpredictability*, in which it is understood that the individual loses control of predicting how much he or she will use once drug-taking has begun. Thus, while Jellinek (1952) early on stated that a small quantity of alcohol would set up a demand for more alcohol and that this demand would last until the individual was too intoxicated or too sick to drink more, only a few months later he clarified his position by stating that it may take an alcoholic weeks of drinking before total loss of control develops. Thus, it was not inevitable that one or two drinks would lead to drunkenness. This misunderstanding about loss of control is also used often as part of the denial process by an individual that he or she is an alcoholic. By pointing out that he or she can often stop after only one or two drinks, the individual justifies his or her position by saying that alcoholics are unable to stop. Thus, the sense of loss of control can be best described as the inability of the chemically dependent individual to choose *invariably* whether or not he or she will use and the inability to regulate *predictably* how much will be used (Nace 1987).

Since the pharmacologic effect of the drug may be a stimulus to loss of control, as will be discussed later in the chapter, abstinence remains the cornerstone of treatment efforts, since it removes both the possible pharmacologic effect and the continuing psychological effect.

Personality Regression

The pathological effect of mood-altering chemicals often includes an impact on personality functioning, particularly in the area of regression.

Regression, a return to an earlier developmental mode of psychological functioning, may be conceptualized as a shift in psychological defenses from those which are characteristic of the more mature individual to those which are characteristic of the less mature individual. These less mature defenses include acting out, passive-aggressive behavior, and somatization (developing physical complaints), as opposed to the more mature mechanisms of suppression, humor, or anticipation (Vaillant 1971).

While the effects of chemical dependency are often confused with various personality disorders, it is important to recognize, first, that personality disorders are often common antecedents of chemical dependency and, second, that the use of mood-altering chemicals may lead to personality changes independent of a preexisting character disorder. Thus, the individual who is chemically dependent often seems to have a personality disorder during the active phases of the illness, although not all individuals continue to show character pathology when sober (Nace 1987).

The personality changes which occur as manifestations of chronic drug abuse are modifications of the preexisting personality structure. Sometimes the drug nurtures latent or mild pathological features and brings such features into full expression. In other cases, the changes in personality and behavior are in pronounced contrast to the individual's previous basic characteristics.

Some of the manifestations of personality regression in the individual who is chemically dependent result from the rapid, predictable, and pleasurable pharmacologic action of various drugs. As is well known, any experience that has such euphoric effects is highly reinforcing. In consequence, the person's ability to delay gratification and to tolerate frustration is weakened by this experience of immediate gratification. As a result, certain specific traits or behaviors are then observed, including grandiosity, impatience, decreased tolerance of frustration, impulsivity, and passivity. These traits which will be described more fully in chapter 4, are often quite uncharacteristic of the individual, and confuse and frustrate the person's friends. Grandiosity, an exaggerated sense of self-importance, is shown by an inordinate need for attention and by the expectation that the individual deserves it. This attention may be expected because of the individual's qualities or strengths or because of his or her suffering. This sense of grandiosity also causes individuals to develop unrealistic expectations of themselves, expectations which often lead to greater guilt and an increased sense of inferiority. In addition, grandiosity often results in a sense of self-sufficiency which can interfere with the individual's receiving help for the disease.

Impatience, the tendency to want to do everything in a hurry, is frequently observed at the beginning of treatment. The individual wants to receive treatment, and become drug-free, in a very short time. A decreased tolerance of frustration is often evident in the anger, anxiety, or despair which results when individuals do not receive their requests as quickly as they desire. Impulsivity involves those behaviors which fail to take into account the consequences of actions. Thus, the person over-responds to situations and makes snap decisions without giving sufficient thought to the consequences of those decisions. Passivity is characteristic, because drugs provide a high yield for very little behavior. Thus, activities which involve sustained effort and discipline—even though they may result in a natural "high"—are undervalued, because they require too much effort. Thus, in treatment, the individual must have a sufficient time in a drug-free state before any regressive effects of drugs can be separated from preexisting character pathology.

Denial

While a variety of defense mechanisms are often used as part of the individual's attempt to alter reality, the chemically dependent person is likely to make denial the prime defense of his or her behavior. Denial is used to block the efforts of those who point out reality to the individual and to justify continued use. At the same time, denial commonly invokes anger, discouragement, frustration, and distancing for those who have approached the individual. By avoiding a recognition of the destructive effect of his or her use of drugs, the chemically dependent person protects the self from lowered self-esteem.

Individuals who are new to the area of chemical-dependency counseling need to recognize that denial, being largely unconscious, is different from lying and deceit. The individual is protecting the self at a very safe level, free from conscious experiencing, as a means of protecting the ego. In addition, denial protects the option to continue to use, which for the addicted individual is the essence of life. Denial also is a means of protecting the individual from a sense of personal hopelessness. All of these are part of an attempt to preserve ego integrity. Since the individual feels as if he or she cannot cope without drugs, does not want to live without drugs, and can't stop using anyway, the importance of denying that he or she has a problem in using magnifies. To recognize one's helplessness over drug usage is to acknowledge the necessity to quit, which is beyond the individual's grasp. Since this results in too much psychological pain, the mind mercifully prefers the illogical alternative of denial.

Denial acts, then, to ward off the painful feelings of helplessness over the inability to control the use of drugs and to block an accurate appraisal of the consequences that using has had on the individual's health, social relationships, and job performance. Thus, while rationalization, projection, minimalization, avoidance, and delaying are also used as attempts to justify, conceal, or preserve using, denial is a more prominent approach, because it blocks the need for the use of the other defense mechanisms entirely.

In addition, three major distortions—blackouts, repression, and euphoric recall—serve to ward off or distort the reality of the individual's using and, thereby, contribute to the process of denial. Blackouts, which are a physiologically induced state of amnesia, result in the individual not remembering what he or she did while under the influence. Repression, which is similar to a blackout in that the individual represses memories that are painful or conflicted, does not result in a total loss of memory of an experience. Euphoric recall is the experience of remembering only the positive feelings associated with using, without bringing to mind the behavioral consequences, partially because the euphoric effects are more closely associated in time with using than are the painful consequences. Thus, denial is reinforced by the distortions of cognitive processing that occur from the effects of drug use, as well as by the defensive thinking and behavior stimulated by the individual's need to maintain ego integrity and adequacy.

Conflicted Behavior

Nace's sixth construct of alcoholism is conflicted behavior. The variety of behaviors which result from a dependence on drug use involve pathological patterns of using, as well as such other behavioral manifestations as deterioration in job performance, child or spouse abuse, reckless driving and/or accidents, and an aggressive deterioration in judgment, sense of responsibility, and sense of values.

In many ways, these behavioral manifestations have the same effects on family and friends as does denial. Anger, contempt, frustration, and rejection are frequent responses. These individuals, however, often are unaware of the conflict which arises within the chemically dependent individual. He or she really does believe that love permeates the relationship, yet continues to behave in a manner that suggests that the relationship is no longer important. Thus, prior standards and expectations are repeatedly ignored and guilt, shame, and a sense of worthlessness develop, and another cycle begins. Each manifestation of the illness results in a lowering of the sense of self-worth, which leads to feelings of inadequacy, which can only be dealt with by using.

As Nace points out, it is only by recognizing the pervasive and primary effects of psychological dependence in the experience of individuals who are chemically dependent that an understanding of the disease concept can emerge. This construct, along with those of craving, loss of control, personality regression, denial, and conflicted behavior, helps shape the disease concept and clarify the nature of the illness.

The idea that chemical dependency is a disease does, of course, have its detractors. Some criticize the disease concept because it can be used by those who are chemically dependent as a cop-out. They suggest that the disease concept undermines the responsibility of the individual and provides excuses for the individual to continue using without accepting responsibility for such use. Others point out that there are certain social, ethical, or political advantages to calling chemical dependency a disease. Fingarette (1988) has been a leading critic of the disease concept. He suggests that a key factor for continuing the myth of "disease" is the widespread presence in the treatment and lobbying communities of paraprofessional staff members who define themselves as "recovering alcoholics." He goes on to suggest that this group, which often has not had the benefit of scientific or professional training, tends to be relatively unconcerned about the issue of scientific validity. Rather, he suggests that they believe that the experiences and anecdotal information they offer as evidence for their beliefs constitute positive proof of their claims. However, while Fingarette is correct in saying that the field of treatment for chemical dependency is widely populated by individuals without professional training, this argument does not provide any evidence that the signs and symptoms, the identified pathogenesis, and the psychological constructs which have been identified in this chapter are any less valid. While many individuals in the field might be identified as paraprofessionals, a large number do have professional training and are concerned about the use of the most valid and reliable information concerning the etiology, characteristics, and treatment of the disease.

GENETIC FACTORS

The nature-versus-nurture controversy over the etiology of chemical dependency in general and alcoholism in particular has been replaced by a recognition that both sets of factors are important. A number of studies have examined various genetic factors in the etiology of alcoholism. In general, four types of studies have supported the idea of a genetic influence on alcoholism. These include, first, the studies of the familial nature of alcoholism, that is, the manner in which it tends to run in families. Second are the animal studies, which support the importance of inherited factors in the organism's decision to drink and in the decision related to the quantity consumed. Third are studies of twins, which demonstrate a two times greater risk, or more, of alcoholism in an identical twin of an alcoholic than in a fraternal twin. The fourth, and most compelling, source of evidence are adoption studies in the United States and Sweden. These studies have revealed a fourfold or higher alcoholism risk for the children of alcoholics adopted at birth and raised without knowledge of their biological parents' problem, when compared with children of nonalcoholics adopted at birth. As a result, research is being done now in an attempt to identify the genetically mediated biological factors which contribute to this alcoholism risk (Schuckit 1984).

While there is little question that alcoholism, and for that matter chemical dependency, tend to run in families, the issue of whether this familial influence is a result of heredity or environment continues to be difficult to answer. Schuckit and Duby (1983) demonstrated a possible familial factor in the metabolism of alcohol. In the metabolism study, nonalcoholic relatives were found to produce higher levels of blood acetaldehyde to a standard oral dose of alcohol, when compared to an age- and sex-matched control group. This suggests that a biological predisposition to alcoholism or to alcohol abuse may be inherited, just as learning how to drink, how to abuse alcohol, when, and for what reasons may be related to one's family experiences. Certainly conceptions of excessive alcohol use and abuse are learned in the family context, as well as in the more general cultural environment of individuals. Whether it be heredity or environment, the fact is that alcoholism does run in families. The child of an alcoholic is more likely to become alcoholic. Studies have shown that up to half of the descendants of alcoholics become alcoholics themselves. For this reason, the focus of research has turned to animal studies, to carefully controlled studies of twins, and to adoption studies to try to isolate the influence of heredity and environment.

Animal studies have, until recently, shed little light on the issue of genetic factors in alcohol and other drug abuse. Just as different individuals have a different reaction to the taste and effect of alcohol, rats and mice have been found to have the same range of likes and dislikes. Some strains of mice, for example, are teetotalers and apparently find alcohol's taste or effect unpleasant. Others are heavy drinkers and will consistently choose an alcohol solution over water or a sugar-and-water solution. And other mice are more mixed in their likes and dislikes and can be compared to the typical social drinker who will occasionally sip one or two drinks.

The preference for alcohol is widely believed to be regulated by complicated chemical activities in the brain. As far back as 1968, rats dramatically reduced or completely stopped drinking alcohol when given a chemical substance which depleted the brain's supply of serotonin, a brain amine responsible for relaying messages from one brain cell to another. While serotonin appears to increase the animal's preference for alcohol, the brains of those strains of rats which seek alcohol contain higher levels of serotonin than the brains of alcohol-avoiding animals. Further, drinking alcohol increases the concentration of serotonin in the brains of alcohol-preferring animals, but does not increase the concentration in the brains of alcohol-avoiding animals.

In addition, tetrahydropapaveroline (THP), the product of the interaction of acetaldehyde and dopamine, also affects how much an animal will drink. In tests where THP was injected into the brains of rats, it caused those that normally avoided alcohol to drink excessive amounts, even to the point of unconsciousness; they also suffered withdrawal symptoms and would continue to drink as though to avoid them. This result indicates that preference for alcohol is not even a necessary factor, since rats which at first refused to drink could be made to drink addictively when THP was injected into their brains. Thus, at least two brain amines—serotonin and THP—have been shown to be related to addictive drinking.

Since it is not possible to employ scientific investigational methods using an experimental model to examine the issue of separating nature and nurture, it is necessary to locate persons with particular life experiences and then compare them to people with other backgrounds. One way of doing this is to study twins. Goodwin (1985) has worked extensively on the topic of alcoholism and heredity. Although many of his studies have used data from Sweden (because detailed records of marriages and births, and other data, make it easier to trace families), his work seems to be consistent with findings in studies performed in the United States. One early study was based on a large sample of twins; in each set, one twin was known to be alcoholic. The researchers determined if each pair of twins was identical or fraternal, and then interviewed the twin brother or sister of the known alcoholic. The findings supported the prediction that the other twin in identical sets would be more likely to be alcoholic than would the other twin of fraternal sets. However, since this was not always true, there did appear to be an environmental factor involved.

Hrubek and Omenn (1981) examined the medical histories of 15,924 pairs of male twins listed in the National Academy of Sciences–National Research Council Twin Registry for alcoholism or alcohol-related diagnoses. The group was composed of pairs of twins who had served in the United States armed forces and were all at least 51 years old at the time of the study, so that most subjects would have passed through the highest risk period for alcohol problems. Not only were identical twins significantly more likely to have been diagnosed as alcoholic, they were also more frequently recorded as having suffered from such alcohol-related illnesses as alcoholic psychosis and liver cirrhosis. This study, with its large sample, has been used to support the idea that there is a substantial genetic effect in determining whether or not one becomes alcoholic.

In a rather different type of study, involving 15,007 same-sex pairs of high-school students who were twins, Loehlin and Nichols (1976) also found that their data supported a genetic component to alcohol abuse and, to a lesser extent, normal drinking behavior. Both alcohol-abuse and normal-drinking hereditary estimates were substantially greater for men than for women. However, this study did involve a sample of teenagers who had not yet passed through the greatest risk period for alcoholism. Also, later adult abuse was not included in the study.

A third study (Clifford et al. 1981) focused on female alcoholism. Clifford found, as had Loehlin and Nichols, a smaller genetic effect on female drinking, and also noted that the genetic-environmental model fit was less satisfactory for females than for males. They attributed the latter to the existence of a competition effect between female twins, with the result that if one drank heavily there was a tendency for the other to drink less. All in all, some studies show a substantial genetic effect, some show little effect, and others are equivocal (Searles 1988).

The other method for studying the question of nature versus nurture with human subjects is based on adoption. Conceptually, this technique permits one to assess genetic and environmental factors independently by comparing the relationships of adopted siblings, nonadopted siblings, biological parents, and adoptive parents. Thus, genetically dissimilar individuals reared in the same home yield a direct estimate of shared environmental factors, whereas genetically related individuals reared in uncorrelated environments provide an estimate of genetic influences. This method of studying genetic factors in alcoholism theoretically yields the most powerful and convincing evidence. However, because of the difficulty of undertaking this kind of research, there have been few studies which relate directly to the etiology of alcoholism.

The two most important groups of researchers—Clonninger, Bohman, and Sigvordsson (1981) and Goodwin, Schulsinger, Hermensen, Guze, and Winokur (1973)—conducted their research in Scandinavia because of the extensive, centralized medical and personal records kept on the entire population. This gave them access to considerable data on both the biological and adoptive relatives of adoptees.

Goodwin's studies were based on the idea of finding children who were born to an alcoholic mother or father, but who were put up for adoption very shortly after birth and thus were not raised by their biological parents. He then compared these children in later life to a corresponding group of adopted infants whose biological parents were not alcoholic. Since both groups of children were adoptees, any relationship between alcoholism and being an adoptee should be the same for both groups and would, in effect, cancel itself out in comparisons between them. Goodwin chose to study only male children, and in 85 percent of the cases the biological alcoholic parent was the father.

The difference in the incidence of alcoholism for the two groups was statistically significant. The rate of alcoholism among the adoptees who had an alcoholic biological parent was 3.6 times greater than that among the adoptees whose biological parents were not alcoholics. In addition, Goodwin and his associates found that even longtime environmental exposure (over 14 years) to an alcoholic parent did not increase the risk of becoming an alcoholic.

In fact, no identifiable home environmental factors led to an increased or decreased risk for alcoholism.

Clonninger and his colleagues gathered data in Sweden on 862 men and 913 women adopted at an early age by nonrelatives. This even larger sample size was made possible by the greater number of available records. He found that both genetic predisposition and postnatal environmental factors influenced whether or not an individual became an alcohol abuser. As a result, his studies have been found to suggest that there are multiple pathways to alcohol abuse, that men and women do not exhibit the same patterns of abuse, and that there is a distinct type of severe alcohol abuse which is highly inheritable and found exclusively in men. All in all, the adoption studies, much like the studies of twins, suggest that there are genetic factors which are involved in the etiology of alcoholism, but that there are environmental factors at work also. To state it differently, Goodwin and Guze (1974) concluded after a thorough review of family, twin, adoption, genetic-marker, and animal studies that while genetic factors could not be ruled out, they could be ruled in.

METABOLIC FACTORS

Acetaldehyde has been identified in several studies as a major villain in the onset of alcoholic drinking. Lieber (1976) reported that his research had found that the same amount of alcohol produced very different blood acetaldehyde levels in alcoholics than it did in nonalcoholics. Since much higher levels were reached in alcoholics, he theorized that this unusual buildup was caused in part by a malfunctioning of the liver's enzymes.

Schuckit and Rayses (1979) performed studies confirming that in alcoholics the breakdown of acetaldehyde into acedate is performed at about half the speed of the metabolism in the nonalcoholic individual. This may also explain the accumulation of acetaldehyde in the alcoholic's bloodstream.

However, neither of these studies could determine whether the enzyme malfunction preceded the heavy drinking or was a result of heavy alcoholic intake. In other words, does the alcoholic drink too much because his or her body is somehow abnormal, or does the body become abnormal because the alcoholic drinks too much? Both Lieber and Schuckit did further studies and obtained results similar to those of Schuckit and Rayses. They both had findings which indicated that the metabolic abnormality exists prior to heavy drinking. Like alcoholic parents, the children of alcoholics (who before the experiment had never drunk alcohol) were unable to convert acetaldehyde to acedate at normal speed. Thus, heredity was clearly implicated in these studies, and addiction to alcohol may, in part, be traced back to this liver-enzyme malfunction which results in a buildup of acetaldehyde throughout the body. These large amounts of acetaldehyde then interact with the brain amines to form active compounds with some morphine-like properties, which in turn trigger the alcoholic's need to drink more and more alcohol to counter the painful effects of the progressive buildup of acetaldehyde. In addition, these findings may also be related to the previously reviewed studies which showed that animals injected with THP changed from alcohol-avoiding animals to alcohol-preferring animals.

Other studies, including those by Nathan and Lisman (1976), suggest that the risk for developing acute alcoholism could increase if the individual were less able to moderate drinking because of an impaired ability to estimate intoxication at a given level of alcohol content in the blood. There is some evidence to suggest that alcoholics are less able than others to estimate their blood-alcohol levels after drinking. Schuckit (1982) found that the alcoholic had a lessened response to the acute effects of modest alcohol doses, which might in turn impair his or her ability to tell when it is time to stop.

With this finding in mind, another study addresses the possibility that whether or not one is an alcoholic might affect the quality or intensity of intoxication. The study (Schuckit 1984) suggests that young men with a higher future risk for alcoholism may be unwilling or unable to pay attention to their surroundings when they are becoming intoxicated, which may support the possibility that they feel less intoxicated because they pay less attention to how they are feeling or responding to their environment.

The findings reviewed in this section supply some interesting leads for further research, while providing some potential answers for the influence of genetic mechanisms on alcoholism. Certainly the animal studies, the studies of twins, and the adoption studies, along with the research involving metabolism and the effects of alcohol on electrophysiological differences, provide solid evidence that there is a genetic factor in alcoholism, though the extent of that influence is still unclear. More evidence is needed to determine if the same kind of genetic influences are found in those who are addicted to drugs other than alcohol.

BEHAVIORAL THEORIES OF CHEMICAL DEPENDENCY

While the general field of psychology and its application to a variety of problem areas has seen a tremendous increase in an emphasis on cognitive-behavioral concepts during the past three decades, the field of chemical-dependency treatment has been slow to look at, and examine critically, the application of those concepts. Although there has been a long history of the use of chemical-aversion therapy to induce a conditioned aversion to alcohol, this approach has been largely abandoned. Instead, a variety of models have been developed, which have become more sophisticated and more closely tied to research findings as they apply to individuals who are chemically dependent. Behavioral views on alcoholism and other drug addictions have added cognitive elements as mediating variables to the learning factors considered responsible for the development of abusive drinking. While these ideas are often seen as threatening to the disease concept and to the traditional views of chemical dependency, acceptance of contemporary behavioral views of the problem does not require rejection of other etiological factors, whether sociocultural or genetic and physiological (Nathan 1984). The behavioral position, instead, is that while learning may play a major role in the addiction of some individuals, it does not necessarily do so in the absence of other important etiologic factors.

The behavioral view of how an addiction is acquired is based on some basic concepts, or behavioral formulations. These include:

1. The complex of discriminating stimuli that are present for any person at any time.
2. Behavioral options, which include appropriate and inappropriate drinking responses in a particular environment.
3. Any consequence of a behavior that increases the probability of the reoccurrence of that behavior.
4. Punishment, which is any event that results in a decrease in the rate of occurrence of the behavior.

Thus, a behavioral view of chemical dependency focuses on the behavioral effects of stimulus events and on reinforcement and punishment schedules which may increase or decrease the likelihood of any appropriate behavior. The best-known, most influential, and most controversial versions of the application of learning theory to alcoholism are given in Mello (1972, 1983) and in Sobell and Sobell (1978). Rather than developing a theory of alcoholism, they made attempts to apply operant methods of conditioning to either determine the alcoholic's preferred pattern of drinking or to modify the alcoholic's drinking style to produce a normal pattern of social drinking. The Sobells' effort to teach alcoholics to drink socially provided the conclusion that increasing the alcoholic's awareness of internal cues would permit him or her to return to social drinking that would be both appropriate and nonabusive. Their findings after 2 years were impressive and influential. A 10-year reevaluation (Pendery, Maltzman, & West 1982) confirmed that their original deduction was incorrect. Those patients who had recovered had achieved stable abstinence, but thirteen of the fourteen remaining patients had either died or repeatedly relapsed to alcohol dependence. However, the major contribution of the Sobells' study was to focus attention on the use of learning theory in treatment of alcoholism. The Mello studies led to the conclusions that (1) alcoholics did not display loss of control in free-drinking programs; (2) alcoholics never consumed all of the alcohol supply that was provided them; (3)

alcoholics could initiate periods of abstinence and could control the amount they drank; (4) the amount alcoholics drink could be manipulated by a work-reinforcement schedule; (5) abstinence could therefore be bought; (6) alcoholics would taper off and control their drinking; (7) some alcoholics can drink socially; (8) alcoholics do not display craving and loss of control as these have been previously described; and (9) alcoholics will continue to drink even after alcohol produces negative, dysphoric effects for them.

Bandura (1969) provided a developmental framework regarding alcohol use and abuse from a social-learning-theory standpoint, which assumed that all drinking, from incidental social use through abuse and alcoholism, is governed by similar principles of learning, cognition, and reinforcement. Since that time, a list of principles has emerged from theoretical-empirical developments. These principles offer an understanding of psychosocial and cultural predisposing influences on drinking, as well as the interactive role of predisposing individual differences that may be either biological or psychological and genetic or acquired. These influences help to describe experimentation in alcohol abuse, as well as subsequent use, and suggest that abuse is likely to occur under conditions that overwhelm effective coping ability and reduce the individual's perception of efficacy. Then the consequences of abusive-drinking episodes in themselves can lead to further drinking, while recovery depends upon the individual's ability to acquire general coping skills and the self-control skills required to manage drinking. Thus, alcohol abuse is seen as a method of coping with the demands of everyday life. As such, it is related to those approaches which focus on tension reduction and stress-response dampening, as well as to expectancy theory.

The tension-reduction model assumes drinking to be a learned means of reducing conditioned anxiety that is present in the environment. Thus, the existence of a state of tension energizes the drinking response, and the relief of tension provided by alcohol or other drugs reinforces the drinking or using response. However, Cappell and Greeley (1987), after a thorough evaluation of recent work on the application of tension-reduction theory to chemical dependency, concluded that this model does not work as a single-factor explanation, because alcohol and other drugs do many things besides reduce tension. They did conclude, however, that the tension-reduction model is valid within a relatively circumscribed portion of the overall model of drug use, and that it makes its greatest contribution as a crucial component of more complex models.

Developing out of the tension-reduction model was the stress-response-dampening model, which focuses on a drug's effects on the individual when he or she is stressed. Sher (1987), for instance, argues that alcohol dampens the physiologic response to stress, subjectively alleviating stress and thereby reinforcing drinking in similar stressful situations. He focuses on the psychopharmacologic approach to chemical dependency, examining the psycho-physiologic effects of drugs and the possible direct and indirect pharmacologic mechanisms involved. He also emphasizes the importance of nonpharmacologic cognitive effects (i.e., expectancies) and the role of individual differences in the way the individual is sensitive to the stress-response dampening of a particular drug. Thus, he considers the stress-response-dampening model to be a psychobiological minitheory that is part of the larger context of cognitive-social learning theory.

In the past decade, there has been an increasing interest in the impact on the individual's drinking behavior of their expectations about the effects of alcohol. This has led to the use of expectancy theory in attempting to better understand the effects of alcohol and other drugs on individuals. The concept of expectancy refers to the anticipation of a particular set of effects from the use of a drug. Researchers in expectancy theory have focused their work on four areas: (1) initiation of alcohol and other drug use, (2) maintenance of drinking and using behaviors, (3) acceleration of drinking or using in some individuals, and (4) continuing use of alcohol and other drugs, even when the consequences have become physically and behaviorally destructive. Donovan and Marlatt (1980) found that specific expectations about alcohol developed through peer and parental modeling, direct and indirect experiences with drinking, and media exposure. A first set of expectations relates to mood alterations. A second expectation is enhanced social interaction and a feeling of control or power. A third group has arisen from traditional views of alcoholism and relates to the expectation of the alcoholic to feel craving sensations and thus feel compelled to drink.

Various research based on these concepts has led to findings supporting the idea that the belief that one has consumed alcohol appears to be more important than whether one actually did consume alcohol, at least in terms of the following behaviors: subsequent drinking in alcoholics, social anxiety, sexual responsiveness, aggression, delay of gratification, mood states, motor abilities, assertiveness, and such cognitive processes as attention and recognition memory (Nathan 1984). Sometimes the expectations about the impact of alcohol diverged from its actual effects, while at other times the two converged; the process was seen to vary as a function of subject sex, research setting, or experimental design.

Finally, the relapse-prevention model of Marlatt and Gordon (1985) has received a great deal of emphasis during the past few years. This construct, which might also be called an addictive-behavior model or a self-control model, is derived from the principles of social-learning theory, cognitive psychology, and experimental social psychology. For them, addictive behaviors are viewed as overlearned *habits* that can be analyzed and modified in the same manner as other habits. In addition, addictive behaviors are presumed to lie along a continuum of use, rather than being defined by such discrete or fixed categories as excessive use or total abstinence. These overlearned addictive behaviors are seen as maladaptive habit patterns which are performed during or prior to stressful or unpleasant situations; they are maladaptive to the extent that they lead to delayed, negative consequences in health, social status, and self-esteem.

Marlatt and Gordon respond to the criticism that to accept their model of learned addictive behaviors is equivalent to blaming the user and making that individual personally responsible for his or her condition by pointing out that since addiction is defined as a powerful habit pattern with an acquired vicious cycle of self-destructive behavior locked in by the collective effects of classical conditioning and operant reinforcement, the addicted individual is not to be held responsible for this behavior in the sense that he or she is to be blamed for being chemically dependent. Thus, Marlatt and Gordon believe that their position on "responsibility" is very compatible with the same notion as viewed in the traditional disease concept. Table 2.1 presents an outline of the differences between the self-control model and the more traditional disease approach as outlined by Marlatt and Gordon. They suggest that the two models hold contrasting basic assumptions about the etiology and treatment of addiction problems on a number of levels, including an understanding of locus of control, treatment goal, treatment philosophy, and treatment procedures. Their model presents one additional fresh approach that may provide a broader and more harmonious perspective on the basic nature of addictive behaviors and how to treat them.

While Denzin (1987) has criticized the application of behavioral principles in understanding alcoholism, those who are interested in increasing the effectiveness of treatment programs for various types of chemical dependency may need to examine critically these concepts and ideas as a means of determining which of them will be appropriate for use in the treatment program. Actually, the diversity of models for understanding alcoholism and chemical dependency, which is sometimes seen as a cause for despair, may also be seen as a sign of healthy growth of the profession of chemical-dependency counseling. This diversity may have come about because individuals have had different experiences and have described those experiences in different ways. George and Cristiani (1990) point out that such differences might be compared to the fable of the blind men attempting to describe an elephant. One, touching the leg of the elephant, described it as a big tree trunk. Another, touching the body, described it as big like a house. A third, touching the tail, believed that the elephant was something like a long rope. And the fourth, who touched the elephant's trunk, described the elephant as being like a large fire hose.

Table 2.1   The Self-control and Disease Models: Alternative Approaches to the Treatment of Addictive Behaviors

TOPIC	SELF-CONTROL MODEL	DISEASE MODEL
Locus of Control	• Person is capable of self-control	• Person is a victim of forces beyond one's control
Treatment Goal	• Choice of goals: abstinence or moderation	• Abstinence is the only goal
Treatment Phi-losophy	• Fosters detachment of self from behavior • Educational approach	• Equates self with behavior • Medical/disease approach
Treatment Pro-cedures	• Teaching behavioral coping skills • Cognitive restructuring	• Confrontation & conversion • Group support • Cognitive dogma
General Approach to Addictions	• Search for commonalities across addictive behaviors • Addiction is based on maladaptive habits	• Each addiction is unique • Addiction is based on physiological processes
Examples	• Cognitive-behavioral therapy (outpatient) • Self-control programs • Controlled drinking programs	• Hospital treatment programs (inpatient) • Aversion treatment • AA + Synanon

Source: From *Relapse Prevention* by A. G. Marlatt and J. R. Gordon. 1985. New York: Guilford Press.

As different views of chemical dependency are clarified and integrated, professionals in the field will gain a more thorough, comprehensive view of the total, most effective means of counseling and treating drug abusers. This integration and understanding cannot come too quickly.

SUMMARY

Although chemical dependency has had clearly understood and recognized symptoms for centuries, there is still a lack of comprehension of how and why it occurs. While there are data to support a variety of explanations, the predominant theory describing the etiology, natural history, and consequences of the disorder is still the disease concept as described by

Jellinek. Supporters of this view point out that there is a specific set of signs and symptoms, that there are clear-cut stages or phases in the development of the disorder, and that there are specific drinking and using patterns that are characteristic of chemical dependency. In addition, chemical dependency includes a psychological dependence, an intense craving, a loss of control, and personality regression.

The importance of genetic and metabolic factors in chemical dependency has been identified. Likewise, an increasing emphasis on behavioral explanations has provided further understanding of the disorder. While these theories are generally in conflict with the disease model, they may eventually be seen as providing information that may enhance the disease model and develop into a comprehensive construct that more accurately describes the disorder and the variations among those who have become addicted.

3 ——

Codependency:
Characteristics and Treatment

Jill Symmonds-Mueth, M.A., M. Ed.

INTRODUCTION

There are many stereotypes of an alcoholic home: holes in the walls, empty liquor containers, a dirty and disheveled appearance all around. But alcoholism also hides behind starched chintz curtains, expensive interior decoration, and an apple pie baking in the oven.

Regardless of the appearance, one experiences an uneasiness in the home of a chemical dependent. "There was a tension so thick you could write your name in it," one grown daughter of an alcoholic father remarked about the uncomfortable, just-below-the-surface anxiety which permeated her home.

"I used to hate Sunday afternoons," recalls Tom*, a 37-year-old son of an alcoholic father and a Valium-dependent mother. "We would all be doing something around the house: watching television, studying, doing chores. But actually we would be more involved in watching each other out of the corners of our eyes. I couldn't really concentrate—no one could. The least little thing anyone did might trigger such hysteria that we were afraid to hardly make a move."

Chemical dependency affects all family members to varying degrees. In a violent and explosive atmosphere, children and spouses live with fear as the alcoholic or drug addict becomes increasingly abusive. In more passive family systems, members learn to live with punishing silence and withdrawal.

The events portrayed in this chapter are not found in every home. Chemical dependency is different within each family, and no two families or even members of the same family will demonstrate the same characteristics of the disease (Ackerman 1987). What is true, though, is that chemical dependency, whether it be in the form of alcoholism or other drug abuse, has a tremendous effect on the family. That effect also appears to escalate through the stages of chemical dependence until the family is as consumed with the chemically dependent person as the chemically dependent person is with drugs or alcohol.

As with chemical dependence, codependent family members follow predictable patterns of dysfunctional behavior as the drinking or drugging behavior progresses. Kinney and Leaton (1987) have outlined six stages of family response to alcoholism:

1. *Denial*—The problem does not exist, or, if it does, there are a number of logical explanations.

2. *Attempts to eliminate the problem* (also known as "bargaining")—There obviously is a problem, and the family is recognizing that drug use is not situational or normal. Pleading, bartering, and veiled threats may enter into the repertoire of defenses of the family. Such actions as pouring liquor down drains and flushing chemicals down toilets are common in this stage.

*The anecdotes reflect real individuals; the names used are fictional to respect confidentiality.

3. *Disorganization and chaos*—Balance in the family is gone. Finances may be deteriorating as the chemical dependent spends more of the family's resources on using. Children may be having full-blown trouble at school. The spouse may seek help on his or her own.

4. *Reorganizing in spite of the problem*—The spouse and children will mutually divide up the roles that the chemical dependent has in an attempt to get back to a normal family life. Consistent, conscientious efforts to "change" the addict are dropped as fruitless.

5. *Efforts to escape the system*—Family members may resort to geographic or emotional distancing. Separation or divorce may or may not occur. Children, if able, may opt to leave home.

6. *Family reorganization*—If divorce or separation occurs and the nonaddicted spouse retains custody of the children, then the chemically dependent member might not be present every day. If recovery has begun, the substance abuser has to be reintegrated into the family as a "different" member (i.e., as a sober person). This may cause conflict as family roles become reassigned and new boundaries are defined to accommodate this change in the existing system.

A family may become "stuck" in just one of these stages in a never-ending drama, or they may progress through all with amazing and heart-breaking speed. They may also vacillate on two or more of the stages, depending on the number of crises that arise.

THE FAMILY AS A SYSTEM

In the interconnected pain of chemical dependence, the chemical dependent is not the only symptom bearer within a family system. In order for the chemically dependent person to continue to drink or use drugs, a complicated pattern of behaviors—frequently called "enabling"—must begin for the rest of the family.

Enabling is that process of interactions and roles that the family takes on to lessen the pain caused by substance abuse. Wegscheider (1981), a therapist of chemical dependents and their families, sees enabling as a family process propagated through covert rules that allow the chemically dependent person to continue to use drugs. The members may say that there is nothing they truly want more than the person to stop drinking or using, but their behavior with the chemical dependent and with each other only covers up the abuse. Not surprisingly, this process does much more harm than good, in that it allows chemical dependency to continue and eventually escalate.

To illustrate: In order for the alcoholic mother to keep drinking, her husband must work and care for the children. If the children are old enough, they may take on the majority of the home responsibilities for the father so that he does not have quite so much to do when he gets home from work. "By the time I was 7, I could cook full meals, clean the house, and take care of my little brother," says Susan as she describes what "old enough" meant in her family.

Clearly Susan was "Daddy's little helper." As he explained to her, "Sometimes Mommy doesn't feel well all day and you can really do her and me a big favor by..." The list of "favors" grew with her years and pretty soon Susan was running the entire house.

As enabling gets into full swing the responsibilities of the chemical dependent dwindle more and more; the rest of the family take on those tasks exponentially. Eventually, the only real "job" the family will give the addict is to drink or use drugs. Not to be misleading, all families do not fall into such dire straits with a substance abuser in the home. There are many people, termed "functional," whose lives and the lives of whose families do not appear impaired by their use; financial hardship, employment jeopardization, or difficulties with the law have not occurred—and might not ever. This is not to say that the *quality* of all their lives is not suffering. Perhaps eventually the more serious consequences of their drug abuse might appear.

"It never dawned on me that my dad's drinking was the source of much of the unhappiness in our home. Everything looked great. We had plenty of money, his business just kept getting better every year, he never missed any days of work, we all did terrific at school and in the town we lived in. Everybody he knew thought he was the greatest, but to me, he was just a mean son-of-a-bitch. It just never hit me that it had anything to do with drinking since he was *always* drinking. Until he went into treatment, I don't think I ever knew him without some sort of booze in him," recalls 29-year-old Anthony.

An unspoken cooperative effort on the part of the family allows the drinker to keep on drinking, the drug addict to stay addicted. Fear of losing this familiar system, however painful and dysfunctional it may be, keeps the family locked into place.

It is here that the need for "homeostasis" is seen (Becvar & Becvar 1982, Okun & Rappaport 1980). While homeostasis is actually a biological term meaning a state of equilibrium produced by a balance of functions, there is no better definition of what goes on in the family. To put it another way, the family returns again and again to dysfunctional behavior, not because it is particularly comfortable, but because it is *familiar*. The members will unwittingly and unknowingly sabotage the actions of any member who attempts to break away from his or her accustomed role.

"In my family," tells Robert, a 19-year-old son of an alcoholic father, "the minute my father came home we were all on stage. My mom would be the worrier and none of us kids would dare upset her any more. This made my sister retreat to her room and my brother turn on the television. I did whatever needed to be done: fix dinner, help with homework, do housework. My littlest sister, though, would be the charmer. She would tell the most outlandish stories. It was amazing how she knew just the right time to do it, too!"

This is not so amazing after all: These children played predictable roles in their strict home. Robert's family, like many others, had a vested interest in keeping things going just the way they were. The family drama Robert alludes to happened just like clockwork when Dad walked through the door.

If recovery is sought, a new balance must be struck to regain a feeling of familial composure. However, it is not a simple matter of the chemical dependent just changing roles (dependent for sober). A whole new "person" is added about whom no one really knows much and, least of all, trusts. Many family members still see the ghost of an unpredictable and sometimes dangerous person in those with new-found sobriety.

What an extraordinary amount of effort on the part of all the members of the chemically dependent family! But it is familiar, and familiar is comfortable, even though we have seen that "comfortable" is a relative term. No one is willing, or has the knowledge, to "step out of the system" and refuse to participate (Becvar & Becvar 1982). Further elaboration of the roles in the system follows in this chapter.

THE RESPONSE TO CHEMICAL DEPENDENCE

The enabling that has been described in the previous sections is part of the larger picture of codependency. Just as the alcoholic or drug abuser is dependent on his or her drug of choice, the family is obsessed with the chemically dependent person (Steinglass, Tislenko, & Reiss 1985). Al-Anon (the organization of self-help for friends and families of chemically dependent persons) espouses the disease concept of codependency, using strategies similar to those of Alcoholics Anonymous. Their beliefs indicate that the chemical dependent is addicted to a drug and the codependent(s) is (are) addicted to the chemically dependent person.

Other theorists see codependency as "symbiosis" rather than a disease process (Brown 1988, Weiss & Weiss 1989). Codependents, in this theory, are seen as being stagnated at earlier developmental stages of life and are unable to proceed and disengage themselves from their chemically dependent and codependent family members. Their reactions to life situations are seen as "normal" (although impaired by adult standards) in light of very "abnormal" situations in their earlier lives.

Regardless of the theory of codependency, family members act in ways that are not in their best interests. Others in the substance abuser's life can (but perhaps with some regret) sever the ties with him or her and go on: A boss can find another employee, a friend can arrange to spend more time with others. But family members are caught in a debilitating bind. Depending on how long the dependency has been going on, the spouse and children will have a difficult time at best in gaining physical or emotional independence.

The spouse loves this person—or thought so at one time—and that knowledge is a powerful magnet in their dyad. The children are confused by the events that occur. They wonder (at their varied levels of comprehension) why things are not comfortable or even tolerable. They are the true victims of the impaired system, because they are not capable of going anywhere to escape.

"When I finally came to grips with the fact that my father's alcoholism had indeed played a part in the way I look at things today as an adult, I had several rude awakenings. The worst of which was that I was ten times more angry at my codependent mother than at my father. She had the ability to take us out of that situation and she chose not to because she didn't want us to be from a 'broken home.' Believe me, that would have been a joy compared to what we endured," remarked 30-year-old Janet.

The layers of denial peeled off, one by one, as Janet looked at herself. It was at a friend's suggestion that she examined her father's drinking. At first she scoffed, refusing to believe that her problems with that had not died with him some 10 years earlier. After attending several Adult Children of Alcoholics meetings (a branch of the Alcoholics Anonymous and Al-Anon organizations), all the years of turmoil surfaced and allowed her to see that nothing had really changed. She was still dealing with the world in the same ways she had when she was a child. She was still "reacting" to the chemical dependency instead of "acting" as a mature young woman. Janet's struggle is to be a long one. Others like her will discuss their struggles with recovery later in the chapter.

Other children grow up through their family's dysfunction and eventually become old enough to leave it by going to college, off to work, or marrying. They also find themselves ill-prepared to meet the real world. As is reported by this 45-year-old son of two alcoholic parents: "It was like I grew up in a foreign country. No one had taught me what I needed to get along in life. Since the time I left for college, I have spent so much time watching other people to see what 'adults' were supposed to act like. I am always asking myself, 'Is this normal?' Most times, I still don't know."

Denial

The first stage of codependency is that of denial. Denying that the chemical dependent is using as much as he or she does is a typical scenario. Coming home drunk at 8:00 P.M. will be interpreted as "He just stopped off for a drink after work and got to talking." There are few spouses who actually believe that "one drink" can have that much of an effect or time warp on their mate, but they nevertheless dismiss inebriation as situational or "just this once."

Denial for codependents goes through progressive stages. In all codependents it arises from the need to not have happening what is indeed happening. "I simply would not believe that my son was chemically dependent," says a 45-year-old mom at her third Al-Anon meeting. "No matter what I found in his room or in his pockets at laundry time, and no matter what his clothes smelled like on Saturday morning, I could not believe that my baby was capable of getting mixed up with drugs. We are a good family."

This need to appear happy and well-adjusted drives denial even further down. The 14-year-old sister of the addict just described says "He's my hero. I can't believe that those creeps he hangs around with put him up to this." She credited an unsavory group of teens with whom he had been spending time recently with his drastic change of behavior. And her speech reveals yet another face of denial: the willingness to project unfavorable behavior onto others rather than attribute it to the chemical dependent. Perhaps the popular discussion of "peer pressure" by parents and educators is more a manifestation of denial than any real temptation for healthy children to deviate from acceptable family norms (Kaufman & Borders 1984).

As the progression of denial goes further, entire sets of thinking can be discarded. People who have lived with a chemical dependent for a long time find it increasingly difficult to call up any feelings at all because they have shoved down the unpleasant ones for so long. Some of the earliest recovery for codependents is just the ability to feel a feeling—any one at all: joy, sorrow, anger—and to be able to connect it to themselves.

Most rationalizations offered by the drug abuser take the focus off him- or herself and put it elsewhere. The bitterness and hatred that the chemical dependent may feel internally can spew out in venomous accusations and comments toward family members. Codependents actually do begin to question themselves about the accuracy of their observations and statements regarding chemical use as they see it; some rationalizations of denial seem plausible, and repetition enhances them. They begin to believe the negative things the substance abuser is saying about them and start to question their core worth. After a prolonged period this perceived worthlessness causes them to deny the most important thing—that they are lovable, intelligent, people who deserve to take care of themselves.

Bargaining

Frequently bargaining is just as unhealthy as denial, but it does shake up the system. In order to bargain—or, as Kinney and Leaton (1987) put it, "attempt to eliminate the problem"—one must see an actual problem to begin with and believe that one has the power to solve it. The chemical dependent is confronted with the charge that his or her drinking or drug use is out of hand and that something has to be done. What that something is is anybody's guess as families struggle again and again with the best solution. Spouses put on pressure to cut down on drinking, stop associating with known abusers, and strike other bargains of reciprocal favors in attempts to eliminate the increasingly frequent out-of-control substance abuse.

Whether they believe it or not, the mate of a chemical dependent might first offer that he or she doesn't believe chemicals are causing the family problems. They may revert back to denial ("Chemicals really aren't the problem") or to manipulation ("Even though I'm lying, I'll tell him that booze isn't the problem") in an effort to get the chemical dependent to some sort of therapy. The sober spouse feels so impotent and unimportant that he or she believes the actual message has to come from someone else in a position of authority (counselor, clergy, social services) before the dependent person will seek help. The abuser attempts, at least on the surface, to convince the codependent that the codependent is crazy—that therapists are for crazy people. If the chemical dependent *does* agree to go to therapy, a real dilemma develops for the spouse: If he or she has manipulated the chemical dependent to get some therapy to talk about "the kids" or "the marriage," then how will he or she raise the question of drug abuse without outwardly betraying the mate? If it is blatant, there is a chance that the chemical dependent will flee in an attempt to remain with the chemicals. A lot of sober spouses go into therapy with crossed fingers—with hope that the therapist will be sharp enough to see the problem as it is without it being verbally spelled out. The real tragedy is that if the therapist is not clued in, either by information or by clinical insight that chemical dependency is the problem, therapy becomes yet another smokescreen for the drug abuser. "See, I went to therapy like you wanted, and nothing has changed. You're the one that needs help. Now just leave me alone." (In other words, "I've held up my end of the bargain.")

Again, another double-bind becomes evident. If the therapist is knowledgeable about chemical dependency, and questions drinking or drug abuse, then the chemical dependent can accuse the codependent of "telling lies." Once more, therapy becomes abortive. From this discussion it should be apparent that knowledge of chemical dependency and the codependent family system is of utmost importance in a therapist's repertoire of skills.

Disorganization and Dysfunction

A great deal of denial and bargaining can be intertwined with the next phases of the breakdown of the chemically dependent system. It is in this phase of disorganization and dysfunction that the ever-sought-after homeostasis is disappearing. It is harder and harder for the family and the chemical dependent to maintain the image that all is well. The crises are coming closer together, and the spouse spends most of his or her time "putting out fires," which may include financial problems, trouble with the authorities, loss of employment, and difficulties with the children in school.

FINANCIAL TROUBLES

Money may become a real issue, with less and less to spend on living expenses and more being drawn out for chemical use. The spouse who is not working or has a less than adequate job may have to resort to many avenues just to get the bills paid. An extra part-time job, borrowing from institutions, friends, and family, or even withdrawing money from children's accounts are not uncommon behaviors.

"I always knew how bad things were if I came home from school and we didn't have electricity or phone service. I used to dread the end of the month because that's when the disconnections happened. I thought we were rich when three months passed with lights, phone, and gas all working at the same time!"—Rosalie, a 31-year-old daughter of two alcoholic parents recalls.

She continues, "I never told my friends that my baby-sitting money usually disappeared. They got to use theirs for spending money, but I lied and told them that my parents were very strict and made me save all mine. It got to be that I'd just hand it over so my mom wouldn't have to worry so much. She'd give me these IOUs, but we both really knew that she could never pay me back."

LEGAL DIFFICULTIES

Trouble with the law also characterizes this Disorganization and Dysfunction phase with some chemical dependents. Much time may be spent processing "Driving Under the Influence" (DUI) charges. Families can be caught in a seemingly endless cycle of bail and bond. Again, financial difficulties surface here, with the exorbitant expense of legal fees and court costs for the chemical dependent. Those family members still in denial will rationalize that it is best to spend their money on a "smart lawyer" to get their chemical dependent out of jail and out of a suspended license. The charges are sometimes dropped or reduced to "Careless and Imprudent Driving," and the substance abuser is out on the road again to either kill or be killed. Two or three DUI citations reduced to this lesser charge are not uncommon for the chronically chemically dependent—moreso, if the family is in an upper socioeconomic level.

Once again, one sees that the family is reacting to the chemical dependency without stepping out of the system. Such a step out would be to leave the chemical dependent in jail, or at least make bail contingent on immediate evaluation by a substance-abuse clinic. This will be discussed more fully in the treatment section of this chapter.

EMPLOYMENT PROBLEMS

The chemical dependent may lose his or her job because of excessive tardiness, absence, or ineffectiveness. A string of jobs may make the substance abuser unemployable, which further feeds his or her sense of guilt and worthlessness. The family may enable this by working harder themselves, getting extra jobs, and all "chipping in" to see that the bills get paid.

If the chemical dependent maintains employment, it may be because the spouse or the children will again enable him or her by calling in sick for the abuser or making excuses to bosses and co-workers. Once again, they deny that a worse problem than a lost job is the chemical dependence that allowed it to happen.

Some persons are also very functional despite their chemical dependence; they never lose, or worry about losing, their employment. This is sometimes the most confusing of all to the family, as witnessed by Cindy, a 32-year-old recovering child of an alcoholic father:

"My dad is probably the most functional alcoholic in the world. Not only has he never lost employment, he has never even missed a day of work. All the while we were growing up he would use this against my mother in an endless game of logic. In the end, by some twist, she would have to admit that if he truly had a drinking problem the prestigious company for whom he worked would not only not have hired him in the first place, but would not see fit to keep advancing him as the years passed. He eventually died of his disease, and I wonder about this today. Was he truly so brilliant that his alcohol consumption made no difference in the quality of his work? Maybe his associates and clients liked him because of all his drinking and entertaining! Did the company keep elevating him to positions of greater importance because they were reluctant to call him on his drinking behavior? I guess I will never really know the answers to these questions, but I do know that he could have been a much better father and husband if he had not been a chronic alcoholic. And I might have been a much better daughter."

PROBLEMS AT SCHOOL

This phase of substance abuse and codependency is truly brutal for children. Unable to concentrate, they may find themselves, although bright, unable to make passing grades. The most stalwart and intelligent of children may have difficulty working up to potential when they wrestle with incomprehensible anxiety. The mere thought of leaving home each day unsure of what will happen while away, a dread of unexpected disasters waiting at home, and a pervasive and free-floating anxiety are but a few examples of the internal conflicts that beset these children.

That same nameless anxiety can drive other children of chemical dependents to excellence. Afraid of letting their guards down, or even of making a "B," these youngsters' school work garners glowing reports from teachers.

"It was my job to do well in school," remarks a 30-year-old engineer with a bright future. "No one would ever suspect anything could be wrong at our house if I was bringing home all 'A's,' or participating in every team sport, club, or organization. The truth was, it gave me a good chance to get out of the house a lot. I have a tough time saying 'no' to anyone."

While this young man obviously didn't have time for disciplinary problems, they are characteristic of other children (Reilly 1984). The inability to concentrate mentioned earlier and failing grades may result in an "I don't care" attitude that leads to a vicious cycle. A chemically dependent parent who pays little attention and a distracted sober parent who may do even less thus seal the fate of these youngsters academically. If attention cannot be gotten from teachers, parents, or peers with excellence, then acting-out behavior will do the trick. These children become virtual maestros of disobedience in an effort to be noticed for something.

Still again there are children of chemically dependent families who become school problems in exactly the opposite way. These are the kids who are so shy and withdrawn that they literally wish to slip through the woodwork. For them, school is an excruciatingly social experience which at any time might flag something as wrong at home. These "lost children" plod along as best they can with few friends and little interaction in the classroom.

Most children in the school setting do not fall into such neat categories; they combine all the characteristics. What the codependent children do have in common, though, is a fierce and overwhelming desire to appear "normal," even if they have not the foggiest idea what that is.

"Once I stepped on that schoolbus, I was determined that no one would know what had happened the night before at my house," said Judy, 28. "It was only this year that my best friend told me that she had known all along! For 18 years I thought I had done such a good job!"

Above all, the family secret must be kept. Anger is easily aroused in either parents or siblings when a child dares to expose the dysfunction. If the family is in true denial about the chemical dependency, then last night's bloody argument, Susie's withdrawn nature, or Bobby's fight in the lunchroom will appear unrelated. Other exhausted, worried parents will be overly harsh or critical of teachers and administrators in efforts to protect their family from "outside harm."

It takes skilled and educated teachers to recognize the varied faces of codependency: the brave scholar-athlete, the patience-trying scapegoat, the disappearing wallflower, the standup comic. Perhaps what is needed most in our educational institutions is the consistent caring that may win these children's confidence so that they may recognize a resource for help (Ackerman 1983). Ability to detect and deal with the children of chemical dependents is a must for a school counselor. Many excellent resources are available today to help enlighten both the educator and counselor.

Reorganization

Homeostasis is the strongest of forces. When all the props are knocked from beneath the chemically dependent family, there are frantic attempts to get back into balance. This leads to the next phase of codependency, which can aptly be called Reorganization with new roles.

These new roles that the family members find themselves conforming to appear very gradually. Situation by situation, the spouse and children are molded into actions and reactions that are characterized by the following descriptions (Wegscheider 1981):

Chief enabler—usually the spouse of the chemically dependent person, and may be chemically dependent as well. This individual has a vested interest in and is charged with keeping status quo regardless of the level of pain.

Hero—usually the oldest child. He or she takes responsibility for the family's outward appearance to others and for maintenance of as near-normal functioning as possible within the family.

Scapegoat—usually a middle child. He or she is constantly getting into minor or major trouble. This child serves to take the focus off the problems in the system and the chemical dependent.

Lost child—typically a middle or youngest child. He or she seems to disappear into the woodwork. Along with the hero, this child serves as a foil to the scapegoat.

Mascot—usually the youngest child. Constant displayer of humor or jest. May also be the eternally ill or frail child. He or she takes the focus off the system and its gravity.

Before more thorough discussion of these thumbnail sketches, it is important to understand that there are no true characters in a chemically dependent family. The hero will have characteristics of the mascot at times. The lost child may alternate with the scapegoat, depending on the number of crises generated by the system. The chief enabler is called "chief" because, while the others are certainly enabling the chemical dependent, he or she may be considered a costar. Any of the birth-order children will serve as the chief enabler if there is not another parent or if the other parent is acting out one of the other roles. If a child is the chemical dependent, then there may be more than one chief enabler, depending on parenting styles.

There may certainly be more than one of any of the roles in a given family. "In my family of eight children," says the 30-year-old daughter of a chemically dependent mother, "we had one real hero, one real scapegoat (who eventually became chemically dependent), and all the rest of us were lost children. Nobody even knew we existed except when everybody had to be fed."

She did recognize that in her subsystem of lost children there was a hero (herself) and a mascot. There was too much competition in the bigger family for the lost-child hero to compete with the actual one. The lost-child mascot only felt safe enough to be funny with his siblings, with whom he commiserated. The kind of humor she said she noted in that youngest brother was shared only rarely and only with a few. He was much too threatened to ever expose any of his real self to the entirety.

THE CHIEF ENABLER

The chief enabler is usually the spouse of the chemical dependent. More often than not it is a woman, although an increasingly large number of females are being treated for chemical dependence, which places their abstinent or social-drinking husbands in the role.

Characteristics of the chief enabler include excessive worry, guilt, intense need for control of all situations, and low self-esteem (Wegscheider 1981; Steinglass, Bennett, Wolin, & Reiss 1987). Fear seems to be the overriding factor that guides thoughts and actions. Fear that the situation will continue as it is—or, even worse, escalate—does not allow chief enablers the luxury of not participating in the system.

The planning and rescuing go on ad infinitum—"What will happen if he gets arrested? I will just go pick him up." "What will happen if the bills are not paid? I will just go borrow the money." "What embarrassment she will cause at the school play! We just will not go. Janie will understand." The well-meaning lies, the calculated deception, the planning aimed at survival, are endless in the lives of chief enablers.

It is not as if this person deliberately sets out to do these things; enabling is a debilitating loss of self. Little by little, the sober spouse takes responsibility for everything—including the chemical dependent's own right to "hit bottom" and find help. It is all done through love, or devotion, or preservation of the family and does not on the surface look harmful. The chief enabler takes control.

With the chief enabler in charge, feelings are often taken away from the children in the family. Denial of the problems caused by excessive chemical use does not allow fear, anger, confusion, or doubt to be expressed. These feelings are driven deeper and deeper into the members until retrieving them is almost impossible.

"My mom would ask me how things were at school," reported 28-year-old Marcie. "But all she wanted to hear was the good stuff, so that's all I told her—even if it meant lying. She nor I never stopped to pay attention to the fact that adolescence was a horrible time for me. I knew it was not all right for me to tell her what emotional troubles I was having for fear she would think it had everything to do with Daddy's drinking."

This example shows that natural family developmental stages are masked by codependency and chemical dependency. The struggles associated with mid-life transitions are often exacerbated by the normal problems of adolescence (Hansen & Liddle 1983). Most parents experience a considerable degree of tension as their teens wrestle with their own search for independence, while they themselves are attempting to take stock of their own lives. This, however painful, is an entirely natural process in families developing through time together (Okun & Rappaport 1980, Hansen & Liddle 1983). Add to that the insurmountable problems that active substance abuse and codependency inflame, and the home becomes a powderkeg.

The chief enabler is so concerned with the family running as smoothly as possible (with no violent outbursts of affect) that normally stormy times are hidden. The essential preparation for independence done by younger adolescents and the necessary leave-taking done by young adults is never addressed.

"My mom acted like I was a traitor when I finally left for college," remembers 20-year-old Jeff. "She made me feel like I was abandoning the ship! My friends' parents weren't having such a hard time with their kids leaving—like it was something that everybody normal did. Me, I didn't know what 'normal' was. And what was even scarier, I knew my mom didn't either."

Adolescence and the launching of older children from the home are indeed normal crises in the lives of families. That is not to say that they are not troublesome for all. No parent or child truly remains unaffected. However, for the chief enabler, this seems to be a particularly horrific time. He or she is facing mid-life stressors at the same time that the children are needing support in their own growing up and growing out struggles (Scarf 1987). Dealing with the throes of the adolescent rebellion of the scapegoat or the desertion of the family by the talented hero is sometimes more than can be tolerated. Without the help of a spouse or a great support system outside the home, many chief enablers find themselves not knowing which way to turn. They may arbitrarily and angrily lash out, creating an artificial confrontation that allows the children a "justification" to leave home. It is easier to separate in anger than to go through a natural grieving process that allows people to be emotionally closer to each other. When both children and parents have spent their entire lives not acknowledging feelings, much less discussing them, this appears to be the most viable option.

"I will never forget the day I moved out of my parents' house to start my first official job. I needed some help moving and it was done in stony silence. I got to thinking after they had left how weird it had been, especially with my mom. Here I was so excited and so scared about everything and I couldn't even talk about it. For months I had wanted to share my fear of actually graduating and becoming responsible to an employer. I had to do most of my sharing about previous job interviews with a friend, and I was angry that I could not do that with my mom. Everybody else was! It was like in her mind, if we never talked about it, it just wouldn't happen," recalls Peggy, the 28-year-old daughter of a chemically dependent father and a codependent mother.

Another young adult remembers a similar situation: "My [codependent] mom started on Valium about the time we all hit high school. It was different at first, her being calm instead of screaming. My [alcoholic] dad was pretty uninvolved—actually, that's quite an understatement. Anyway, when my oldest sister left for college we all thought my mom would freak out. But she didn't—I think she just took more Valium. My sister was pretty hurt that no one seemed to notice her [being] gone. Of course, I may be wrong, because we never talked about it."

With such a bleak picture painted of the chief enabler, one would not think that there were any positives. Although enabling has its emotional, physical, spiritual, and mental drawbacks, it also has "rewards" (Rothberg 1986, Wegscheider 1981):

Control—The chief enabler, particularly if not a drug abuser, is in complete control of all situations, dominating the spouse and the children. Everything that is thought, said, felt, or done (except chemical use) runs through the chief enabler, like messages through a switchboard. Being the head of the house is indeed a powerful feeling. Everything runs much more smoothly when one person is in charge of everything—and everybody.

Capability—Although it is a very expensive way to get approval, the chief enabler has everyone in awe of how he or she runs the household, holds down a job, takes care of the children, and still stays married to the chemical dependent. For the chief enabler, being a martyr is one way to get recognition. True skills may go unnoticed by everyone, including the chief enabler, in his or her effort to keep the balancing act of codependency afloat.

Powerfulness—Feelings of watching a SuperMom or SuperDad are evoked in observing a classic chief enabler. He or she sends the erroneous verbal and nonverbal message to the substance abuser and the codependent children, "Never fear! I am here!—I'll fix it! I'll get it all accomplished!"

Because of the strengths of the chief enabler, the drug abuser is given "permission" to be chemically dependent, shielded from the reality of the drinking or drugging world. Bills will be paid, children will be cared for, bosses will be appeased. What a relief!

To the children, the chief enabler is the all-protecting cloak. They don't have to (and are not allowed to) feel, think, or act for themselves. Situations are handled effortlessly by someone else, so there is no desire to act alone. There is a catch here, though. While children may feel safer having Mom or Dad think and feel for them, nascent and undeniable needs to feel, think, act, and react keep cropping up. The powerfulness of the sober parent versus these undeniable human strivings is frequently a subject for the offsprings' internal battles.

Add to that the children's own observations of others in the world (peers, neighbors, etc.), taking responsibility for their own feelings and actions creates a terrible double-bind. How can one emotionally desert the parent who many times has literally sheltered one from harm in order to be an individual? The chief enabler will use this knowledge consciously or unconsciously to maintain a well-meaning but suffocating hold on the system.

On the other hand, the life of the chief enabler is far from rosy. Things have to become immensely intolerable before he or she will get the help the family so desperately needs. Usually it is begun by some sort of major disaster (or a series of relentless smaller ones) that upsets the system enough to let in a little light. The level of stress that this person is used to functioning in would be enough to put anyone in the grave—and often it does just that.

In addition to the extreme sense of overresponsibility already discussed, one may also see other characteristics of chief enablers. He or she may wear the face of the distraught martyr who will spill all to anyone who cares to listen, but rejects all suggestions or help. At the base of this is a real fear of change.

The chief enabler is also prone to hypochondriasis in an effort to be noticed. On the other side of the coin are real physical ailments (stress-related and otherwise) frequently ignored in an effort to keep doing what needs to be done.

"Tremendously angry" is yet another way that this codependent might be described by others (Reilly 1984). What is frightening is to know that however composed the person is on the surface, a volcano of rage exists underneath.

THE HERO

Typically the role of hero is usually assumed by the oldest child in the family. Characteristically, the hero feels protective toward the younger siblings and the sober parent, and so maintains the posture of family "savior."

Many of the same traits that are found in the chief enabler appear in the hero. The need for control and the willingness to take it, the demonstration of extraordinary capability, and the self-inflicted responsibility to be larger than life allows the hero to take on any and all problems that arise. It is no wonder that the chief enabler and the hero frequently have such a close relationship. That is not to say that it cannot be adversarial; fierce competition can erupt when each tries to solve dilemmas in his or her own way.

If the chemically dependent parent is out of the routine decision-making process of everyday living, then a cross-generational alliance can occur (Minuchin 1974). In this coalition, a parent and a child band together to make decisions about the rest of the family, rather than there being one strong and separate parental unit doing so (Haley 1973, Minuchin 1974, Haley 1976). The chemically dependent "absent" parent becomes a child at best, a guest at worst, isolating and withdrawing from most family activities.

This crossing of generational boundaries presents some real problems for the hero in later life. The adult responsibilities too soon expected and assumed rob him or her of childhood. However, it is not to be denied that a great sense of self-esteem rises out of the knowledge that the hero is counted on so much and that the rest of the family looks to that individual for approval. The outside praise that the hero receives for being "the best" at school, sports, or community activities also allows him or her to mask the painful inadequacies really felt. For, in the end, he or she is powerless over the chemical dependency, and guilt for that is abundant.

Heroes give an outward appearance that all is well with the family. It is their express duty to look good and to promote the myth of health for consumption by friends, family, school, and neighborhood.

"I never knew what to say to friends and neighbors after the police would come to pick up my brother for dealing dope. The lights would be flashing and the people peering out of their windows to see yet again what was going on. There's only so many times I could make the excuse of 'traffic tickets' or 'questioning him about another friend.' Inside I felt sick, embarrassed, and utterly furious. Thinking back, my best grades seemed to happen right after these episodes. I guess I thought I had to try anything to make the family look good," recalls David, a 30-year-old hero in recovery for codependence.

Winning outside approval is time consuming. Heroes have little left over for deep contemplation of the real situation at home. That sad striving to prove something to others eventually becomes the hero's only way to feel good. Heroes become familiar and comfortable at too early an age with perfectionism, forever giving in to the need to do something perfectly in order to feel accepted.

Heroes are frequently described by other siblings as "bossy." While there may be times when the younger brothers and sisters welcome the protective arm of this "pseudo-parent," more often than not they resent him or her. This resentment is not reserved strictly for the hero, but is spread to the parents, as well, because of the inadequate rearing they are getting from another child.

Later in life, the hero may mourn his or her lost childhood, realizing that it has been skipped over entirely. There seems to be an overall pervasive rigidity to all they do and an absolute inability to have fun. It is not unusual therapy for a hero-adult to be given such tasks as playing on a playground, buying a favorite stuffed animal, or allowing themselves to really cry about hurt feelings.

Heroes may fall prey to the same physical and psychosomatic illnesses that befall the chief enabler. Overextension of mind and body in an attempt to meet all the needs of everyone causes them to neglect their own needs for food, sleep, and exercise. Resistance to disease and emotional disability are lowered as they struggle to use denial in a different way. This time, the denial is not about the substance abuse itself or even the family system, but rather that, being superhuman, they simply do not need basic care. This may be further reinforced by the family, who has the same denial.

"Once when I was 13, I went a week with a toothache so bad I just cried all the time. My mom would say, 'Just take some aspirin. It can't be that bad.' I thought I was just being a crybaby. Well, I took so much aspirin, it eventually caused a temporary hearing loss. When she finally took me to the dentist, major damage had set in and I needed to have a lot of dental work. But, I was so glad to finally be out of pain that I forgot, or maybe actually didn't even know, that I had a right to be angry. That is until about two years ago."

These are the words of a 32-year-old woman who is in treatment for codependency. She also remembered that horrible sore throats, colds, and other childhood diseases were never seen by a doctor. "It will be better tomorrow," was the constant watchword of her codependent mother. It is no wonder that she as a hero-adult has to exert conscientious effort to receive regular medical and dental care. What she also remembers was not wanting to be "less" than her chief-enabler mother, who also suffered through illnesses without medical attention. Thus the symbiotic and dysfunctional union of the hero and the chief enabler is evidenced with this pair in their denial of natural physical frailties.

THE SCAPEGOAT

Many families who seek therapy do so for a reason other than the chemical dependent. The scapegoat plays a very important, but personally painful, part in the system. It is this child who unwittingly becomes the "identified patient" rather than the chemical dependent or any number of other codependents in the family. While the rest of the members may be doing things that are just as unhealthy, the scapegoat tends to step outside societal norms too often. These are the children who may be constantly in trouble at school, in the community, and probably with the law.

Scapegoats are usually male and a middle child (Wegscheider 1981). It appears that the first born, whether male or female, usually becomes a hero, and the last born, regardless of sex, becomes a mascot or placater. A great deal of positive attention is given to these two roles, and so acting-out behavior is sought by a middle child to achieve the same end. "Attention is attention is attention," whether it be negative or positive. If a child cannot get it for being funny or responsible, then the other avenue open is to be the worst that one can be. And scapegoats are most assuredly that!

Constant calls from school administrators, the local police, or parents of peers keep the family ever moving from one disaster to another with this child. This person, instead of being chastised, should be given congratulations for the marvelous job they are doing on behalf of the family (Haley 1980). They are taking over the focus of the family pain! Everyone has all but stopped thinking about and reacting to the chemical dependent. They now have a new place to concentrate their attention—this rotten kid who can't stay out of trouble and "causes such worry."

"My mom didn't cause half the trouble that my brother did when we were growing up. At least she stayed at home when she was drunk. My brother was everywhere and into everything. We would just hold our breath on a Saturday night when the phone rang, wondering what he was up to now. It took me a much longer time to get over the anger I had for my brother's behavior than for my mom's booze and pills."

What this now 27-year-old hero of the family did not know about his seemingly worthless brother was that he loved his mother more than anyone knew and would willingly, time and time again, take the heat for her. What he also did not recognize was that the worst of times for his brother well paralleled the most severe for their mother. An intricate and well-orchestrated dance was taking place all those years between the mother and the scapegoat. When the mom's use of chemicals and alcohol escalated, she was saved by an equal amount of acting-out frenzy by her scapegoat son. All of this was done nonverbally and completely unbeknownst to either party or to the rest of the family, who served in their own right to keep it all going.

Many scapegoats are very familiar with the legal system by the time they reach adolescence. Statistics for juvenile offenders reared in chemically dependent homes indicate that by the time they reach the teen years, these children are "twice as likely to receive a psychiatric diagnosis for recidivist behavior than their more compliant counterparts" (Goodwin 1976). The "recidivist" diagnosis is a form of therapy in that the scapegoats are at least recognized as having problems, even if the real cause is not actually suspected.

Another symptom that this child is directly in line for is that of chemical dependency (Steinglass et al. 1987; Clair & Genest 1987; Jurich, Polson, Jurich, & Bates 1985; Reilly 1984; Wegscheider 1981). Since this person seeks his or her recognition outside the family, he or she becomes an easy target for use and abuse of chemicals with peers—many of whom are acting out their own scapegoat roles. This child finds out all too soon that substances dull the pain of home and make it easier to relate. They may have assembled their friends in a sort of "family" since they feel so unloved in their own nuclear one.

They often have isolationist tendencies in spite of their bravado, and the chemicals make the insecurities they feel and the inadequacies they have projected onto themselves disappear. Either sex may become chemically dependent or sexually promiscuous. Accidental death or suicide may result from their daredevil attitude and total conviction of their lack of worth.

The scapegoat and the hero are paradoxically the most interchangeable of all the roles. While it would appear at first blush that the "truly good" and the "truly bad" natures of these people would not be so compatible, it is.

Since the hero is usually the first born, if he or she leaves the family often sees it as a betrayal, regardless of the reason. The scapegoat is directly in line to step into the abandoned shoes. The family naturally has a different reaction to this "new" person—usually favorable. The scapegoat now has no one with whom to compete for positive attention, thus making it easier to become the new savior of the family. The ousted hero cannot regain his or her former position, and is treated as the new black sheep of the family. For a number of heroes, it is the first time that they have tasted freedom without undue responsibility for others. This tempts them to act out more, thus fulfilling the piece of the family system that has longed for a new scapegoat. The system is once more complete, but with a slightly different cast. Homeostasis is once more regained and the family is unhappily "happy" once again.

The scapegoat is hard evidence that such families cannot be treated in therapy individually with any expectation of cohesive results. If ever there was a reason to treat an entire family, it is here, with this child creating the presenting problem. His or her behavior, almost without exception, is the result of an unhealthy family system rather than recidivist actions grounded in nothing. If treated individually in therapy, the problems do not disappear, they just change focus. Someone else in the family will step in to renew the lost chaos and once again the microscope will be off of the chemically dependent person.

THE LOST CHILD

A number of members are now participating in the family problems surrounding chemical dependency. The substance abuser is busy with drink or drugs; the chief enabler is occupied with expertly coping; the hero is consumed with achievement-oriented behavior; the scapegoat is busy absorbing the dysfunction of the family through deviant behavior. Enter a new character, who seems destined to be lost in the crowd. That is exactly what happens. This is the role of the lost child, and it is occupied primarily by children who come later in the birth order (Wegscheider 1981).

This role can be compared to the feeling one gets upon arriving in the middle of a joke. Unless a person is terribly bright (or has heard it before), it is difficult to reassemble the set-up to make sense of the punchline. In the case of the lost child, no one rushes in to make sure he or she is understanding what has transpired up to the point of this individual's arrival. The family secrets are extremely well guarded, and the last thing that will happen is an in-depth explanation of the problems that have already occurred. The family, through denial, is lost about what is transpiring anyway, so it is not just a matter of not telling for the sake of not telling. By the time the lost child comes into view, many patterns have emerged, crystallized, and hardened into the cement that binds the family together in dysfunction.

This role is not as specific in its purpose as are those of the chief enabler, the hero, or the scapegoat. This is not to say that lost children do not play a part in enabling the chemical dependent—quite the contrary. It is their withdrawn and disappearing nature that allows both the chemical dependent and other members of the family to think that the drinking or drugging is not as far-reaching as it is. Because people rarely see the lost child, it is easier to think that substance abuse is not harming him or her. We see then that this role, however innocuous it appears to others, is just as responsible for the preservation of the drug abuse.

There are some identifiable characteristics that lost children share. A reclusive personality and an inability to deal with social situations typify these people all through their lives. A sense of being unloved pushes them into a feeling of being responsible for the whole painful system in the home. Another trait may involve a tendency to be overindulgent, leading later in life to their becoming chemical dependents, overeaters, or both. A fierce independence and seriousness of nature is also seen in these little ones who allow parents to believe that they need scarcely any rearing. Finally, an inability to recognize either true potential or problems is fairly common.

To look at a lost child, one might believe that he or she is practically nonexistent. These children would literally love to disappear into the woodwork to avoid any type of interaction with others. They find solace in their own company because it is ignored in the larger nuclear family, and find themselves playing alone more often than not. At a younger age many of them have imaginary friends with whom they do everything. They often are creative individuals, given their propensity to be alone and their need to manufacture satisfaction for themselves.

As a result of their reclusive personalities and withdrawn natures, lost children demonstrate a remarkable lack of social knowledge that follows them throughout their lives. "To this day I have many problems associated with people and how I should act around them," says one identified lost child, now 31. "My parents never had what one might call social friends. My father had his drinking buddies and my mom chose to never socialize, so I did not know how to be a friend. Instead, I spent most of my growing up being afraid of other children, even if they were nice and seemed to like me. My mom never trusted anyone and I think that rubbed off on me. Now as an adult, I frequently make excuses to get out of social situations. I absolutely cannot 'small talk.' Thank God I found my wife, who prefers to stay at home with me and hates those cocktail party encounters as much as I do."

It is indeed fortunate that there are lost children to marry other lost children. This young man not only sought out but married a person who was comfortable with the same behaviors with which he grew up. A way of permanently assuring that his introverted nature could continue was thus sealed in the bonds of matrimony. His wife, not strangely at all, had a very similar background. What a sense of acceptance and belonging they filled in each other after all those terrible years of being lost!

A rather fierce independence may become part of the lost-child personality; they are frequently capable of taking care of themselves at a very young age. Tragically, no one offers to take that away from them. The chief enabler is so caught up in the very obvious dramas that are being put on by the chemical dependent and the scapegoat that a child who requires very little care taking is a blessing. Unfortunately, one cannot rear oneself adequately and so needs—emotional, physical, psychological—go badly unmet. They may as adults appear to be surviving quite nicely, still requiring little from others. It is here, though, that they frequently become frozen—surviving, but not really living.

These children are often prone to self-absorption and overindulgences. They may use food to stuff down their pent-up emotions and loneliness and are prone to weight problems. As adults, they are also subject to chemical abuse in a search for more sophisticated or longer-lasting ways to deal with their solitude. Drug use may also be an easier way for them to grapple with the problems of social acceptability. Overspending may also haunt these children-turned-adults in later life, as they purchase items not because they think they deserve them but because of a need to remedy the past.

Always fearful of what might happen, these little ones are in constant search of somewhere to hide when the fireworks start. The sad thing is that even when there are good interactions in the family or in the classroom, their internal unavailability closes them to the chance of making a connection.

These children are subject to illnesses (psychosomatic or real), as are heroes and chief enablers, but for different reasons (Wegscheider 1981). Frequently ignored by parents, being ill or "accident prone" forces a bit of individual attention that all children crave regardless of birth order or their role in the system. The scapegoat finds getting that attention more palatable in a negative way, the hero through achievement and perfection, but the lost child is unable to compete in either of these arenas. A lot of trips to the emergency room, even if physically painful, is still time that does not threaten to get lost in the shuffle of other people's needs. While this might seem like drastic action for a child to take in order to get his or her parents' time, one must remember that it may not be entirely volitional.

An overdeveloped sense of personal responsibility surfaces in the lost child. While this characteristic is most commonly found in the hero, it is for different reasons. The hero fervently tries to control outcomes so that logical and natural consequences do or do not occur. He or she then feels responsible for either the wanted or the unwanted outcome. The lost child may take the nonverbal "rottenness" of the situation and ascribe it to his or her own personality. Because of a pervasive feeling of being unloved and ignored, lost children begin to believe that *they* are the reason bad things are happening in the home. Just as no one rushes in to rear them, no one bothers to sense that here is a child who is feeling terrible about himself or herself. When one spends the majority of one's time tucked away in a safe place, it is difficult for others to gauge something to be troubling.

The difference in the perceptions concerning responsibility lies in the presence or absence of validation from others. The hero has been acknowledged for his or her many capabilities—indeed this person's very role in the family lies in doing things well or outwardly appearing acceptable to others. Even the contempt shown to scapegoats for terrible behavior acknowledges their legitimate place in the family. The only thing the lost child receives is the very clear message that whatever he or she does is inconsequential because there are other problems with which to contend. That total lack of validation—even acknowledgment of being a person—is readily absorbed into the lost child's ephemeral self-concept. The result is a child who desires to be alone, preferring it to rejection, and who willingly will take the sickness of the system and ascribe it to himself or herself without a verbal complaint.

Lost children may also be recognized by their seriousness. Lowered self-esteem, reinforced by little positive regard from others in the family, does not allow them to relinquish their inner grasp of responsibility. At a young age this is pretty serious business to contemplate, much less internalize. Lost children learn their social knowledge from substandard models and many times suffer the consequences with peers. After just a few painful encounters, attempts may cease, leaving him or her content to stay on the sidelines, internally wishing that things could be different.

Just as with the other roles, lost children appear to be stuck in their particular groove, unable to move right or left. Therapists have a difficult time helping these clients to realize their true potential because they have run away from themselves for so long. It is also hard for these clients to believe that they even have a potential worth exploring after all the years of self-deprecation. On the other side is the lost child's reluctance to see problems as truly severe. Denial is most frequently used by these children who, being absent in mind or body, don't allow themselves to believe the seriousness of the dynamics of the chemically dependent home. Later in life, they may spend the greater part of therapy bringing to the surface knowledge and feelings intricately buried. Andrea, a 20-year-old lost child, observes:

"It seems like I will never be over this. In some ways I wish I had never come into therapy. If I hadn't, I never really would have known how lonely and unloved I felt as a child. But I guess it has been a real gift, too. I now have a couple of true friends because I have been able to show them all the parts of myself that I have come to understand. I *do* things differently now because of therapy. The pain is still there but I have to trust that it will not always be."

THE MASCOT

Everyone knows a mascot. He or she is the funniest person at the party, the one who knows just when to add a bit of levity to a serious conversation, and the one who is frequently the most irreverent. All this masks the very real pain inside that is born from being raised in a chemically dependent home.

Of course, it would be erroneous and simplistic to believe that everyone who shares these entertaining characteristics is necessarily a relative of a chemically dependent family. However, these have been identified as being most prevalent in those children and children-turned-adults who held the place known as the mascot in dysfunctional families.

The mascot shares many similarities with children in the other roles. Being funny is very positive in our society, and so he or she shares that reinforcement with the achievement-oriented hero. The mascot, through his or her antics, takes the focus off the chemical dependent, thus aligning himself or herself with the scapegoat. While the lost child detests the limelight, the mascot seems destined to be in its center; both, however, are convenient ways to escape the reality of the situation.

Since the mascot is usually the last child, the parents tend to be overprotective. He or she is encouraged not to grow up, to stay the baby of the family. The secrets that abound in a chemically dependent home are never shared with this child. Indeed, he or she is even lied to about what happens. While this is well-meaning strategy by parents and older siblings, the harmful potential of complete disregard for the mascot's innate sense of what is right and wrong is ignored. Time and time again, fears are allayed, only to surface again with the next incident.

One of these well-intentioned lies is "Everything is all right. There is nothing to worry about." While we have seen that the other children hear this, too, it seems most prevalent with the mascot, who is being protected at all costs. Even the other children get in on it to guard the baby. This can have serious ramifications later in life. Lisa, now 32, tells this story of being a mascot:

"I tried to think back as to when I first questioned my own sanity. Even though I have always thought I wasn't 'just right,' I think it was when I was 9 that I really began to think that there was something truly wrong with me. My parents had had a knock-down drag-out argument which led to them physically abusing each other. I had heard the thuds below my bedroom and the sounds of breaking glass. When I asked my mother the next morning why she had a black eye and my dad had a cut on his forehead, she made up this outlandish story that ended in perfect logic. But even with all I had heard, I simply couldn't believe other than what she was telling me. After that I began to be wary about most of my own thoughts—I thought I was nuts. The last thing I did was share them with anyone."

This was a child caught in a maze of double-binds attempting to make some sense of mixed messages and downright lies. Coming from a large family, the older children colluded with the parents in protecting her from the situation. In the end, though, what they could not shield her from was her perceptive mind's own coping mechanisms to alleviate dissonance; she was admitted to a hospital for psychiatric treatment at 17. But, she was indeed not crazy—quite the contrary. The result was a series of very bizarre behaviors on her part which placed her in the role of the identified patient rather than her parents.

There are other characteristics of the mascot. These children are given to showy and inappropriate behavior in any setting. They are frequently treated by the medical community for "hyperactivity" when younger because they absolutely cannot contain their actions and minds at school (Wegscheider 1981). They are described by others as amusing, but very shallow, causing serious social problems throughout their lives. Early experimentation with drugs and alcohol is also a real danger for them as they attempt to do anything for approval. Sexual promiscuity may also come about as a result of their bid for attention, along with inappropriate styles of dress and action.

As with the scapegoat, a mascot may be the first person to receive treatment for acting-out behavior. Teachers, administrators, and parents may see this child as a mass of energy ready to explode and unable to be contained. While this is how their pain is manifested on the outside, on the inside they are constantly watchful and on guard. They are frequently the most perceptive of the group of family members, waiting for unspoken cues. When situations become tense and out of hand, they jump in at any cost to save and to amuse.

John, age 34: "Once when I was in high school, I was on the verge of being suspended for disrespectful behavior. As a matter of fact, one more incident and I was out the door. I was in class and a really heated argument broke out between the teacher and another student about a grade or something—it had absolutely nothing to do with me. I even thought to myself, as I began to crack jokes out loud, that I probably was going to get bounced for this. But, I just couldn't stand the yelling. I defused the situation all right; I was out for ten days. I think I felt worse for my mom, who just cried when the school told her. She had so much to contend with and I had just made it worse. I tried to just lay low at home for a while, but that was the longest ten days of my life."

Mascots learn very early that behaving immaturely will get the attention they need. As a result, they feel quite at home outwardly displaying behavior designed to relieve the tension of the situation. The purpose is twofold. First, the focus is, for a brief time, taken off of the chemical dependent. Second, by the distraction, the spotlight is off the enabling process as well.

The mascot only knows this type of behavior and so uses it generously in all settings—appropriate or not. At school he or she is constantly chattering, distracting, and amusing other children. This person may be as bright or brighter than the hero, but since he or she is constantly on the go, true potential is hard to measure. In the community, the mascot will be the one in the middle of everything; not necessarily to accomplish anything, but just to be noticed.

This child finds solemn occasions unbearable and very hard to understand as yet another double-bind occurs. He or she usually ends up getting punished for behavior that a few minutes ago brought tears of laughter.

Mascots' friends call them shallow and unpredictable, which is no wonder, given their style of coping with unpleasantness. To be a good friend one has to be able to laugh and to cry appropriately. It seems that mascots have not learned to do the latter and at times find themselves not only unwilling, but unable, to respond adequately.

"I used to feel like the biggest heel," says Gerald, a 27-year-old recovering mascot. "My friends in high school would be going through some really rough times with parents, or girls, or grades, and all I could do was joke about it. I got punched a couple of times but it never did any good. Even now, in the middle of the worst thing that could possibly happen, my mind comes up with the most inane and amusing thoughts. I don't think I know how to think bad thoughts. I also don't think that any of the guys I called my friends really thought of me as their friend. I always found out about stuff happening that they didn't tell me."

One can only surmise the frustration that Gerald's friends felt when, trying to share intimate feelings, they were dismissed in laughter. It is a shame that no one knew, or cared to look deeper into, Gerald, to see someone who hurt as badly or worse than anything they could imagine; a person so devoid of knowledge of himself and others that the only thing he could do was use humor as a weapon. Gerald was terrified of feeling any empathy for his acquaintances, for in that lay all the questions that he was not allowed to ask in his own family.

Heroes, scapegoats, and lost children hold no corner on the market in propensity for chemical dependency. Mascots become keenly aware of the power of mood-altering substances and of their ability to make unnamed feelings go away. They are seduced by anything that will allow them to not feel, for it is in feeling that problems arise. If a quick joke or acrobatic stunt doesn't do it, then a fast drink or well-timed pill will. Chemically dependent mascots are forever stuck in childhood, having had the pain of growing up masked by alcohol or other drugs. As a result, they never learn to deal with adult emotions, fears, or responsibilities. They seek out mates who will enable their chemical dependency and keep them safe from the world like their family did.

There is another face that the mascot may hide behind that is completely different from the amusing one described up until now. In place of the acting-out, or silly and amusing behavior, another type of mascot may demonstrate psychosomatic or stress-related illnesses in abundance. While none of the roles is exempt from this, it may fall to the mascot to actually *be* the illness that pervades the family. This child is nonverbally sent out to portray, as a mascot for a sports team would, a single image of the family for identification to others.

Unfortunately, the medical community which treats these children and adults rarely recognizes the red flags of codependency. Instead, each illness is treated individually without probing further and possibly identifying patterns of the family system. Allergies, asthma, ulcers, migraine headaches, and imaginary ailments for which there is no ready cure keep the family from focusing on the chemical dependency and codependency. Because the mascot has been so babied and protected, the family has a built-in "sponge" in this person to absorb all the dysfunction, love, and care anyone and everyone can give—care that desperately needs to be divided up among all the other hurting people in the family.

"From the time my brother was born until his death [at 29 from chemical dependency], he had every illness in the book at least once," remembers Kerry, age 31, hero of his chemically dependent family. "I remember my mom taking him to the doctor almost every week for something or other. The things that he suffered from the worst were migraine headaches and allergies. Now that I'm in recovery, I can look back and see that his worst headaches were right after something bad had happened at home. He suffered unmercifully from allergies to everything, too."

Kerry continues: "To this day I have a lot of bitterness toward doctors. I know they can't know everything and that their patients have to be able to volunteer information to help them make diagnoses, but it seems as if they don't even try to find stuff out. My family was, and is [Kerry is the only one in recovery for codependency], a walking example of chemical abuse and codependency. It seems like it ought to be required for them to take classes like this before they get out of medical school."

Just as with the other roles, the mascot unknowingly plays his or her part in enabling the chemical dependent to keep using. If this person suddenly decides to "get well" (or die, as in Kerry's brother's case), another will unwittingly step into the abandoned role to maintain the precarious homeostasis.

RULES OF A CHEMICALLY DEPENDENT FAMILY

No organization can run effectively without regulations governing its behavior. Likewise, no family can function without a set of rules, overt or covert, to delineate the behavior of its members. It is through these rules that boundaries are formed between individual family members, between such dyads as the parents, between siblings and parents, and between the nuclear and extended family members (Minuchin 1974). These boundaries may be described at the extremes as diffuse or rigid, depending on the rules set up to create them (Minuchin 1974; Friedman, Utada, & Morrissey 1987). For the most part what will be discussed is a rigid and tightly boundaried set of rules most characteristic of the closed system chemically dependent families usually occupy.

Briefly, a family with diffuse boundaries has difficulty separating from each other; parents are not separated from older children, who are not separated from younger siblings. It may appear as "one big happy family," and no one is comfortable with individual space and thought. Contrastingly, a family with rigid boundaries allows little information about feelings to pass between generations or individuals. An invisible wall is erected around everyone, and no one is comfortable communicating and sharing feelings.

Healthy families fall somewhere in between. The parents are a solid and discrete unit with the responsibility to guide and nurture youngsters. Expression of feelings is encouraged. Most important, children are taught the value of *connection* to their family because they are respected first as individuals.

Overt rules are those that are outwardly spoken or demonstrated. For instance, a family may have it in their system that the younger members must always show respect for the older members. This will be openly discussed and modeled in day-to-day living, with punishments doled out according to the infractions that occur.

A covert rule concerning this might be that older members of the family are to be shown respect *except* if they are chemically dependent. A child growing up in such an environment will have a difficult time understanding such disparity, especially since covert rules are never discussed. Time and time again, they will be punished for not showing respect for their parents or older siblings, all the while watching Mom or Dad ignore, chastise, and demean a chemically dependent grandparent.

While rules form in reaction to specific or recurring events in each chemically dependent family, there are a few that appear to be characteristic of most (Wegscheider 1981, Black 1981, Woititz 1983, Smith 1988).

Rule 1: Maintaining homeostasis should be the most important thing to all family members.

Preservation of the system is supposed to be at the forefront of everyone's thoughts, actions, and feelings. Anything that gets in the way of this should be disregarded and discouraged as being detrimental to the united front the family must show. A fuller treatment of this rule can be found in the earlier section discussing the family's response to the chemical dependency.

There are three common principles that form in families who are covertly determined to keep the status quo alive regardless of the degree of dysfunction occurring in the family (Black 1981):

1. *Don't talk.* This maxim sets up rigid boundaries between the members themselves, as well as the outside world. If no one is let in on the family secrets, then there is a better chance that things can continue as they unhappily are. Children are afraid of discussing their thoughts about what is occurring at home for fear that the family will be broken up if too much is known. Additionally, the members have been covertly, and even perhaps overtly, told that family business should remain so and is not for outside consumption.

There is no greater reinforcement for this than the amount of *nontalking* that is done within the home itself. Each child, according to his or her role in the family, reacts differently to this.

As a consequence of the "don't talk" rule, shame is prevalent in these children, regardless of role or birth order. No one is willing to openly discuss what is shameful to them. In the case of the chemically dependent family full of secrets, children frequently do not know what they should be ashamed of, but it must be pretty bad if no one talks about it. Fossum and Mason (1986) define shame as "an inner sense of being completely diminished or insufficient as a person. It is the self judging the self" (p. 5).

Perhaps more explanatory of these children who are so unaware of the reason for their feelings, these authors go on to say that shame is "the ongoing premise that one is fundamentally bad, inadequate, defective, unworthy, or not fully valid as a human being" (p. 5).

Instructed firmly, either verbally or nonverbally, about the evils of discussion, these children take upon themselves this unfounded feeling of being bad and shameful—a feeling that can last throughout their lives.

2. *Don't trust.* It is difficult to trust someone if you can't talk with them. This implicit rule acts as additional insulation against outsiders. Family loyalty is held up as the paradigm of virtues, even when that loyalty should have been long abandoned. Children see parents ever wary and watchful of situations where outside influences could possibly alter the carefully guarded thinking patterns in the home. Schools and communities are not to be trusted as anything more than "meddling." The little ones grow to mistrust each other, and eventually themselves, unable to rely on their own instincts to help them in dangerous situations.

Additionally, because of chemical dependence, a crucial trusting bond between parent and child (eventually to translate into that between child and the world) may never be formed (Smith 1988). This occurs in human beings in the period of life from birth to age 2. If trust is not nurtured then, and is further eroded by later deliberate acts of distrust, then a very important chunk of growing up is bypassed. While not impossible to correct in adulthood with therapy and support, it lays down the foundation for a person who, only with a great amount of conscientious effort, will be able to think others trustworthy. Using such exacted effort actually belies

the very word trust, so it is difficult to discern whether this is a recoverable human trait once denied.

3. *Don't feel.* Perhaps this is the most detrimental of all the covert rules that maintain this family system. It is also a logical outgrowth of the two listed above, as children see that demonstration of feelings, both good and bad, is superfluous and unwanted. All feelings do, they are told, is to rock the boat and threaten to disturb the tenuous patterns established. Eventually they become so used to shoving them down that they become buried forever with the need to talk and the abandoned trust.

One can observe a child-turned-adult of chemical and codependent parents and almost see feelings longing to escape. They will be unnamed, having been so long denied, and emerge in a cavalcade of tears and anguish before they are acknowledged. Or they will sit, dormant and festering, for an entire lifetime, never to be acknowledged or felt, hidden with the greatest of sophistication. For without help, a codependent child unfamiliar with feelings becomes an adult whose only knowledge of himself or herself is what those binding family rules have taught.

Rule 2: No one has the right to behave differently.

Chief enablers, heroes, scapegoats, lost children, and mascots must remain so. No one is allowed to step out of the appointed role. But, if they dare to do so, they need to find another place quickly before the system is threatened. Chemical dependents and chief enablers, particularly, propagate this rule that actually allows them to stay firmly slotted.

When changes do occur, usually the person will pick a role that is close in character to his or her own. A mascot may trade places with a lost child, both escaping the reality of the situation. A deserted hero slot might be filled with a scapegoat longing to replace his or her negative reinforcement with positive reinforcement. A chief enabler who simply decides to walk out of the entire situation may return to find an angry hero filling the vacancy. In this case, the family may have just inherited another scapegoat, should the chief enabler's return be permanent.

Rule 3: Someone or something else is responsible for all ills—not chemical dependency.

This need to assign and then shift blame to people and things outside the dysfunctional family system is very characteristic of chemical dependency. Although the judgmental attitude of the chief enabler may make it appear as though responsibility is being laid onto the chemical dependent, this actually is not the case, and denial is the reason. For whatever terrible things happen in the home as a result of drug abuse, the real criticism will be given to fate, and its inexorable hold on the family. In essence, the family is doomed to live in unhappiness simply because "that's the way things happen in life." The chief enabler and the chemical dependent may have unwittingly picked each other to continue a legacy of disappointment and distress begun many generations ago in their own families (Scarf 1987, Baruth & Huber 1984).

THE FAMILY-RECOVERY PROCESS

Although research in chemical dependency extends back many decades, it has only been in the last ten years that families of alcoholics have been diligently treated as having specific difficulties linked with the environment in which they live(d). The slowness to recognize their importance comes not from callousness, but from a general inability of researchers to label behaviors and feelings without something more concrete upon which to attach them. In essence, treatment for codependent family members has taken a back seat to treatment of the active chemical dependent because there was not something more tangible to measure (i.e., drinking behavior).

Two current methods of codependency treatment will be discussed: the disease model, which is predominant in most treatment centers, as well as in Alcoholics Anonymous and such related organizations as Al-Anon; and the developmental-symbiosis model, which is the subject of some of the most recent literature (Weiss & Weiss 1989, Brown 1988).

The most widely acknowledged and used treatment method for chemical dependents has been that of the disease model. From there, it has been an easy jump in the minds of treatment professionals to assign a similar disease process to codependency, which has led to millions of codependents coming into their own "recovery" process. Treatment centers counsel them in "Family Programs," and Al-Anon and Adult Children of Alcoholics meetings flourish throughout the country.

In line with the disease model of codependency, family members are treated as if the disease of chemical dependency has invaded not only the substance abuser but them as well. In essence, the body, mind, emotions, and spirit of each person in the family has been as greatly damaged by alcohol or other drugs as that of the chemical dependent. Although there are a host of actual stress-related physical illnesses that may beset a codependent living in such an environment, the major emphasis for recovery is placed on healing the emotional, mental, and spiritual aspects of the person.

In most treatment centers, and in all Al-Anon programs, the Twelve Steps of Alcoholics Anonymous are employed as a guideline for recovery for codependents. By using these steps, healthy changes in day-to-day (and at times, minute-to-minute) living are possible, which result in a more sane life style. Participants are encouraged to see how their own past behavior, both with the chemical dependent and with other members of the family, kept the substance abuse and codependency going.

According to this model, everyone is suffering from the same or a similar disease. A focus of the disease model is personal responsibility for recovery from it. Therefore, codependents must do what is necessary to ameliorate their own problematic behavior. This can best be described by discussing the codependents in the various roles they play in the family.

With the substance abuser clean and dry, the chief enabler in recovery will have to take responsibility for changing his or her compulsive need to control people and situations. This is not to say that this past behavior is being negatively evaluated; quite the contrary. Controlling served an important purpose to the family and perhaps even saved the lives of the children. But it also enabled the chemical dependent to keep using. Now is the time to begin to recognize this and to change behavior patterns to more healthy ones.

Similarly, heroes must be shown how their actions enabled the drug abuser to continue and allowed other family members to place them in the role of savior. Feelings about what has happened to them as children growing up must be resurrected, however painful. Heroes wrestle daily with guilt over not being able to control the chemical dependent's use. They must be helped to understand that they were not as responsible as they might have felt themselves to be.

Scapegoats must be allowed to see themselves as intrinsically good people rather than as dysfunction absorbers. This is difficult for any therapist or support group to do, since they will be fighting against years of constant criticism, received from others, self-inflicted. So ingrained are negative thoughts and patterns of action that at times it will seem impossible to replace them. Overcoming scapegoats' nightmarish fear of everything, that for so long has been held at bay, will open them up to all the potential that awaits.

Lost children must be helped to not be so isolated. For them, trust is a major issue with all people with whom they come into contact. The rest of the family will need to get to know them in order to show that the world is really not such a scary place after all. Their emotions went into hiding along with their physical beings, and so bringing feelings to the surface and out may take much effort, particularly on their part. For in the end they, as all other codependents, must *want* to feel.

Mascots will need support in harnessing their ebullient (or hypochondriacal) nature so as to react more appropriately with the world. These people are so incredibly observant that they become excellent candidates for recovery if they allow themselves to turn that skill inward. To risk looking internally at the troubled soul that drives them to constantly be at the center of attention is painstaking work. Finally, to help them "re-parent" themselves appropriately allows them the necessary growing up they have been denied.

Another model of codependency treatment, developmental-symbiotic, appears diametrically opposed to the disease model in many ways. First, the words *disease, illness,* and *sickness* are never used. Codependents are seen as behaving in a manner representative of arrested developmental growth stemming from a drug-abusive environment. Their codependent behaviors, although not in their best interest, are seen as *normal* reactions to the very *abnormal* situations in which they grew up. Second, codependents are seen as being symbiotically tied to their families of origin, unable to progress through the natural stages of the life cycle to become functional and independent adults. Symbiosis, as discussed by Brown (1988) and Weiss and Weiss (1989), refers to an unhealthy dependent relationship between family members. In essence, codependents are normal, not sick, people who need assistance in individuating themselves from their families in order to progress through life as self-sufficient adults (Bowen 1985). When one can go back and heal damaged and developmentally immature parts of the self, relationships with others can grow.

Therapy using this model concentrates on identifying an earlier part of growing up where one became "stuck" and progressing through the subsequent stages to the present. For example, Weiss and Weiss do a great deal of "nurturing the child within" work by bringing codependents back to painful feelings of early childhood. Through physical and emotional techniques, clients are encouraged to act out and feel earlier stages of development; permission is given to be "that hurt and angry four-year-old." The natural maturing process can then begin to unfold and clients can react in more realistic and autonomous ways with friends and family members.

Regardless of the philosophy that guides a therapist working with codependents, there are three important steps that codependents must go through in order to attain some peace with what has gone before and to shape what will come after (Smith 1988).

1. *Identification of problems and abuses of the past.* By bringing out into the open pain and ineffective coping mechanisms of the past, a codependent can then move on. What matters most here is not actual facts but perceptions. For in the end, everything that matters to anyone about his or her life has more to do with how something appeared and the feelings surrounding it than with actual reality.

2. *Expression of the pain.* In order to heal properly, emotional wounds, so long repressed, must now be discussed openly and honestly. In this stage of therapy the rules of "don't talk, don't trust, and don't feel" (Black 1981) must be shattered. Anger, grief, and shame over events of the past are revealed and dealt with. The codependents going through (not around) this very painful state will emerge much better able to handle the same feelings that will occur in the future without suppressing them in their previous dysfunctional ways.

There are few therapists who put an actual timeline on this second stage of recovery. While therapy may be labeled as "brief" (contracted for a few sessions and then reevaluated for continuation or dismissal), ongoing support from organizations like Al-Anon, Alateen, or Adult Children of Alcoholics (ACA) should be suggested. Even therapists who adhere more to the developmental-symbiotic model of therapy for codependents see Al-Anon's and ACA's broad base of support as helpful to their clients. These groups also give codependents gradual practice in trusting other individuals with personal issues.

In addition, counselors themselves must understand (regardless of their personal belief system) what an Al-Anon group will come to mean to their clients. Helping clients explore the information presented will go a long way in allowing them to leave therapy when the time comes for dismissal. It is from these groups that codependents get a healthy dose of reality testing from others who have been through the same experiences. As one recovering alcoholic, also an adult child of alcoholic parents, puts it: "I go to AA for my sobriety, and ACA for my peace as a human being. I couldn't get along without either one. They keep me *living* instead of wallowing in the past."

There are many families where only one or a few members reach out for help for their codependency. In many of these cases, the drug abuser does not desire sobriety, but for these codependents living with the family's problems has gotten to be too much to handle. It is vital for counselors to remind these brave souls that they are in recovery for their own codependency, *not* to get anyone else into recovery. Attitude and behavioral changes in them, as a result of professional treatment or Al-Anon, may indeed help other family members to see that there is a better life than that which has gone before. But, just as every chemical dependent must reach his or her own "bottom" of despair, so must the other codependents. Stressing the *individuality* of everyone's program of recovery is imperative.

3. *Understanding, forgiving, and abandoning the "victim" life style.* These may be seemingly impossible tasks to the newly recovering codependent, but they grow easier to handle with time and much support. It has been discovered, though, that an incomplete job done in stage two does not allow this final stage to occur. Many codependents find such relief in being able to openly admit to the identified problems of stage one that they "skip" directly to stage three without ever really feeling the pain. In short, they revert back to their old roles in dealing with issues, which was to stuff unpleasant feelings or minimize their importance.

Codependents must be helped to see that their expression of such feelings will not destroy the family, but that refusing to give them their due probably will. An example of this would be the person who has received therapy for a number of years but does not appear to be making any real progress. The same issues, perhaps disguised a bit, keep them stuck in a never-ending process of identification and letting go without really doing the latter. In attempting to "save the family" from the grief of their bitterness, they doom themselves to living in pain forever.

Again, this is where the support groups excel. Regular sharing of feelings with others knowledgeable of the chemically dependent system allows the gradual growth of the ability to stop being the victim of it.

"There is so much I don't even need to say at [Al-Anon] meetings. But, I look around and people are nodding their heads in agreement to unspoken feelings! Some have had worse lives than I, but everyone just *knows*. I have never before experienced such complete understanding. I am a firm believer in therapy from professionals—that is how I found ACA in the first place. I still will go to a counselor whenever issues are incredibly hard for me to solve even with my [ACA] program. But for day-to-day support, I have found it here," reports a 29-year-old adult child of an alcoholic, in recovery for the past 6 years.

A current dilemma facing all therapists, and one which affects the consumers of psychotherapy, is deciding which therapeutic model will be the most effective for codependents. Adding to this dilemma (or indecisiveness) is that research indicates that all therapeutic models have about the same success rate. The question then becomes, "Is it the model or the therapeutic relationship that affords the most impact" (Yalom 1975).

With this in mind, it is important to remember that regardless of either of these important elements, the recognition of the personality characteristics of codependents is paramount. Also, one must keep in mind the pervasiveness and far-reaching effects chemical dependency and codependency have. Today, clients who come for therapy who have had some brush with the disease far outnumber those who have not.

But a therapist cannot treat effectively something of which he or she is not aware. With so many continuing-education programs and so much literature about codependency and chemical dependency in the profession today, there is little excuse for the therapist to not avail himself or herself of the abundance. While one may have other areas of expertise in counseling, being able to assess the need for and properly refer clients to someone who specializes in substance abuse and codependency issues is critical.

ADULT CHILDREN OF CHEMICAL DEPENDENTS

As long as there have been chemical dependents, there have been children of chemical dependents. The passage of years simply does not erase the many problems that stem from growing up in a drug-abusing home. Some common problems placed in the laps of therapists and support groups by these adults have their roots in identical nightmares of their younger selves. There are several characteristics that are common to all regardless of roles. These will be explored first, followed by short and more specific descriptions of what sets the hero, scapegoat, lost child, and mascot apart as adults.

People Pleasing

A pervasive inability to trust one's feelings because of the inconsistencies with which one was raised stands out in most adults brought up in chemically dependent atmospheres. This shows up as "people-pleasing" behavior. Children of chemical dependents are unaware, or unable if they are aware, to listen to what their instincts are telling them about what is right or wrong for them. These people cannot say no to anyone and overextend themselves beyond human capability.

Fear of Abandonment

An extreme fear of abandonment does not simply go away with more life experience—if anything, it is intensified. This is manifested in either clutching and dependent behavior or in an inability to form attachments of any kind. Both of these reactions to very real emotions serve to drive others away from this very paradoxical person who finds it so hard to give or receive love in a healthy manner. This is seen in all the roles and among both men and women.

Dysfunctional Relationships

Friends, lovers, and spouses are usually picked because of their similarity or complementarity of personality (Baruth & Huber 1984). Examples might be lost children as friends, a mascot and a lost child as lovers, or a hero drawn to a chemically dependent work situation. These people seem to attract and be attracted to other chemical dependents and codependents in order to play out the roles to which they have become so accustomed. It is not as if one goes out in conscious search of another dysfunctional person. But by the very repetitive nature of family systems, the propensity for constant involvement with either a chemical dependent, a codependent, or both is very high.

Fear of Failure

A lack of balance to life follows these children-turned-adults far into their future. At the bottom of this is the fear that all they do or will do will fail. As children, no amount of effort or action made the parent stop drinking. This "failure," coupled with a child's lack of understanding of the problem, makes the remainder of their days caught up in no-win situations. Men appear driven to achieve more and more even though their sense of failure is unending. Many women choose executive paths for the same reason.

Another pattern for women emerges, however, in that it has been more societally acceptable for them to live out their lives considerably below their talents for fear of that same failure. An "easy" life, perhaps one without a career, is seen to be better than a more fulfilling and challenging one as a way of avoiding pain and reinforcing this failure premonition. These patterns of constant over- and underachievement are seen in all the roles that have been explored in this chapter.

Overwhelming Guilt

Guilt for so many things underlies a great deal of the maladjustment of adulthood these children face. The wish that their parents were dead, begun but never openly admitted as a child, persists (or intensifies, or is sublimated) at an even more damaging level. If the parent does indeed die, then deeper scars develop with the lost hope of resolution through confrontation.

Resentment

Guilt and anger toward the sober parent are also present. The realization that life did not have to be spent in a chemically dependent home causes resentment to build. The thought that the child was powerless to do anything about the problem, but the sober parent was not, is a major source of contention in adulthood. An adjustment to divorce, however painful, seems more palatable when thinking back on the years of hell surviving in an unstable and unhappy home. As adults, these people sometimes feel resentment toward everything and everyone tracing back to this original pattern.

Rigidity

Should they manage to achieve some amount of stability in their own homes and occupations, the need to maintain that control may make them rigid and unbending in their approach to spouses, children, employers, and employees. Adult children of chemical dependents are generally unspontaneous in their life styles as a defense against the chaos that reigned in their childhood years. They often vow never again to live with such tension as that associated with never knowing what was going to happen next.

Fear of Confrontation

As a result of a vow to avoid confrontation at any cost, children of drug abusers learn intricate ways to stuff emotions until they are unrecognizable. These might be the people who are proud that they "never fight" with their spouse or friends. The anger that arises in any normal close relationship is never acknowledged, let alone dealt with, as they try more and more elaborate denial systems. This is particularly the case with heroes.

Immaturity

Opposite difficulties with control are found in the other roles, but with the same results. Often when scapegoats, lost children, and mascots want or need to be in control, they find themselves short on experience. If the parents have been overly critical, negligent, or overprotective, proper instruction in decision-making strategies is never conveyed or modeled for emulation. Scapegoats, lost children, and mascots appear unable to take responsibility, but by default rather than by an unwillingness to do so.

Compulsive Behaviors

All adult children of chemical dependents, as discussed in previous sections, face almost insurmountable odds of becoming substance abusers themselves. Alcohol and drugs dull the pain of their previous existence and allow them to feel more "normal" in their dealings with people and social situations. If a child grows up in a home with one chemically dependent parent, the chance that he or she will suffer the same fate has been widely reported as being as high as 85 percent. With both parents involved in drink or drugs, the figure climbs to 90 percent. What appears to be a genetic predisposition toward chemical dependence is a topic that is now receiving attention in chemical-dependency research. More information should help to educate families and professionals regarding future generations.

A list of common personality characteristics of adult children of chemically dependent or dysfunctional families appears below. The information in the preceding pages regarding varying roles in the family—and different coping styles that resulted from those roles—should more clearly explain any apparent contradictions among some or all of the following (Symmonds 1984, Woititz 1983):

1. An overdeveloped sense of responsibility *or* one of total irresponsibility.
2. A fear of anger or authority, leading to an unwillingness or inability to confront others.
3. A low sense of self-esteem or worth (regardless of many accomplishments, *or* itself the reason for accomplishing very little).
4. A generalized oversensitivity to the actions and feelings of others. This allows the person to not deal with his or her own feelings because he or she is focusing on others.
5. Difficulty being spontaneous or having fun, *or* not being able to be serious in the face of any situation.
6. Terror of abandonment. This causes one to hang onto a relationship at any cost *or* to adopt an externally carefree attitude to mask the internal emotional paralysis arising from the fear of being rejected and alone.
7. Harsh judgment of self and others (with forgiveness coming last, if ever, to self).
8. An addiction to excitement. This can take the disguised form of such other compulsive behaviors as chemical dependence, gambling, lying, or workaholism. This may also characterize the individual who appears content to "live dangerously" with procrastination and forced deadlines.

9. An inability to make commitments in either everyday or long-term emotional situations. The person who is continually late for appointments and engagements with others may be subtly manifesting this behavior.
10. An overly dependent personality. This may be characterized by clinging and smothering behaviors *or* by an overly independent personality, as demonstrated by extreme difficulty with interpersonal relationships.
11. Generalized feelings of being different from others but an inability to describe "normal."
12. Constant seeking of affirmation from others, which may be demonstrated by compulsive lying.
13. An inability to express feelings because of intellectualization or basic unawareness of their existence.
14. Regimentation in all tasks *or* lackadaisical attitude toward people, places, and situations.
15. Inability to care for self emotionally and sometimes physically because of deep denial of need for proper nutrition, rest, and health care.

More extensive lists of characteristics have been compiled by various support groups around the country. However, the list above gives an overall picture of adult children of chemically dependent families. It also appears to be extremely accurate, as clients like Roy say:

"The first time I saw that list I felt like someone had socked me right in the stomach. Here I was in black and white. I never dreamed anyone else felt the way I did, much less had the guts to write it down. It was like someone had been reading all my mail for the past thirty years and knew me better than I knew myself."

More specifically, heroes, scapegoats, lost children, and mascots have their own particular brands of dysfunctional behavior. Also, there is not a person on earth who fits the neatly stereotyped categories presented here. Heroes have deep psychological pockets resembling those of lost children. Scapegoats have, just under the surface, the desire and capability to become heroes if ever given the chance. Mascots easily exchange places and feelings with both lost children and scapegoats. In short, one cannot look at a list, make a character judgment, and not see other roles peeking out. Human personality is so complex that it would be impossible for therapists to categorize it so. What one can gain from knowing this information is an overall flavor of the person, and perhaps how he or she might be inclined to act in a situation, given the role previously adopted in the family.

Heroes as Adults

Heroes in adult life are still seen as "well-adjusted" and as "having everything all together." This child was ignored, except for the good he or she did the family, and was subsequently left in adulthood with many unmet emotional needs. "An entire population of children of alcoholics grew up looking so good and acting so perfectly that they themselves were astounded at what they had accomplished" (Black 1980).

Hero children as adults may find the need to be in control so overwhelmingly great that they continue the pattern, unable to enjoy life or to be less serious. Because they shoved back feelings in order to perform duties for others, they now find they cannot express themselves even when they want to. Hero adults become resistant to intimacy with others because of mistrust, leaving them nowhere to turn when their "in control" world goes awry. Their feelings of emotional isolation, so strongly felt in childhood and reinforced by the chief enabler, continue for life, without help and support.

Scapegoats as Adults

Inappropriate behavior in personal and social situations does not readily leave the scapegoat. He or she, as an adult, may still be living in the rebellious acting-out of younger years. Many scapegoats have had several encounters with law enforcement by this time. They may be seriously involved with their own chemical dependence and have found friends and mates to enable and support their habits.

On the other side is the scapegoat who never really got into any particular trouble, but still served as the end of the pecking order in the family. These people as adults may still seek out situations in work and relationships that allow them to be used and abused by others. These are the persons who are blamed for everything because they lack the emotional wherewithal to not accept it. Their fragile self-esteem does not allow them to behave differently without a great deal of help and support from others. These scapegoats, too, are prime targets for chemical dependence, but, even more likely, for a host of stress-related illnesses.

Lost Children as Adults

This child withdrew from others to protect himself or herself from the craziness of home life. As an adult, a rather unhealthy situation may arise because of the inability to master the arts of engagement and decision making. Rolling with the tide is what these people do best. When forced to make commitments based on logical and directive thinking, they are adrift.

Lost children are frequently drawn to other people with problems (such as chemical dependency) as lovers and friends because they can continue the flexible adjuster role they have perfected in their own nuclear families. These relationships will be bound by nothing substantial because no one will be making decisions.

Mascots as Adults

In still another vein is the placater-child, the mascot-turned-adult. Such persons, like the heroes, will find it difficult to ask for help for basically the same reason. They have always been so responsible for other people's happiness that they have lost the ability or the words to take for themselves from others. As a result, they have no practice in getting their own needs met or even identifying what those needs might be.

They, too, are likely to marry a chemical dependent so they can continue their loving and supportive role. Somewhere down the line their unfulfilled desires and constant sacrifice meet them head on and anger effuses from every emotional pore. Since their whole life has been spent diffusing these negative feelings in everyone else, it is infinitesimally more difficult for them to own them.

The two forms of mascots we saw as children are still in place as adults. Some are still committed to comedic behavior; others are enmeshed in real and imagined illnesses. Both types allow the person to remain out of the actual situation of living by placing the focus elsewhere.

The clown refuses to see things with adult eyes, continuing his or her problems with social relationships. This person, as when he or she was a child, is the first to be called to a party and the last to be called whenever disaster strikes. This one-sided interaction with others forces the adult mascot into shallow and emotionless experiences that doom him or her to continual adolescence.

The perennially ill mascot is likewise devoid of healthy social interaction and therefore never able to truly recognize his or her worth as a person to others. After awhile, those around him or her refuse to be on the receiving end of a litany of maladies, and this mascot is forced into a form of isolation. When actual or more serious disease or illness does happen, people are more likely to ignore the very great need to communicate that these individuals have. A return to the chemically dependent system and the parents who were forever there for them, shielding them from all harm, is sometimes the only relief. Thus the adult mascot of this variety is kept forever a special child.

GRANDCHILDREN OF CHEMICAL DEPENDENTS

The effects of drug abuse and codependency are far-reaching. Recent literature suggests that not only do children of chemical dependents have a considerable legacy with which to deal, but *their* children do as well (Smith 1988, Balis 1986, Cook & Winokur 1985, Stabeneau 1985, Goodwin 1976). The second generation passes on characteristics of codependency to their offspring in much the same way that they themselves inherited their characteristics. Adult children of chemical dependents (whether chemically dependent themselves or not) convey a message of victimization and codependent patterns of behaving to their offspring, regardless of their efforts in the opposite direction. Moreover, roles identical to those previously described in the chemically dependent nuclear family become present in the homes of codependents trying to raise their families as best they can. An important figure in the identification and treatment of future generations of chemical dependents, Smith (1988) saw numerous problems such people encounter in dealing with life.

A distorted family image, propagated by the second generation, yields inappropriate perceptions for the third. Being reared by perhaps sober parents, these children are told only good things about their ancestors. Little is shared about their grandparents as parents, but tension is high, as reluctance to discuss such matters is evident.

With no logical source for problems (e.g., blatant chemical dependency), these grandchildren feel as if they themselves are responsible for whatever misfortunes life gives out. They blame themselves for everything and are unaware that they have not been taught adequate coping strategies. An inability to discuss such issues with codependent parents (who are incapable of empathizing with their children's pain) exacerbates the situation.

Grandchildren of drug abusers are best at forming superficial relationships. With little real sharing of feelings witnessed in their codependent home, the third-generation child is short on skills in forming and maintaining intimate relationships.

The grandchildren of chemical dependents have difficulty asking for help. They see their codependent parents in similar straits and have a tendency to continue this pattern. They do not wish to become even more of a burden to their parents, who already seem overwhelmed by the world, and therefore think they have to solve all of life's mysteries on their own. This attitude is manifested in a different way by children who are so overparented that they grow up never needing to ask for help because everything is done for them.

A struggle with compulsive behaviors is frequently found in this population. Growing up with codependent parents, the children may see other compulsions besides chemicals. Work, food, spending, or relationships all serve as convenient outlets to the same purpose as the grandparents' chemical dependency.

In a codependent home, many of the same secrets are kept as in the original chemically dependent home. Grandchildren are very confused about this because in their own home there may not have been any blatant dysfunction that needed secretiveness. They only know by example that most concerns of the family are not discussed among themselves or with others.

Further generations of codependents are prone to episodes of depression and anxiety. In reaction to the wild mood swings of their untreated codependent parents, the grandchildren find themselves mired in the same unpredictable situations. This is compounded because there is not any actual and observable cause for them to feel bad. Their guilt for "being depressed over nothing" perpetuates the cycle.

These grandchildren can be described as possessing strong family loyalty. Needing the family's approval more than anything is an overwhelming characteristic of grandchildren of chemical dependents. They are indoctrinated into the "don't talk, don't trust, don't feel" rules (Black 1981) very early in life, doing anything not to violate this for fear of being abandoned by their good parents.

Because they come from what look like "trouble-free" homes, grandchildren who become chemically dependent themselves are ashamed of bringing such a scourge to their "spotless" family name. If they know of their grandparents' difficulties with substances, they feel guilty for bringing them back into the family after they had been removed the generation before.

Overall, homes where chemical abuse takes place, and those in which untreated codependency dominates, are more similar than they are different. Both can be described as being closed systems (Goldenberg & Goldenberg 1985, Becvar & Becvar 1982, Okun & Rappaport 1980).

There are some elements inherent in the definition of a closed system that are particularly applicable to chemically dependent and codependent families. First, there is little transmission of information to the outside environment for fear of exposing the family to criticism and judgment. Unresolved wounds from the original home seem less painful if left alone and a new life attempted. Second, the members are unable to "heal" themselves and are unwilling to let outsiders in to help because of many painful trust issues. A third common characteristic of both homes is the idea of fate being a strong determiner and the family as being externally controlled. The grandchildren are taught to *react* rather than *act* in their own interest, since this was a coping strategy used by their codependent parents while growing up. Finally, time and additional stress tends to break apart the system rather than increase its intricacy. Addition or subtraction of members, as well as stressors placed on everyone in normal life-cycle events (child launching, marriage, retirement) cause many more problems for these homes than for one described as more "open" in its approach to life. Lack of communication between members further perpetuates the notion of "us against them," closing off the family or families even more.

Therapy for grandchildren of chemical dependents consists of many of the same things that are done for their parents who seek help. The rules of the family are broken with permission, feelings buried under secrets are revealed, and finally these clients can see a reason why they felt the way they did growing up. Just like the codependents of the generation before, though, constantly ruminating on past history does little to allow acceptance of responsibility for the future. Therapists must help grandchildren to not become enmeshed in self-pity, but to look forward to the future with new understanding and new decision-making capability.

Such support groups as ACA have much to offer the grandchildren of chemical dependents. Open discussion of feelings, support from other members, and acquiring the courage to try new behaviors and attitudes help them to grow and to change. It is in this generation that the vicious cycle of codependency can begin to be broken. A treated grandchild of a chemical dependent has a much better chance of raising his or her children with less codependent behavior than ever before (Smith 1988). An open, honest, and loving atmosphere is not a good environment for chemical dependency or codependency to grow. Problems that naturally arise in the normal development of individuals and families have an excellent chance of being dealt with and dismissed rather than being buried for resurrection by succeeding generations.

SUMMARY

Chemical dependency is not the only problematic pattern of behavior that exists within a family. Constant adjusting to it by the members creates an overlying maladaptation known as codependency. Each member of the family finds a niche (chief enabler, hero, scapegoat, lost child, or mascot) most fitting with his or her personality or birth order. In an attempt to survive a very abnormal environment, the members may demonstrate arrested developmental growth and have great difficulty functioning independently of the nuclear family. The family system, no matter how strained, is to be preserved at all costs, and elaborate rules are created to this end. The family is seen as a protective system, paradoxically guarding what is making them the most unhappy because of the fear of change.

Children of chemically dependent parents demonstrate the behaviors of codependency with their own children just as if they were still living with the drug-abusing person(s). Thus, codependency is passed from generation to generation, even if actual chemical dependency is not. However, persons filling all the roles we have discussed are also prone to drug abuse through indoctrination of behavior and lack of adequate coping styles.

The most widely used treatment of either chemical dependence or codependence is the disease model. Through this, clients and their families are taught that chemical dependence and its accompanying codependence are diseases that invade the body, mind, emotions, and spirit of the family. Taking responsibility for actions done under the influence of drugs *or* codependency thus makes it possible for individuals, as well as entire families, to move ahead in their lives and to break cycles of unproductive living. A newer theory, the developmental-symbiotic model, suggests that codependents are normal but developmentally stunted individuals. Codependents need assistance extricating themselves in healthy ways from their families of origin to become autonomous and more fully functioning people.

Recognition of the pervasiveness of alcohol and other drug abuse and its effects on the family are in demand by consumers of psychotherapy. Therapists should avail themselves of further education in the field of chemical dependence and codependence so as to suggest the most helpful strategies or to make appropriate referrals. Clients should be encouraged to join ongoing support groups (AA, Al-Anon, Alateen, ACA), particularly those who need to have a broad base of support in daily living.

FOR FURTHER READING

Al-Anon's twelve steps and twelve traditions (1981). New York: Al-Anon Family Group Headquarters.

Alcoholics anonymous ["The big book"] (1976) (3rd ed.). New York: Alcoholics Anonymous World Services.

Curran, D. (1983). *Traits of a healthy family*. Minneapolis, MN: Winston Press.

Eisenberg, S., and Patterson, L. E. (1979). *Helping clients with special concerns*. Boston: Houghton-Mifflin.

Friends in Recovery (1987). *The twelve steps for adult children of alcoholics and other dysfunctional families*. San Diego, CA: Recovery Press.

Hart, L. (1987). *The winning family*. New York: Dodd & Mead.

Johnson Institute (1979). *Chemical dependency and recovery are a family affair*. Minneapolis, MN: Johnson Institute.

Satir, V. (1972). *Peoplemaking*. Palo Alto, CA: Science and Behavior Books.

Viorst, J. (1986). *Necessary losses*. New York: Ballantine.

Wholey, D. (1984). *The courage to change*. Boston: Houghton-Mifflin.

Woititz, J. G. (1985). *Struggle for intimacy*. Pompano Beach, FL: Health Communications Press.

4

Diagnosis and Assessment of Chemical Dependency

OVERVIEW

Introduction
Recognizing Behavioral Patterns in Chemical Dependency
   Physical Symptoms
   Behavioral Symptoms
   Emotional Symptoms
   Social Symptoms
   Spiritual Symptoms
Laboratory Pattern
Screening Instruments
   DSM-III-R
   The Twenty-Questions List
   Michigan Alcoholism Screening Test (MAST)
   Adolescent Alcohol Involvement Scale
   Problem Drinking Scale (PDS)
   Alcohol Use Inventory (AUI)
   The Comprehensive Drinker Profile (CDP)
   Cocaine Assessment
   Minnesota Multiphasic Personality Inventory (MMPI)
   MacAndrew Alcoholism Scale
Summary

INTRODUCTION

An evaluation of the existence, and severity, of chemical dependence is essential in the early stages of treatment to confirm the need for therapy, as well as to gather data that will be useful in the treatment process. Accurate diagnosis and assessment improve the chances of effective treatment, since it ordinarily depends on a comprehensive analysis of the nature, causes, and effects of an individual's problem.

A comprehensive assessment allows the counselor to recognize that individuals who are chemically dependent are not all alike, but have diverse and multifaceted contributing and resulting problems. This leads to the counselor gathering information about the individual so that a personal treatment plan can be developed that is consistent with his or her specific needs. In this chapter, assessment will be examined as a process that may be subjective (looking at behavior patterns) or objective (using various screening instruments). In most cases, both types may be necessary for developing a comprehensive profile of the client.

RECOGNIZING BEHAVIORAL PATTERNS IN CHEMICAL DEPENDENCY

Before individuals who are chemically dependent can be treated, there must be some recognition that a problem exists. This realization by other persons close to the user usually results from certain changes in behavior that suggest that something is happening within the individual's life. Sometimes this is misunderstood as depression, a mood disorder, or some other behavioral problem.

Although there are specific signs and symptoms that indicate probable chemical abuse and possible chemical dependency, it is important to differentiate among the patterns of use of mood-altering chemicals. The brief definitions that follow may provide some basic guidelines in assisting counselors in developing their own meanings for the words.

1. *Use.* The ingestion of a mood-altering chemical with the goal of somehow altering one's state of consciousness. (May or may not cause problems.)
2. *Misuse.* Using a mood-altering chemical with some adverse physical, psychological, social, or legal consequence (e.g., getting high, getting stoned, getting drunk, etc.).
3. *Abuse.* Chronic, recurrent misuse of mood-altering chemicals.
4. *Dependence.* A state characterized by a strong urge or craving to change one's state of consciousness through the use of a mood-altering chemical, with the development of tolerance and of withdrawal symptoms (physical or psychological) upon removal of the drug (Lawson, Ellis, & Rivers 1984, 37).

The symptoms of chemical dependency can be divided artificially into six areas of impact, or symptoms: physical, behavioral, emotional, social, spiritual, and other.

Physical Symptoms

Physical symptoms involve changes in the person's physical health as the result of his or her abuse of mood-altering chemicals. These include the use of alcohol and other drugs as medication, perhaps to get to sleep or to relieve stress. They also entail the kinds of physical difficulties outlined in chapter 2 that often result from the abuse of various drugs. The individual may experience problems with his or her liver, heart, or stomach because of the effects of the drugs being used. He or she may also have bruises and injuries that were acquired while drinking or using. Because the user often does not eat properly, neglecting food in order to focus on drugs, the caloric intake becomes limited and he or she becomes physically run down. As the tolerance for illnesses, like colds or flu, decreases, the person is often unable to work or to perform other responsibilities. Additional physical symptoms can include blackouts, increased tolerance for the preferred drug, decreased sexual drive, tremors, and an overall deterioration in physical health.

Behavioral Symptoms

Chemical dependency brings on major changes in the user's behavior. One area of change has to do with the drug itself. The individual becomes preoccupied with drinking or using, spending much time thinking about the next occasion that he or she will be able to use. This preoccupation, however, may be accompanied by an avoidance of conversation about alcohol and other drugs. While the person may have formerly boasted about getting high or getting intoxicated at parties, now he or she is not likely to talk about it. If someone else brings up the subject, the individual may become angry, fearing that the person will talk to him or her about the using that is being done. This avoidance generally results from a fear that he or she has become chemically dependent. In addition, the individual often changes his or her drinking patterns, perhaps going days without using, because of a need to prove that no addiction exists. After the individual has been "on the wagon" to prove that he or she can handle drinking, then that person is likely to change the drinking pattern again to show that he or she can drink without having the same old problems. This may involve changing drinks (e.g., from whiskey to beer), shifting locations, changing the times for drinking, or even switching from one drug to another. But no matter how many changes are made, the individual becomes immersed in the same old problems. Such alterations may also include having a drink or a joint to start the day, a tendency to gulp drinks or to sneak extra "hits" on a joint, or to hide drugs so that he or she will not have to worry about ever being in a situation where they are not available.

In addition, other behavioral symptoms appear. The individual frequently begins lying about his or her alcohol and other drug use. Knowing that this use is above normal and feeling ashamed of it, individuals either lie verbally ("No, I haven't been drinking") or lie by acting as though they aren't really high. Broken promises or commitments occur. Individuals fail to show up for social engagements. They are unable to make decisions. Perhaps most dangerous of all is an increase in aggressive behavior, which may include the physical abuse of the self, as well as the physical, and verbal, abuse of others. Frequently, such aggression results from the person's belief that others are the cause of his or her problems; thus, the individual strikes out against them with verbal and/or physical abuse. The often-used WART analogy stands out— "with alcohol, repeated troubles." Most of all, the user becomes unpredictable in his or her behavior.

Emotional Symptoms

As individuals progress in their movement toward chemical dependency, emotional changes occur. Feelings of remorse or guilt are very common as the person experiences a sense that his or her using and primary reasons for using are out of control and no longer fit the norms of his or her previous drinking patterns. In addition, the individuals regularly recognize the kinds of problems that their using is creating for their friends and family and feel guilt about this as well. Unfortunately, the remorse or guilt experienced is not enough to stop their using. At the same time, users develop unpredictable mood swings. They may, on the one hand, be very loving, helpful, and giving (to the point of doing special things for the family and bringing lavish gifts home and acting especially perfect). However, the unpredictability of these mood swings also means that the individuals may then, with little warning, show irrational outbursts of anger, intense jealousy, irrational resentment, and a lack of interest in what others think or feel. In addition, chemically dependent people often become very grandiose in their behavior, buying things they don't need, giving exceptionally lavish gifts to friends and family, picking up the check at bars and restaurants, and generally acting in a very extravagant manner.

Social Symptoms

Chemically dependent individuals generally withdraw from their family and friends, developing either a tendency to be alone most of the time, so that they can use without fear of being criticized, or making new friends whose common interests revolve around the use of mood-altering chemicals. Thus, the social relationships that had been important to the individuals deteriorate, partially as a result of the withdrawal, and partially as the result of their friends being somewhat confused and embarrassed by their new behavior. A need to use before social events, to get them ready, and after social events, perhaps having a "few for the road," develops. The person becomes uncomfortable at any kind of social gathering where alcohol or other drugs are not being used. The primary criterion for whether or not to attend a social occasion becomes the possibility of drinking or using. In addition, problems at work or at school develop as the individual's interest deteriorates and attitudinal problems develop. There may also be an increase in legal problems, whether it be public intoxication, driving under the influence, or reckless driving.

Spiritual Symptoms

This may be the most clearly defined change in the individual. As the person progresses in his or her dependency on alcohol and other drugs, the importance of these mood-altering chemicals increases to the point that they are more important than anything else. The individual becomes so dependent on drugs that he or she will lie or steal to maintain the supply, and a virtually total breakdown in his or her values and ethics results. As will be shown in chapter 7, the individual's values and ethics are the core of his or her spirituality. At the same time, individuals become attracted to others whose life style and value systems are considerably different from what they have been used to. In a sense, using with "inferiors" is an attempt to excuse the person's own behavior by comparing him- or herself to others who appear, on the surface, to be worse off. With these changes in various areas of the individual's life comes a growing rigidity in life style; this rigidity often includes the individual's feeling the need to drink or use at specific times during the day or night and feeling frustrated and uneasy if events preclude use at that time. The person's self-imposed rules begin to change, but do so in a way that does not tolerate interference with his or her drinking or using time. As a result, there is a growing loss of control. Blackouts, binge drinking, morning drinking, and repeated broken promises all increase. The individual becomes much less predictable as to whether he or she will be available for family holidays, will have problems caused by alcohol-impaired judgment, and will be sociable in a variety of settings.

LABORATORY PATTERN

In addition to an assessment of behavior patterns, proper use of lab results can also assist in diagnosis and management of drug use. The most widely used test is the measure of alcohol level, which indicates the individual's state of intoxication at the time of testing. In addition, a standard urine drug screen will detect trace amounts of such chemicals as opiates, cocaine, Quaaludes, barbiturates, nicotine, and a number of tranquilizers. In addition, urine tests can screen for marijuana products, but do not indicate the degree of intoxication or confirm recent exposure as other drug screens do. The presence of cannabinoids in the urine only means that the individual has used marijuana sometime in the recent past. The urine screen is sensitive, reliable, and requires only a small quantity of urine; samples may be stored for long periods.

SCREENING INSTRUMENTS

DSM-III-R

Although the *Diagnostic and Statistical Manual of Mental Disorders* (DSM-III-R, APA, 1987) is not a screening instrument as such, it does list some specific diagnostic criteria for determining if an individual is suffering from a form of chemical dependency. Using the general heading "Psychoactive Substance Use Disorders," the DSM-III-R divides them into ten categories, each of which is further divided into the classes of *dependence* and *abuse*. The nine categories which the DSM-III-R identifies relate to the use of alcohol, amphetamines, cannabis, cocaine, hallucinogens, nicotine, opioids, phencyclidines (PCP), and sedatives or hypnotics. Polysubstance dependence, psychoactive-substance dependence not otherwise specified, and miscellaneous dependence or abuse are also indicated.

Wanberg and Horn (1987) have divided the various criteria used by the DSM-III into three general categories; they are also appropriate for the DSM-III-R. These categories include the pattern of pathological alcohol use, impairment of social and occupational functioning, and tolerance or withdrawal secondary to alcohol use. A difficulty in applying the categories is that tolerance is difficult to identify reliably, and individuals who must report the information on which the criteria are based are often unreliable, either because of denial or a lack of information. The actual diagnostic criteria for the various psychoactive-substance-dependence disorders are presented in table 4.1. The additional diagnostic criteria that are needed to change the diagnosis from one of dependence to abuse are shown in table 4.2.

The Twenty-Questions List

Probably the most used screening instrument is the Twenty-Questions List, originally developed at Johns Hopkins University Hospital in Baltimore, Maryland, to determine whether or not an individual was alcoholic. The questions are given to the individual being evaluated and ask for a self-report on the effects of drinking on his or her life. Areas of the individual's life are scrutinized in specific ways, including friends, family, work, cravings, emotions, health, and self-confidence. The twenty questions, shown in table 4.3, are a good preliminary screening device, but, again, there is the possibility that the self-report may be distorted by the individual's denial.

Table 4.1   Diagnostic Criteria for Psychoactive Substance Dependence

---

A. At least three of the following:
   (1) substance often taken in larger amounts or over a longer period than the person intended
   (2) persistent desire or one or more unsuccessful efforts to cut down or control substance use
   (3) a great deal of time spent in activities necessary to get the substance (e.g., theft), taking the substance (e.g., chain smoking), or recovering from its effects
   (4) frequent intoxication or withdrawal symptoms when expected to fulfill major role obligations at work, school, or home (e.g., does not go to work because hung over, goes to school or work "high," intoxicated while taking care of his or her children), or when substance use is physically hazardous (e.g., drives when intoxicated)
   (5) important social, occupational, or recreational activities given up or reduced because of substance use
   (6) continued substance use despite knowledge of having a persistent or recurrent social, psychological, or physical problem that is caused or exacerbated by the use of the substance (e.g., keeps using heroin despite family arguments about it, cocaine-induced depression, or having an ulcer made worse by drinking)
   (7) marked tolerance; need for markedly increased amounts of the substance (i.e., at least a 50% increase) in order to achieve intoxication or desired effect, or markedly diminished effect with continued use of the same amount
   Note: The following items may not apply to cannabis, hallucinogens, or phencyclidine (PCP):
   (8) characteristic withdrawal symptoms (see specific withdrawal syndromes under Psychoactive Substance-Induced Organic Mental Disorders)
   (9) substance often taken to relieve or avoid withdrawal symptoms
B. Some symptoms of the disturbance have persisted for at least one month, or have occurred repeatedly over a longer period of time.

CRITERIA FOR SEVERITY OF PSYCHOACTIVE SUBSTANCE DEPENDENCE:

   Mild: Few, if any, symptoms in excess of those required to make the diagnosis, and the symptoms result in no more than mild impairment in occupational functioning or in usual social activities or relationships with others.

   Moderate: Symptoms or functional impairment between "mild" and "severe."

   Severe: Many symptoms in excess of those required to make the diagnosis, and the symptoms markedly interfere with occupational functioning or with usual social activities or relationships with others.[1]

   In Partial Remission: During the past six months, some use of the substance and some symptoms of dependence.

   In Full Remission: During the past six months, either no use of the substance, or use of the substance and no symptoms of dependence.

---

[1]Because of the availability of cigarettes and other nicotine-containing substances and the absence of a clinically significant nicotine intoxication syndrome, impairment in occupational or social functioning is not necessary for a rating of severe Nicotine Dependence.

Source: From *The Diagnostic and Statistic Manual of Mental Disorders* (*DSM-III-R*), American Psychiatric Association. (1987). Washington, DC: Author. Reprinted by permission.

Table 4.2 Diagnostic Criteria for Psychoactive Substance Abuse

A. A maladaptive pattern of psychoactive substance use indicated by at least one of the following:
   (1) continued use despite knowledge of having a persistent or recurrent social, occupational, psychological, or physical problem that is caused or exacerbated by use of the psychoactive substance
   (2) recurrent use in situations in which use is physically hazardous (e.g., driving while intoxicated)
B. Some symptoms of the disturbance have persisted for at least one month, or have occurred repeatedly over a longer period of time.
C. Never met the criteria for Psychoactive Substance Dependence for this substance.

Source: From *The Diagnostic and Statistical Manual of Mental Disorders* (*DSM-III-R*), American Psychiatric Association. (1987). Washington, DC: Author. Reprinted by permission.

Table 4.3 Are You an Alcoholic?

To answer this question, ask yourself the following questions and answer them as honestly as you can.

	YES	NO
1. Do you lose time from work due to drinking?	____	____
2. Is drinking making your home life unhappy?	____	____
3. Do you drink because you are shy with other people?	____	____
4. Is drinking affecting your reputation?	____	____
5. Have you ever felt remorse after drinking?	____	____
6. Have you gotten into financial trouble as a result of drinking?	____	____
7. Do you turn to lower companions and an inferior environment when drinking?	____	____
8. Does your drinking make you careless of your family's welfare?	____	____
9. Has your ambition decreased since drinking?	____	____
10. Do you crave a drink at a definite time daily?	____	____
11. Do you want a drink the next morning?	____	____
12. Does drinking cause you to have difficulty in sleeping?	____	____
13. Has your efficiency decreased since drinking?	____	____
14. Is drinking jeopardizing your job or business?	____	____
15. Do you drink to escape from worries or trouble?	____	____
16. Do you drink alone?	____	____
17. Have you ever had a complete loss of memory as a result of drinking?	____	____
18. Has your physician ever treated you for drinking?	____	____
19. Do you drink to build up your self confidence?	____	____
20. Have you ever been to a hospital or institution on account of drinking?	____	____

If you have answered YES to any one of the questions, there is a definite warning that you may be alcoholic.

If you have answered YES to any two, the chances are that you are an alcoholic.

If you have answered YES to three or more, you are definitely an alcoholic.

The above test questions are used by Johns Hopkins University Hospital, Baltimore, Maryland, in deciding whether or not a patient is alcoholic.

Michigan Alcoholism Screening Test (MAST)

This test, introduced in 1971, includes a list of twenty-five questions to be answered *yes* or *no*. Requiring only 10 to 15 minutes to administer, it weighs each item on a scale of 0 to 5 and provides a total score which can be used to detect or identify suspected or presumed alcoholics and becomes part of the total data used in making an actual diagnosis. Research has shown that a total score of ten points or more usually indicates that the individual is an alcoholic. Other data, however, suggest that the MAST is "too sensitive" and results in a high rate of false-positive identification. This indicates that a large number of individuals who test as though they are alcoholic actually are not, with one of the problems being the weight given to the individual's having attended an AA meeting. Again, the MAST suffers from the problem of the individuals being truthful in their responses to the clear-cut questions asked. At this point, there is reason to be optimistic about the value of using the MAST with a fair degree of competence, but the MAST must be used as part of the data-gathering process before a diagnosis can be formulated.

Table 4.4   Michigan Alcoholism Screening Test (MAST)

	YES	NO
0. Do you enjoy a drink now and then?	0	
1. Do you feel you are a normal drinker? (By normal we mean you drink less than or as much as most other people.)		2*
2. Have you ever awakened the morning after some drinking the night before and found that you could not remember a part of the evening?	2	
3. Does your wife, husband, a parent, or other near relative ever worry or complain about your drinking?	2	
4. Can you stop drinking without a struggle after one or two drinks?		2
5. Do you feel guilty about your drinking?	1	
6. Do friends or relatives think you are a normal drinker?		2
7. Are you able to stop drinking when you want to?		2
8. Have you ever attended a meeting of Alcoholics Anonymous (AA)?	5	
9. Have you gotten into physical fights when drinking?	1	
10. Has your drinking ever created problems between you and your wife, husband, a parent, or other relative?	2	
11. Has your wife, husband (or other family members) ever gone to anyone for help about your drinking?	2	

(*continued*)

Table 4.4 *(continued)*

	YES	NO
12. Have you ever lost friends because of your drinking?	2	
13. Have you ever gotten into trouble at work or school because of drinking?	2	
14. Have you ever lost a job because of drinking?	2	
15. Have you ever neglected your obligations, your family, or your work for two or more days in a row because you were drinking?	2	
16. Do you drink before noon fairly often?	1	
17. Have you ever been told you have liver trouble? Cirrhosis?	2	
18. After heavy drinking have you ever had delirium tremens (DTs) or severe shaking, or heard voices or seen things that really weren't there?	2**	
19. Have you ever gone to anyone for help about your drinking?	5	
20. Have you ever been in a hospital because of drinking?	5	
21. Have you ever been a patient in a psychiatric hospital or on a psychiatric ward of a general hospital where drinking was part of the problem that resulted in hospitalization?	2	
22. Have you ever been seen at a psychiatric or mental health clinic or gone to any doctor, social worker, or clergyman for help with any emotional problem, where drinking was part of the problem?	2	
23. Have you ever been arrested for drunk driving, driving while intoxicated, or driving under the influence of alcoholic beverages?	2***	
If Yes, how many times?_____)		
24. Have you ever been arrested, or taken into custody, even for a few hours, because of other drunk behavior?	2***	
(If Yes, how many times?_____)		

*Indicates alcoholic response and points for scoring
**5 points for delirium tremens
***2 points for *each* arrest
Scoring System: In general, 5 points or more would place the subject in an "alcoholic" category, 4 points would be suggestive of alcoholism, 3 points or less would indicate the subject was probably not alcoholic.

Programs using the above scoring system find it very sensitive at the 5 point level and it tends to find more people alcoholic than anticipated. However, it is a screening test and should be sensitive at its lower levels.

Most alcoholics score 10 points or more.

Source: From "Michigan Alchoholism Screening Test: The Quest for a New Diagnostic Instrument" by M. L. Selzer, 1971, *American Journal of Psychiatry, 127,* pp. 1653–1658. Reprinted by permission.

Adolescent Alcohol Involvement Scale

The Adolescent Alcohol Involvement Scale was developed in 1979 to use with teenagers to account for variations in use and its effects on the individual resulting from a shorter history of drinking. This instrument takes into consideration that adolescent drinking involves a higher degree of "sneaking around," and therefore questions the individual regarding the methods by which the person acquires his or her alcohol, as well as who he or she drinks with. This scale (shown in table 4.5) is also an effective screening instrument when used with other kinds of information.

Table 4.5   Adolescent Alcohol Involvement Scale

Adolescent Alcohol Involvement Scale, and Scoring Instructions

1. How often do you drink?
   a. never
   b. once or twice a year
   c. once or twice a month
   d. every weekend
   e. several times a week
   f. every day

2. When did you have your last drink?
   a. never drank
   b. not for over a year
   c. between 6 months and 1 year ago
   d. several weeks ago
   e. last week
   f. yesterday
   g. today

3. I usually start to drink because:
   a. I like the taste
   b. to be like my friends
   c. to feel like an adult
   d. I feel nervous, tense, full of worries or problems
   e. I feel sad, lonely, sorry for myself

4. What do you drink?
   a. wine
   b. beer
   c. mixed drinks
   d. hard liquor
   e. a substitute for alcohol—paint thinner, sterno, cough medicine, mouthwash, hair tonic, etc.

5. How do you get your drinks?
   a. supervised by parents or relatives
   b. from brothers or sisters
   c. from home without parents' knowledge
   d. from friends
   e. buy it with false identification

6. When did you take your first drink?
   a. never
   b. recently
   c. after age 15
   d. at ages 14 or 15
   e. between ages 10–13
   f. before age 10

7. What time of day do you usually drink?
   a. with meals
   b. at night
   c. afternoons
   d. mostly in the morning or when I first awake
   e. I often get up during my sleep and drink

(continued)

Table 4.5   (continued)

Adolescent Alcohol Involvement Scale, and Scoring Instructions   (continued)

8. Why did you take your first drink?
   a. curiosity
   b. parents or relatives offered
   c. friends encouraged me
   d. to feel more like an adult
   e. to get drunk or high

9. How much do you drink, when you do drink?
   a. 1 drink
   b. 2 drinks
   c. 3–6 drinks
   d. 6 or more drinks
   e. until "high" or drunk

10. Whom do you drink with?
    a. parents or relatives only
    b. with brothers or sisters only
    c. with friends own age
    d. with older friends
    e. alone

11. What is the greatest effect you have had from alcohol?
    a. loose, easy feeling
    b. moderately "high"
    c. drunk
    d. became ill
    e. passed out
    f. was drinking heavily and the next day didn't remember what happened

12. What is the greatest effect drinking has had on your life?
    a. none—no effect
    b. has interfered with talking to someone
    c. has prevented me from having a good time
    d. has interfered with my school work
    e. have lost friends because of drinking
    f. has gotten me into trouble at home
    g. was in a fight or destroyed property
    h. has resulted in an accident, an injury, arrest, or being punished at school for drinking

13. How do you feel about your drinking?
    a. no problem at all
    b. I can control it and set limits on myself
    c. I can control myself, but my friends easily influence me
    d. I often feel bad about my drinking
    e. I need help to control myself
    f. I have had professional help to control my drinking

14. How do others see you?
    a. can't say, or a normal drinker for my age
    b. when I drink I tend to neglect my family or friends
    c. my family or friends advise me to control or cut down on my drinking
    d. my family or friends tell me to get help for my drinking
    e. my family or friends have already gone for help for my drinking

Scoring Instructions:
The highest total score is 79. An *a* response is scored 1 (except on questions 1, 2, 6, 12, 13, and 14, on which *a* = 0; *b* = 2; *c* = 3; and so on to *h* = 8. When more than one response is made, the one with the higher or highest score is used. An unanswered question is scored 0.

Table 4.5 (*continued*)

Score	Involvement
42–57	"Alcohol Misuse"
58–79	"Alcoholic-like drinkers"

Reprinted by permission, from the *Journal of Studies on Alcohol,* Vol. 40, pp. 291–300, 1979. Copyright by Journal Studies on Alcohol, Inc., Rutgers Center of Alcohol Studies, New Brunswick, NJ 08903

Problem Drinking Scale (PDS)

The Problem Drinking Scale (PDS) was developed by Vaillant (1983) in an attempt to identify the number of alcohol-related problems exhibited by individuals interviewed in a longitudinal study. It can become a method of identifying the seriousness of an individual's drug abuse by examining the number of life problems associated with that person's drinking or drug use. Basically, Vaillant listed a series of problems, all of which were weighed equally, and asked the individual to indicate which of those problems had occurred in his or her life as a result of drinking. Thus, the scale is based on the idea that the number and frequency of alcohol and other drug-related problems define the phenomenon known as abuse and focuses on the number of problems exhibited, rather than on the specificity of those problems. The issues which Vaillant listed include:

1. Complaints by employer.
2. Multiple job losses.
3. Complaints by family or friends.
4. Marital problems.
5. A medical problem.
6. Multiple medical problems.
7. Diagnosis by clinician.
8. Alcohol-related arrest.
9. Three or more alcohol-related arrests.
10. Two or more blackouts.
11. Going "on the wagon."
12. Morning tremulousness or drinking.
13. Tardiness or sick leave.
14. Admission of a problem with control.

In each of these questions, the word "drug" may be easily substituted for the word "alcohol." An individual who scores four or more on the PDS (that is, who indicates that he or she has at least four of the problems that are listed) is considered by Vaillant as likely to be a drug abuser until that individual spends a full year free of problems.

Alcohol Use Inventory (AUI)

A longer, more extensive screening scale for evaluating and assessing drinking behavior was developed by Horn, Wanberg, and Foster (1974). The Alcohol Use Inventory (AUI) is a 147-item, self-administered, quartile-scored instrument. It contains seventeen primary scales, each providing measures of a specific condition of alcohol use and misuse. Six second-order factors define broad dimensions of alcoholism, and the test provides a general factor to determine a conglomerate measure of the use and misuse of alcohol. The scales of the AUI are presented in table 4.6.

Table 4.6   Alcohol Use Multiple-Condition Measurement Concepts: Scales of the Alcohol Use Inventory

---
PRIMARY SCALES

Benefits of Alcohol Use:

1. SOCIALIM—Drink to improve sociability: drinking helps to socialize, make friends, feel less inferior, relax socially, overcome shyness, feel more important, get along with people, relate better to opposite sex, and better express ideas.
2. MENTALIM—Drink to improve mental functioning: drink to be mentally alert, think better, work better, reach higher goals.
3. MANGMOOD—Drink to manage and change moods: drink to let down, relieve tension, to forget, get over being depressed, change moods, because things pile up; swing from periods of happiness to periods of despair.
4. MARICOPE—Drinking follows marital problems: marital problems before drank, spouse unfaithful, spouse jealous, changes in spouse and marital problems have led to drinking.

Styles of Alcohol Use:

5. GREGARUS—Gregarious versus solo use: drink at bars, parties, with friends, not alone, not at home, with opposite sex; most friends drink; most drinking done with acquaintances; usually drink with same group; social life requires drinking.
6. COMPULSV—Obsessive-compulsive drinking: drink throughout day; always think about alcohol; drink same time daily; carry bottle; sneak drinks; bottle by bedside; fear won't have drink.
7. SUSTAIND—Sustained versus periodic use: drink daily; drink weekends and during week; no abstinent periods; intoxicated daily; drinking daily last 6 months or more; do not go on wagon after drunk; long drinking periods.

Disruptive Consequences of Alcohol Use:

8. LCONTROL—Loss of control over behavior when drinking: blackouts, pass out, get mean and belligerent, stagger and stumble, harm to others, suicide attempts, all when drinking; gulp drinks.

Table 4.6   (*continued*)

PRIMARY SCALES   (*continued*)

Disruptive Consequences of Alcohol Use (*continued*):

   9. ROLEMALA—Social role maladaptation: loss of job, live alone, driving offenses, miss work, move a lot, detained by authorities, unemployed, not in a marriage situation, all as a result of drinking.
  10. DELIRIUM—Psychoperceptual withdrawal: fuzzy thinking, see, hear, feel things, weird and frightening sensations, all when sobering up; have had delirium tremens.
  11. HANGOVER—Psychophysical withdrawal: convulsions, shakes, hangovers, physically sick, hot and sweaty, rapid heartbeat, all when sobering up.
  12. MARIPROB—Marital problems in consequence of drinking: spouse angry and irritated over drinking; belittle and argue with spouse when drinking; physically abusive when drinking; spouse nags when drinking; drinking a factor in marital problems.

Self-Concerns about Disruptive Consequences:

  13. QUANTITY—Quantity of daily use when drinking: much wine, beer, spirits a day when drinking.
  14. GUILTWOR—Guilt and worry associated with drinking: worried drinking getting worse, occurring at unaccustomed times; drink causing noticeable fear, depression, anxiety; avoid talking about drinking; make excuses to cover up drinking; guilt after drunk; drinking causes hardships with family and friends.
  15. HELPBEFR—Prior attempts to stop drinking: used Antabuse, have been detoxified, attended AA, sought religion to stop, have sought help many times, used tranquilizers to sober up.

Acknowledgement of Alcohol Use Problems:

  16. RECEPTIV—Treatment readiness: recent crisis led to help; need help now; give month's salary to stop drinking; will do what a counselor suggests; feel that will be able to stop drinking.
  17. AWARENES—Awareness of problems: am sure have problems with drinking; unable to regulate time, amount drunk; realize drinking interferes with living responsibilities.

SECOND-ORDER SCALES

  A. ENHANCED—Drinking to enhance functioning: drink to have fun, to be mentally alert, to have better ideas, to meet people, for ideas to come more freely, to work better, to get along with people, to better express thoughts to opposite sex, to be happier; go to parties to drink; social life requires drinking; most friends drink; do most drinking at bars; most drinking done with friends and acquaintances; encourage others to drink with me; drink to work better.
  B. OBSESSED—Obsessive-sustained drinking: do not drink, sober up and drink again; drinking daily last six months or more; don't go on the wagon; drink during week and on weekends; dwelling on alcohol constantly; keep alcohol close at hand; drink to go to sleep at night; sneak drinks; hide bottles; intoxicated daily; little or no time between drinking periods; carry a bottle; fear may not have drink when need it; long drinking periods; drinking during work day.

(*continued*)

Table 4.6   (continued)

SECOND-ORDER SCALES   (continued)

C. DISRUPTI—Uncontrolled, life-functioning disruption: drinking much spirits, wine or beer each day when drink; as a result of drinking; have had a convulsion, long blackouts, been physically sick, had delirium tremens, passed out, stumbled and staggered, saw and heard things not there, felt things not there, moved from place to place, lived alone, charged with drunken driving, missed work, lost a job, detained for public drunkenness, had medical help to sober up; gulp drinks; drank in morning to relieve hangovers.

E. ANXCONCN—Anxious concern about drinking: drink causes hardships on family, excessive worry, guilt, shame, depression, mood changes, vague fears and anxieties; show resentments when drinking; afraid drinking getting worse, is occurring at unaccustomed times; drink to get over depression, to relieve tension, to forget, to let down, because things pile up; make excuses to cover drinking; avoid talking about drinking; guilt and depression after bout; moods different when drinking than when not drinking; sad when drinking; drink to change moods.

F. RECPAWAR—Awareness of alcohol problem: unable to regulate and control time and amount of drinking; frequency and amount recently increased; drinking definitely a problem now; difficult living without alcohol; present drinking interferes with responsibilities; recent crisis increased awareness of need for help; sure have drinking problem; sought help on own; need assistance now; willing to stay in treatment several weeks; worth more than one month's salary to correct problem; will do anything to stop; will try whatever counselor suggests; am confident can stop drinking.

THIRD-ORDER ALCOHOLISM FACTOR

G. ALCINVOL—Broad alcohol involvement: drinking much distilled spirits; unable stop after one or two; shakes, fuzzy thinking, hangovers, physically sick, noticeable fears, blackouts, see things not there, hear things not there, feel things not there, hot and feverish, rapid heart beat, weird and frightening sensations, miss work, pass out, lose control over what to do, all when drinking or sobering up; drink to relieve hangover; drink in order to feel important, overcome shyness, relieve tension, to forget, when things pile up, to get over depression, to sleep at night; drink throughout day, keep somewhat intoxicated daily; keep alcohol close at hand, constantly think about alcohol, gulp drinks; make excuses or lie to cover up drinking; show marked resentments when drinking; moved geographically to stop drinking; feel depressed after a bout; always have drinks at a bar or party.

Source: From "Assessment of Alchohol Use with Multidimensional Concepts and Measures" by K. W. Wanberg and J. L. Horn, 1983, *American Psychologist, 38*, pp. 1055–1069. Copyright 1983 by the American Psychological Association. Reprinted by permission.

The Comprehensive Drinker Profile (CDP)

The Comprehensive Drinker Profile (CDP) was developed in 1971 as a structured intake interview schedule for assessing alcohol problems.

Since that time, the CDP, having been used and evaluated with a variety of populations, has been revised extensively. It provides an intensive and comprehensive history and status of the individual's use and abuse of alcohol, focusing on information that is relevant to the selection, planning, and implementation of treatment. This instrument (sample questions shown in table 4.7) covers a wide array of important information about the individual and has incorporated the information ordinarily found in the MAST. Unlike other instruments that assess the degree of severity of alcohol abuse, the CDP provides quantitative indexes of other dimensions, including duration of the problem, family history of alcoholism, alcohol consumption, alcohol dependence, range of drinking situations, quantity and frequency of other drug use, range of beverages used, emotional factors related to drinking, and life problems other than drinking (Miller & Marlatt 1984).

The eighty-eight question areas are complex and require that the evaluator be familiar with the information and practice administering the form before using it in real-life situations. However, because the CDP is the most comprehensive, empirically derived instrument of its kind, it can be a very sensitive assessment tool.

Table 4.7   Comprehensive Drinker Profile

Date _____ Interviewer _____

Full name of client _____

                  First   Middle   Last

Prefers to be called _____ Sex (1) _____ F (2) _____ M

A. DEMOGRAPHIC INFORMATION

Age and Residence

   A1. Date of birth _____ _____ _____   Present age _____

                     Month   Day   Year

   A2. Present local address

       Street address or box no. _____

       City or town _____

       State _____ Zip code _____

   A3. Local telephone   Area code _____ Number _____

       Best times to reach you at this number _____

   A4. Name and address of a person through whom you can be lo-

       cated if we lose contact with you (must be different from A2)

       Name _____ Relationship _____

       Street address or box no. _____

       City or town _____ State _____ Zip code _____

       Telephone Area code _____ Number _____

   A5. How did you first hear about this program?_____

       If referred, by whom? _____

                          Name   Agency

(continued)

Table 4.7 (*continued*)

A. DEMOGRAPHIC INFORMATION (*continued*)
Educational History
    A21. Describe your educational background _____
              _____ degree _____ major _____
    A22. Code highest year of education completed _____
    A23. Are you currently pursuing education or training?
          (1) _____ full time (2) _____ part time (3) _____ no classes now

B. DRINKING HISTORY
Development of the Drinking Problem
    B24. About how old were you when you first took one or more
         drinks? _____
    B25. About how old were you when you first became intoxicated?

         _____
         Do you remember what you were drinking? _____
         Beverage _____
    B26. How would you describe the drinking habits of

         ____ your mother?   0 = client does not know
                             1 = nondrinker (abstainer)
         ____ your father?   2 = occasional or light social drinker
                             3 = moderate or average social
         ____ spouse/partner?   drinker
                             4 = frequent or heavy social drinker
                             5 = problem drinker (at any time
                                 in life)
                             6 = alcoholic (at any time in life)

    B27. Do you have any *blood* relatives whom you regard as being
         or having been a problem drinker or an alcoholic?

	Number males	Number females
parents	_____ × 3 = _____	_____ × 3 = _____
brothers or sisters	_____ × 3 = _____	_____ × 3 = _____
grandparents	_____ × 2 = _____	_____ × 2 = _____
uncles or aunts	_____ × 2 = _____	_____ × 2 = _____
first cousins	_____ × 1 = _____	_____ × 1 = _____
Total scores	Males: _____	Females: _____

         Were you raised by your biological parents?
         _____ (1) yes _____ (2) no
         If not, who raised you? _____
    B28. At what age (how long ago) did drinking begin to have an
         effect on your life which you did not approve of? When did
         drinking first begin to be a problem for you?

Table 4.7 (*continued*)

B. DRINKING HISTORY (*continued*)
Development of the Drinking Problem   (*continued*)
_____ age of first problem
_____ denies that drinking is a problem
_____ years of problem duration (age, minus age at first
     problem)
At that particular time in your life when drinking first became a problem, were there any special circumstances or
events that occurred which you feel were at least partly
responsible for its becoming a problem?

_____
_____
_____
_____
_____

B29. Did you arrive at your present level of drinking:
    (1)   _____ gradually over a long period of time?
          How long? _____
    or (2)   _____ by a more rapid increase (over several months
          or less)?

Present Drinking Pattern
  B30. Drinking pattern (check one)
    Determine which of the following categories best describes
    the client's current drinking pattern:

___ (P) _____   Periodic drinker
                  Drinks less often than once a week
                  Is abstinent between drinking episodes
                     Complete episodic pattern chart
___ (S) _____   Steady drinker
                  Drinks at least once per week
                  Drinks about the same amount every week
                     without periodic episodes of heavier drinking.
                     (A heavy episode is defined as one or more
                     days in which pattern fluctuates from the
                     steady pattern by 5 or more SEC's.)[a]
                     Complete steady pattern chart
___ (C) _____   Combination pattern drinker
                  Drinks at least once per week with a regular
                     weekly pattern, but also has heavier episodes
                     as defined above
                     Complete both steady and episodic charts
    If client used to smoke but does not smoke now, how long
    has it been since the last cigarette? _____

(*continued*)

Table 4.7   (*continued*)

B. DRINKING HISTORY   (*continued*)
Present Drinking Pattern   (*continued*)
        Indicate any other use of tobacco (cigars, pipe, chewing). _____

_____

B49. Are you satisfied with your present weight? (If yes, enter
        00. If no, indicate the number of pounds client regards self
        as overweight (+) or underweight (–) using proper arith-
        metic sign.) _____

B50. Describe *all* medications that you currently use, including
        vitamins, birth control, aspirin, etc. [Ask specifically about
        tranquilizers, sedatives, stimulants, diet pills, pain medica-
        tions—by prescription or otherwise. Indicate name of each
        drug, dosage, frequency, purpose, and whether taken by
        prescription (Rx).]

Medication	Dosage	Frequency	Purpose	Rx?
_____	_____	_____	_____	_____
_____	_____	_____	_____	_____
_____	_____	_____	_____	_____
_____	_____	_____	_____	_____
_____	_____	_____	_____	_____
_____	_____	_____	_____	_____

B51. Other drugs card sort

		Specify	Last Use?	Past 3 Mos. Frequency	How?	Dose?
____	amphetamines	_____	___	_____	___	___
____	barbiturates, etc.	_____	___	_____	___	___
____	cannabis	_____	___	_____	___	___
____	cocaine	_____	___	_____	___	___
____	hallucinogens	_____	___	_____	___	___
____	inhalants	_____	___	_____	___	___
____	opiates	_____	___	_____	___	___
____	phencyclidine	_____	___	_____	___	___
____	other drugs	_____	___	_____	___	___
____	Total drug classes used			____ Total past 3 mos.		

B64. Are you currently seeing a counselor, psychologist, or psy-
        chiatrist for counseling or therapy? (If yes, specify.) _____

_____

B65. (Women) Are you pregnant or planning to become pregnant? _____

_____

Table 4.7 (*continued*)

C. MOTIVATIONAL INFORMATION

Reasons for Drinking

C66. What are the main reasons why you drink? In other words, when you are *actually drinking,* what for you is the most positive or desirable *effect* of alcohol? What do you like best about alcohol? _____

_____

C67. Are you aware of any inner thoughts or emotional feelings, or things *within* you as a person, which "trigger off" your need or desire to take a drink at a particular moment in time? _____

_____

C68. Are you aware of any particular situations or set of events, things which happen to you in the *outside world,* which would result in your feeling like having one or more drinks? _____

_____

C69. In terms of your *life as a whole,* what are the most positive *effects* or consequences of drinking?_____

_____

C70. When you are *actually drinking,* what for you is the most negative or undesirable *effect* of alcohol? In other words, what is the thing you like least about alcohol when you are drinking? _____

_____

C71. In terms of your *life as a whole,* what do you see as the most negative effects or consequences of your drinking? _____

_____

C87. Some people say that alcoholism is a disease or sickness, while others say that it is not a disease, but rather is more like a bad habit that a person has learned. Do you see it as a disease or as a bad habit? (If person says "both" have him or her indicate which they would agree with *more.*)
(1) _____ disease   (2) _____ bad habit

Drinker Type Ratings

C88. Now I am going to give you a list of six different types of drinkers and I would like you to tell me which one, in your opinion, best describes you at the present time. (Obtain rating.)
(If applicable): Now I'd like you to tell me the one that you think *your husband/wife* would choose as best describing you. (Obtain rating.)

(*continued*)

Table 4.7 (*continued*)

C. MOTIVATIONAL INFORMATION   (*continued*)
Drinker Type Ratings   (*continued*)

Which one do you think your *closest friend* would choose as
best describing you? (Obtain rating.)
Which one do you think *most people who know you* would
choose as best describing you? (Obtain rating.)
Ratings: Self _____ Spouse _____ Friend _____ Most people _____

1 = total abstainer	4 = heavy social
2 = light social	(nonproblem) drinker
(nonproblem) drinker	5 = problem drinker
3 = moderate social	6 = alcoholic
(nonproblem) drinker	

Compare self-rating with rating for "most people." Is self-
rating:
(1) ____ higher than "most"
(2) ____ equal to "most"
(3) ____ lower than "most"?
Additional comments _____

---

[a]SEC = standard ethanol content. 1 SEC = 0.5 oz (15 ml) of pure ethyl alcohol. 1 SEC = 10 oz
beer, 4 oz wine, 2.5 oz fortified wine, 1.25 oz 80-proof spirits, 1 oz 100-proof spirits.

Note. Sample items from the Comprehensive Drinker Profile are reproduced by special permission
of the publisher, Psychological Assessment Resources, Inc. Copyright 1984 by PAR, Inc. All
rights reserved. The 20-page Comprehensive Drinker Profile Test Administration Kit and
manual are available from Psychological Assessment Resources, Inc., P.O. Box 998, Odessa,
FL 33556; (813) 968-3003.

Cocaine Assessment

Gold (1984) has proposed a self-administered instrument to determine
whether or not an individual is addicted to cocaine. While it suffers from the
same weakness as many other instruments in that it relies on the individual
being truthful about his or her use of cocaine, it has exceptional value because
each of the fifty questions is followed by information about why that question
is important in determining the probability of the individual being cocaine
addicted. Thus, this series of questions (see table 4.8) has an educational, as
well as an assessment, value.

A somewhat different approach is that of measuring addiction by symptoms. The Addiction Severity Index (McLellan, Luborsky, & O'Brien 1980) has
been developed to assess seven areas which are ordinarily affected by an
addiction. Individuals are interviewed and asked to answer a series of objective questions related to the extent of various symptoms for the preceding 30
days, as well as for their lifetimes. The results indicate the severity and
importance of their problems. One weakness is that the questions are fairly
straightforward, and thus the validity of the results depends on the accuracy
of the answers, which may be influenced by an individual's memory problems
as well as by a desire to minimize the addiction.

Table 4.8   Test Yourself for Cocaine Addiction

The symptoms of cocaine addiction are as plain to see as the signals warning that addiction is perilously close. The questions that follow spell them out in detail. Anyone who answers "yes" to as few as 10 of them is teetering on the thin edge of addiction. An affirmative answer to more than 10 is a clear signal that coke has taken over, that the user is addicted and is in urgent need of treatment if he is to have a chance to return to decent health and normal living. As a guide for anyone taking the test, we have provided brief explanations and comments to make clear why an affirmative answer means trouble.

YES	NO		
____	____	1.	Do you have to use larger doses of cocaine to get the high you once experienced with smaller doses? (This means you have developed a tolerance to the drug, that is, that you need more of it by a more direct route to achieve the same effect.)
____	____	2.	Do you use cocaine almost continuously until your supply is exhausted? (This is called bingeing, and it signals loss of control over drug use.)
____	____	3.	Is the cost of cocaine the major factor limiting your use, and do you wish you could afford more? (Your internal controls are virtually gone. The drug is in charge, and you will find yourself doing anything to get it.)
____	____	4.	Do you use cocaine two or more times a week? (If you do, you are in the highest risk group for addiction.)
____	____	5.	Do you have three or more of the following physical symptoms? Sleep problems, nose bleeds, headaches, sinus problems, voice problems, difficulty swallowing, sexual performance problems, nausea or vomiting, trouble breathing or shortness of breath, constant sniffling or rubbing your nose, irregular heart beats, epileptic seizures or convulsions? (Three or more of these indicate severe loss of bodily function related to coke abuse–addiction.)
____	____	6.	Do you have three or more of the following psychological symptoms? Jitteryness, anxiety, depression, panic, irritability, suspiciousness, paranoia, problems concentrating, hallucinations (seeing things that are not there), hearing voices when there are none, loss of interest in friends, hobbies, sports, or other noncocaine activities, memory problems, thoughts about suicide, attempted suicide, compulsive, repetitious acts like combing the hair, straightening of clothes or ties, tapping the feet for no reason?

(continued)

Table 4.8 (*continued*)

YES	NO		
			(Cocaine abuse is causing psychological problems that are not within the individual's capacity to control.)
_____	_____	7.	Have any or all of the problems specified in the previous two questions caused you to stop using cocaine for a period ranging from two weeks to six months or longer? (If not, the acquired disabilities are not strong enough to overcome the addiction.)
_____	_____	8.	Do you find that you must take other drugs or alcohol to calm down following cocaine use? (You are trying to medicate yourself so as to maintain your cocaine habit without suffering the terrible side effects of addiction. You are, of course, flirting with becoming addicted to a second drug.)
_____	_____	9.	Are you afraid that if you stop using cocaine, your work will suffer? (You are psychologically dependent on the drug.)
_____	_____	10.	Are you afraid that if you stop using cocaine you will be too depressed or unmotivated or without sufficient energy to function at your present level? (You are addicted and afraid of the withdrawal symptoms.)
_____	_____	11.	Do you find that you cannot turn down cocaine when it is offered? (Use is out of your control.)
_____	_____	12.	Do you think about limiting your use of cocaine? (You are on the verge of addiction and are trying to ration use of the drug.)
_____	_____	13.	Do you dream about cocaine? (This is related to compulsive use and the total domination of the drug.)
_____	_____	14.	Do you think about cocaine at work? (This is also a part of the obsession with the drug.)
_____	_____	15.	Do you think about cocaine when you are talking or interacting with a loved one? (Obsession with the drug dominates all aspects of living.)
_____	_____	16.	Are you unable to stop using the drug for one month? (This is certainly a sign of addiction.)
_____	_____	17.	Have you lost or discarded your pre-cocaine friends?

Table 4.8   (*continued*)

YES	NO		
			(You are stacking the deck in favor of cocaine by reducing negative feedback.)
_____	_____	18.	Have you noticed that you have lost your pre-cocaine values: that is, that you don't care about your job or career, your home and family, or that you will lie and steal to get coke? (Addiction causes slow but steady changes in personality and the approach to life to reduce intrapsychic conflict.)
_____	_____	19.	Do you feel the urge to use cocaine when you see your pipe or mirror or other paraphernalia? Or taste it when you are not using it? Or feel the urge to use it when you see it or talk about it? (This is called conditioning and occurs after long-term, heavy use.)
_____	_____	20.	Do you usually use cocaine alone? (When addiction sets in, this is the pattern. Social usage ceases.)
_____	_____	21.	Do you borrow heavily to support your cocaine habit? (You can be pretty sure you're addicted if you are willing to live so far above your means to get the drug.)
_____	_____	22.	Do you prefer cocaine to family activities, food, or sex? (This is a sure sign of addiction. Cocaine need overrides fundamental human needs for food, sex, social interaction.)
_____	_____	23.	Do you deal or distribute cocaine to others? (This kind of change in behavior signals addiction because it is an accommodation to the need for the drug.)
_____	_____	24.	Are you afraid of being found out to be a cocaine user? (Addicts usually live a double life, preferring not to choose one or another alternative.)
_____	_____	25.	When you stop using the drug, do you get depressed or crash? (This is a sign of withdrawal—a symptom of addiction.)
_____	_____	26.	Do you miss work, or reschedule appointments, or fail to meet important obligations because of your cocaine use? (The drug has taken over your life.)

(*continued*)

Table 4.8   (*continued*)

YES	NO		
_____	_____	27.	Is your cocaine use a threat to your career or personal goals? Has your cocaine use caused you to lose interest in your career? Has cocaine caused you job problems? Has the drug caused you to lose your job? Has your cocaine use caused you to lose interest in or to have violent quarrels with people you love? Has your cocaine use caused you to lose your spouse or loved one? (You would hardly sacrifice so much if you were not addicted.)
_____	_____	28.	Do people keep telling you that you are different or have changed in a significant way? (Addicted people are indeed different from the way they were pre-cocaine. Such comments are a clue to addiction.)
_____	_____	29.	Have you used more than 50 percent of your savings for cocaine? Has your cocaine use bankrupted you and caused you to incur large debts? Have you committed a crime to support yourself and your cocaine habit? Have you stolen from work and/or family and friends? (If you are not addicted, would cocaine be worth these dreadful problems?)
_____	_____	30.	Do you believe that your cocaine use has some medicinal value in treating a problem you have with energy, motivation, confidence, depression, or sex? (Users who believe this are the most likely to develop addiction.)
_____	_____	31.	Do you think you have had withdrawal symptoms when you stopped using cocaine? (Only addicted persons experience withdrawal.)
_____	_____	32.	If you had $100 to spend, would you spend it on cocaine rather than on something for your house or apartment, on a gift for someone you love, on theater, records, movies, going out with friends or family? (Addicts become so fixated on their drug they can think of nothing else, no one else, and no other form of entertainment.)
_____	_____	33.	Do you think that you are addicted? (If you think so, you probably are.)
_____	_____	34.	Do you use cocaine compulsively despite your recognition that the drug is a very real threat to your physical and psychological well-being,

Table 4.8   (*continued*)

YES	NO		
			relationships, family, and job? (This is addiction.)
_____	_____	35.	Did you ever enter psychiatric treatment or therapy for a cocaine-related problem and not tell the doctor or therapist about your cocaine use or how current or recent it is? (When an addicted person is pressured into getting help, he may not only try to cover up the extent of his drug abuse, but may also use his treatment as a cover for his continued use of the drug.)
_____	_____	36.	Did you have a cocaine problem that was cured either through your own efforts alone or with the help of friends or with professional treatment? (The critical word is "cured." No addict is really cured—rather, he has a remission of a chronic disease that can recur should he become a user of cocaine again.)
_____	_____	37.	Have you ever used cocaine and had hallucinations, a convulsion or seizure, angina (severe pain around the heart), loss of consciousness, the impulse to kill yourself or others? And when any of these side effects passed, did you figure that you would use less next time or use a purer quality of the drug? (These side effects are related to addictive use, but the addict prefers to ascribe them to overdose or to the adulterants used to make the drug go further. He then can continue to use the drug under the illusion that it will be okay the next time.)
_____	_____	38.	Do you leave paraphernalia or a supply of cocaine at work? (This may be a call for help by a person who feels that his or her life is out of his control. It is like a suicide note left so that people will find it and prevent the act.)
_____	_____	39.	Do you sometimes wish that you would be discovered as a user by someone who would see to it that you got into treatment and recovered? (If so, you know you need help and want it.)
_____	_____	40.	Do you use cocaine three times a week or even more often, and still try to maintain an interest in diet, health, exercise, and fitness? (The interest may be there, but the fact is that such heavy use of the drug makes it virtually

(*continued*)

Table 4.8   (*continued*)

YES	NO		
			impossible to act on the interest. There is too great a conflict in values.)
_____	_____	41.	Have you switched from intranasal use to freebasing or intravenous use? (This usually means that tolerance to the drug has developed, and it is very likely that you will binge and become addicted in short order.)
_____	_____	42.	Have you been using cocaine more than once a week for three or more years? (With this much use, any stress, or change in your life, can turn you into a daily user with a high probability of addiction resulting.)
_____	_____	43.	Do you find yourself choosing friends or lovers because of their access to cocaine or their cocaine use? (This kind of behavior usually indicates a life out of control.)
_____	_____	44.	Do you wake up in the morning and wonder how you could have let cocaine gain control over your life? (You are addicted if you have these thoughts.)
_____	_____	45.	Do you find it almost impossible to fall asleep without a drink or sleeping pill or tranquilizer? (You now have a second addiction.)
_____	_____	46.	Since you started using cocaine, have you ever wondered whether you would be able to live without it? (We find that people who raise this question are generally hooked on the drug.)
_____	_____	47.	Have you wondered whether you would be better off dead than continuing to use cocaine? (This question usually suggests an addiction so profound that the addict feels himself terminally ill.)
_____	_____	48.	Have you ever wished that you would die of an overdose in your sleep? (Same as above.)
_____	_____	49.	Do you use cocaine in your car, at work in the bathroom, on airplanes, or in other public places? (You are so desperate you want to be caught— and helped.)
_____	_____	50.	Do you use cocaine and then drive a car within six hours after use? (Cocaine has impaired your judgment and you are out of control. Don't wait to get help until after you have impaired or killed a pedestrian.)

Source: From *800-Cocaine* by Mark S. Gold. 1984. New York: Bantam Books.

Minnesota Multiphasic Personality Inventory (MMPI)

The Minnesota Multiphasic Personality Inventory (MMPI) has been shown to be quite helpful in the assessment of alcoholism (Dahlstrom & Welsh 1960). However, while the MMPI is a self-administered, true-false, 566-item personality test, it requires a trained psychometrician for scoring and interpreting the results. A few specific MMPI profiles have been shown to be consistently associated with alcohol abuse, alcoholism, and other drug abuse (Forrest 1978). The 2-7-4 profile most consistently indicates alcoholism and/or an addictive personality makeup. Forrest (1984) suggests that this particular profile configuration indicates the presence of a personality structure and life style characterized by moderate to severe depression, obsessive-compulsive trends, poor impulse control, anxiety, irrational fears and phobias, irresponsibility, immaturity, and acting out. Forrest also believes that the 4, 3-4 or 4-3, and 4-9 MMPI profile configurations may be associated with alcoholism, alcohol abuse, and chemical dependency. These profiles are usually characterized by an impulse disorder, inadequate personality features, passive-aggressive behaviors, irresponsibility, and immaturity. Obviously, the MMPI validity scales (L, F, and K) must be within normal limits if the MMPI results are to be used as a screening for possible problems with alcohol and/or other chemicals.

MacAndrew Alcoholism Scale

The MacAndrew Alcoholism Scale uses the original MMPI item pool as a means of assessing alcoholism and drinking behavior. In particular, the MacAndrew Scale is designed to differentiate alcoholics from nonalcoholic psychiatric patients. Employing forty-nine items from the MMPI, it has demonstrated good validity and reliability. The MacAndrew Scale is also quicker to administer, if the evaluator uses only those questions which MacAndrew has shown to have validity in identifying individuals who are likely to be alcoholic.

Beyond the diagnostic value of the various screening instruments, they may also be helpful in establishing a treatment plan for the individual who is chemically dependent. Table 4.9 is one example of how a process by which the information gained from assessment can be used in determining the behavior pattern, an appropriate intervention, and a goal or goals for the treatment process.

SUMMARY

This chapter has focused on the process of diagnosis and assessment of chemical dependency in an individual. The expanding recognition of the need to make a comprehensive assessment in order to develop an individual

Table 4.9 Behavior Patterns, Interventions, and Goals

BEHAVIOR PATTERN	INTERVENTION	GOALS
Low self-esteem, anxiety, high verbal hostility	Relationship therapy, client-centered model	Increase self-esteem, reduce verbal hostility and anxiety
Defective personal construct system, ignorance of interpersonal means	Cognitive restructuring using therapies that are directive, such as Ellis, Glasser, group therapy	Insight
Focal anxiety (i.e., fear of crowds)	Desensitization	Change response to same cues
Undesirable behaviors, lacking appropriate behaviors	Aversive conditioning, operant shaping, counter conditioning	Eliminate or replace behavior
Lack of information	Information giving	Give information, have client act on it
Client complaint indicates that social situation is causing difficulty	Organization intervention, environmental manipulation, family therapy	Remove cause of complaint, modify environment
Interpersonal rigidity, poor functioning in social situations	Sensitivity training, communication training, group therapy	Increase interpersonal repertoire, desensitization to group functioning
Grossly bizarre behavior	Medical referral	Medication or hospitalization to protect client from society, ready client for further treatment

Reprinted from *Essentials of Chemical Dependency Counseling* by G. W. Lawson, D. C. Ellis, and P. C. Rivers, p. 66, with permission of Aspen Publishers, Inc., © 1984.

treatment plan has resulted in the development of screening instruments, as well as increased knowledge of those behavior patterns that need to be recognized.

Thus, the physical, behavioral, emotional, social, and spiritual symptoms of chemical dependency are reviewed in terms of identifying their existence and severity. Likewise, a number of screening instruments are reviewed in terms of their value in assessing chemical dependency.

5 ─

Counseling Issues and Techniques

INTRODUCTION

Chemical-dependency counselors are often surprised that the basic techniques and strategies needed to be effective are the same as in counseling other clients. The differences in the counseling process occur because of the nature of chemical dependency and its effect on the individual. One major difference is that individuals who abuse or are dependent on alcohol and other drugs are likely to try to cover up their use and to deny the problem. Even after treatment and the initial admission that they have a problem, these individuals regularly go through periods when they doubt that their chemical use was a problem; their denial becomes a recurring issue.

As a result counselors in this field use confrontation more often than they would in ordinary counseling. It serves to keep the client aware of the chronic nature of chemical dependency and of the continuing need to follow a program of recovery.

This chapter will describe the action-counseling model as a proposed approach to interpret the counselor's skill in a systematic way in order to help move the client toward recovery and personal growth. In addition, those counseling techniques which are particularly valuable in this field will be described.

OVERVIEW OF ACTION-COUNSELING MODEL

While individual counselors need to develop their own personal styles of working with individuals who are chemically dependent, the action-counseling model allows each counselor to emphasize those specific skills or strategies with which he or she is most effective. It really doesn't matter whether counselors see themselves as client-centered or cognitive or Adlerian or behavioral or Gestalt; rather, the action-counseling model provides an overall plan or direction to counseling that will enable counselors to provide maximum help to their clients or patients. Of course, certain techniques are essential to all counselors, regardless of what their theoretical orientation might be.

Action counseling was developed by Dustin and George (1977) as a means of providing structure to the counseling process. The model looks at counseling as having three stages. During stage 1, the counselor establishes a therapeutic relationship, gathers relevant information, and assesses the nature and extent of the individual's difficulty. In stage 2, the client determines the kind of change desired, sets goals for change, and makes a commitment to that change. Stage 3 consists of the action steps and strategies taken to bring about the desired change.

Stage 1 begins with an emphasis on establishing a therapeutic relationship with the client. This is facilitated by the counselor's use of appropriate attending and understanding skills. Such counselor behaviors create a therapeutic environment in which the client is encouraged to explore the various emotional and psychological concerns that may have been related to his or her use of mood-altering chemicals. As this exploration occurs, the client is likely to gain understanding about the self and to move toward the kind of changes that are needed to provide the emotional support desired.

During this process, the counselor uses a variety of counseling skills to facilitate self-exploration and self-understanding. Paying attention to the nonverbal cues the client is giving, linking different areas of concern to show how they relate to one another, and helping the client focus on the major issues that affect his or her life become essential. In so doing, the counselor uses advanced empathy skills, confrontation skills, and immediacy skills. During the entire process, however, the counselor must be aware of the importance of communicating genuine acceptance to the client.

Genuineness may be the single most important aspect of the process. Individuals who are chemically dependent have typically been involved in relationships where no one could trust anyone else. Thus, genuineness becomes the fundamental element in developing the kind of therapeutic relationship that will enable the counselor to be effective. The ability to be oneself without needing to present a professional facade results in counselors not being phoney, not playing a role, and not being defensive. Counselors who are genuine communicate a "realness" in relationships, because they are sensitively aware of their feelings and reactions as they experience them and are honest and direct in their communication with clients. Their external behavior matches their internal reactions and results in their verbal and nonverbal communications being congruent. If they are angry, they say so; if they are frustrated, they let it be known; if they are pleased, they express that pleasure. This type of spontaneous interaction facilitates trust and improves rapport, leading to an increase in treatment compliance. While genuineness is a natural state, it may need to be practiced, since counselors sometimes need to learn to be secure with themselves and open with their feelings, reactions, thoughts, and attitudes.

Genuineness can play an important part in the counseling process. As the counselor listens and responds to the verbal and nonverbal contents of what the client is saying, he or she is also responding to the client as a person. The counselor who can be sensitively tuned in to internal reactions can promote client growth. For example, if the counselor is genuinely moved by the pain and the struggle of the client to find his or her own way, the counselor can share these feelings. Likewise, if the counselor realizes that he or she is having difficulty listening and is, in fact, feeling very uninvolved and bored, the counselor may need to identify client behaviors to which he or she is reacting and to share these feelings in a positive confrontation. While risky, such behavior can be highly facilitative, enabling the client to explore personal issues and behavior that may be interfering with positive relationships.

In addition, being genuine is essential to communicate acceptance to the client. Acceptance, sometimes called warmth or respect or positive regard, includes the communication to another that he or she is prized simply as a human being. It is particularly important in that the counselor is telling the client that in spite of what he or she may have disclosed, the counselor sees the client as being a person of worth and dignity. By doing so, the counselor indicates to clients that they are capable of surviving in a difficult environment and are thus free to choose their own alternatives and to participate in the counseling process as equals. Such communication empowers clients and begins the process of returning responsibility to them.

Expressing acceptance of the person includes acknowledging the individual's feelings as communicated; in combination with empathy, it communicates to the client the essential message "I understand what you are experiencing and I still accept you as a person." This means that the counselor does not discount, deny, or put down the feelings of the client. Rather, he or she must accept the client's feelings and move on toward greater exploration and understanding. Restructuring of cognitive distortion comes at a later time.

Since counselors can think faster than clients can talk, the counselor is able, at the same time that he or she is establishing rapport and gaining an understanding of the client's perceptual view of the situation, to make some tentative decisions about the nature of the problems which must be faced by the client and to collect the necessary information relating to that problem. This can then lead to the second phase of the process.

Stage 2 focuses on identifying some specific goals for change within the client. Although many chemically dependent individuals use the problem situations in which they are mired as excuses for using mood-altering chemicals, the reality of the situation is that most of them do not know how to deal with these problem situations. They lack the insight, judgment, and direction to bring about the kind of constructive change that will contribute to their recovery and lower the likelihood of relapse. Even more important is the sense of hope that can accompany the client's perceiving that his or her life is finally gaining a sense of direction.

Egan (1986) points out that individuals who have a sense of direction in their lives:

1. Have a sense of purpose.
2. Live lives that are going somewhere.
3. Have in place self-enhancing and other-enhancing patterns of behavior.
4. Focus on outcomes and accomplishments.
5. Do not mistake aimless action for accomplishments.

6. Set long-term and short-term goals and objectives.
7. Have a defined, rather than an aimless, life style.

In stage 2, then, the client is challenged to develop new perspectives and to identify goals for change in his or her life. However, as seen in figure 5.1, the most important part of stage 2 is the commitment which the client makes toward change in his or her life. Stage 2, because of that commitment, becomes the turning point of action counseling.

In understanding figure 5.1, it is important to recognize that its direction is downward and inward, that it places the focus within the individual and gains insight into the deepest aspects of the individual's experiencing. Stage 3, however, is upward and outward, as the client begins to take action to bring about the desired change in his or her life. This direction involves changing the focus from the inner experiencing of the client to outward behavior. The key to this process, then, becomes the point at which the individual commits himself or herself to the direction of change that is desired.

Stage 3 is the point at which individuals begin to develop strategies for change in their lives and begin to put them into action. In a sense, the task that is involved in helping clients identify a variety of strategies for implementing

Figure 5.1   The Action-Counseling Model

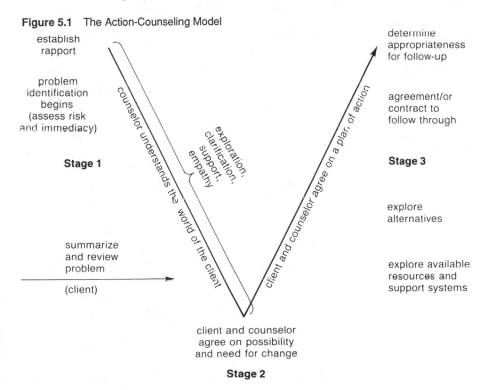

client and counselor
agree on possibility
and need for change

Stage 2

their desired goals; clients then work toward evaluating the strategies and choosing those which have the greatest potential for success. Strategies are then assembled into a plan and implemented.

A variety of counseling strategies are often used during stage 3: relaxation therapy, assertion training, behavioral contracts, and various cognitive techniques. In each case, the behavior goals need to be stated as specifically as possible, along with means of measuring or verifying whether or not the goal has been achieved. This involves the development of realistic targets that are consistent with the goals of the client, and not of the counselor.

SPECIFIC COUNSELING TECHNIQUES

Attending

Attending behaviors are crucial for counselors. They ordinarily involve nonverbal behaviors that communicate to the client that the counselor is involved in what the client is sharing. This concept of physical attending may seem obvious, yet in daily interactions it is often missing. Being with, attending to, and listening to another person can be potent in its effect on the other, communicating warmth and respect for that individual.

In its deepest sense, attending means "being with" the other. The counselor's nonverbal behavior and the many messages it communicates influences clients for better or worse. For example, the counselor's nonverbal behavior can encourage clients to trust, to open up, and to explore the various aspects of their lives that are creating problems for them, or it can promote their distrust and lead to resisting self-disclosure. Perhaps as important, however, is that the quality of attending by the counselor influences his or her perceptiveness in picking up information that is important to the client. Thus, effective attending does two things: It lets the client know that the counselor is with him or her, and therefore establishes good rapport; and it allows the counselor to be in the best position to become an effective listener.

Egan (1986) lists eye contact, adopting an open posture, facing the person squarely, leaning slightly forward, and assuming a natural and relaxed position as being the most important physical attending behaviors. He then summarizes these behaviors by using the acronym SOLER.

First, face the client *squarely*, adopting a posture that indicates involvement. (This entails taking a position with the counselor's right shoulder facing the client's left shoulder and the counselor's left shoulder facing the client's right shoulder.) Such a physical attitude communicates the message that "I'm listening to you and I wish to shut out the other stimuli, verbal and visual, that might interfere with my listening." Turning the body away from another person generally lessens the degree of contact with that person by decreasing the possibility that other stimuli will be shut out. Even when seated in a circle for a group session, the counselor can try in some way to turn toward the individual to whom he or she is speaking. By doing so, the message that "I'm with you now" is communicated. In addition, counselors should also attempt to avoid having a table or desk between them and their clients.

By adopting an *open* posture, counselors are expressing that they are open to the client and to what he or she has to say. Open postures are generally seen as nondefensive, whereas individuals who face someone with arms and/or legs crossed are generally viewed as withdrawing from interaction with others. Such an interpretation may not always be valid, but the counselor must be aware of the message he or she is communicating through physical posture.

Third, *leaning* slightly forward toward the other person signals a greater concern about what he or she is communicating. Many counselors begin a session by leaning back, and then lean forward as the level of interaction intensifies. On the other hand, leaning too far forward may be intimidating to the client, communicating some demand for closeness or intimacy. Thus, leaning forward becomes an important indicator of the involvement between the counselor and the client.

Maintaining good *eye* contact may be as important a nonverbal behavior as anything the counselor can do. In the North American culture, eye contact communicates warmth and trustworthiness. Notice your own reaction to those who do not look at you while talking to you. The reaction is frequently one of distrust or disinterest. On the other hand, observing individuals who are engaged in an intense discussion will point out that in such instances eye contact tends to be the rule rather than the exception. Obviously, eye contact can be interrupted, but looking away frequently is often a clue to one's reluctance to be with and to be involved with the other person.

Finally, assuming a *relaxed* position helps to prevent the kind of nervous fidgeting that can be a distraction to the client. By remaining normal and relaxed, the counselor appears more natural and more real, without losing the sense of involvement. This allows the counselor to focus his or her attention on the client, and also communicates confidence in the self and confidence within the client that the counselor is competent in what he or she is doing.

Empathy

Many writers in the counseling field have discussed the importance of empathy. The significance of understanding what clients are experiencing, and communicating this understanding to them, has been shown to be critical to the counseling process. The ability to enter into and understand the world of the client, to feel deeply, and to communicate this understanding to the client goes beyond the sense of attending. Rather, by communicating an understanding of what the counselor perceives the client to be experiencing, he or she establishes interest and rapport with the client. This becomes a

prerequisite to the counselor's effective participation in other counselor behaviors. By communicating empathic understanding, the counselor provides
relevant, affective, and cognitive information about the client and the client's
experiencing of the world to enable the two of them to develop further insight
into the nature of the client's emotional and psychological concerns. At the
same time, empathic responses provide an opportunity for the client to learn
what it is that the counselor is hearing from his or her verbalizations and to
determine if the counselor is hearing what the client means to say, thus
providing the opportunity for the client to "fine tune" or clarify any misun-
derstandings.

At the same time, the communication of understanding helps to facilitate
the downward and inward direction of stage 1, because the client is encouraged to search more deeply and to disclose more fully those aspects of the self
which may have been hidden from him or her or from others in the past. As
the client comes to feel understood and accepted by the counselor, he or she
feels less vulnerable and therefore more willing to share all aspects of the self.

Empathy basically involves the expression of what the counselor has
identified as being the primary message communicated by the client. The
focus is on the feelings which the client has expressed, with the area of feelings
and the intensity of those feelings being important. Beginning counselors are
often taught to express empathy by stating, "You feel...," followed by the
appropriate feeling word, and then a "because" statement. This encourages
the counselor to focus on the feelings the client is experiencing and to relate
those feelings to the situations or behaviors that underlie the client's feelings.
As counselors become more experienced and fine tune their counseling skills,
they often go beyond the "you feel" formula and develop their own personal
styles in communicating their understanding.

Many chemically dependent individuals, however, are unable to discuss
their feelings easily. Often this is a result of experiences such persons have had
while growing up in which they were taught not to feel by being punished
whenever their feelings were expressed. The punishment may have been
either a verbal reprimand or a verbal discounting of those feelings. In addition,
the chemically dependent individual often represses feelings in an attempt to
counteract their all-too-uncontrolled expression during the using experiences.
Respect for this need to repress the emotions must exist during the initial
stages of counseling. The counselor may begin by emphasizing experiences
and behaviors and proceed only gradually to a discussion of feelings. Sometimes this is done by the counselor stating how he or she might feel in similar
circumstances, communicating not only the right of the client to feel, but also
the right of the client to feel a particular way in a particular situation.

In improving the quality of empathic responses, counselors need to
learn to take time before responding to what the client has said. A brief

Table 5.1 Suggestions for the Use of Basic Empathy

1. Remember that empathy is, ideally, a "way of being" and not just a professional role or communication skill.
2. Attend carefully, both physically and psychologically, and listen to the client's point of view.
3. Try to set aside your biases and judgments for the moment and walk, as it were, in the shoes of your client.
4. As the client speaks, listen for the core messages.
5. Listen to both verbal and nonverbal messages *and* their contexts.
6. Respond fairly frequently, but briefly, to the client's core messages.
7. Be flexible and tentative enough so that the client does not feel pinned down.
8. Be gentle, but keep the client focused on important issues.
9. Respond to the main features of core messages—experiences, behaviors, and feelings— unless there is reason for emphasizing one over the others.
10. Gradually move toward the exploration of sensitive topics and feelings.
11. After responding with empathy, attend carefully to cues that either confirm or deny the accuracy of your response.
12. Determine whether your empathic responses are helping the client remain focused, while developing and clarifying important issues.
13. Note signs of client stress or resistance. Try to judge whether these arise because you are inaccurate or because you are too accurate.
14. Keep in mind that the communication skill of empathy, however important, is a tool to help clients see themselves and their problem situations more clearly with a view to managing them more effectively.

Source: From *The Skilled Helper* by Gerard Egan. Pacific Grove, CA: Brooks/Cole. 1975. Reprinted by permission.

pause before addressing the client provides an opportunity for the counselor to assimilate and reflect on the client's attitude. By doing so, the counselor is free to just listen while the client is talking, rather than worry about the response to be given. In addition, a major empathic skill is that of using relatively frequent, but brief, responses to the client. The counselor strives to take the client's many sentences and compress their message into a response of one or two sentences that is interchangeable in meaning and feeling with what the client has said. Likewise, the intensity of emotion within the counselor's voice and the vocabulary and concreteness of the client's words must be appropriate for the level of the client. Table 5.1 includes suggestions for the use of basic empathy (Egan 1986).

Confrontation

Although confrontation is a highly used skill in the area of chemical-dependency counseling, most counselors find it difficult and are uncertain of the most appropriate way to employ it. Confronting a client's behavior is a sensitive process requiring both a sense of timing and an awareness of the client's ability to handle the information. When confrontation is done well, clients gain insight into their behavior and their relationships with others. Confrontation should only be used in a context of trust and caring, and not as a means of venting anger and frustration.

Generally, confrontation is used to help others become aware of some aspect of themselves, their environment, or their interaction with their environment, of which they are currently unaware. In a sense, this provides an opportunity for the client to examine the consequences of some aspect of his or her behavior. Often, confrontation refers to some form of inconsistency in the person's life: perhaps between what the person says verbally and nonverbally, between what the person says verbally and what the person does, or between what the person says from one occasion to another. By pointing out these inconsistencies, the counselor is opening the door for the client to move toward congruence in his or her behavior.

In addition, confrontation can be used to help clients see things as they are, rather than perceiving them as they would like them to be. By providing an alternative frame of reference, counselors enable clients to clear up distortions in experience. An example of a distorted perception might be "My family has put me in treatment because they wanted to get me out of the way." By pointing out this distorted perception, the counselor becomes free to confront the message by responding to observations that indicate that the family still does love the client, but that placement in treatment was out of concern for the person.

Another use of confrontation is to help clients understand when they may be evading issues or ignoring feedback from others. When a client is evading an issue, perhaps still denying the problem that he or she has with mood-altering chemicals, the counselor might confront him or her with such a statement as:

> You keep saying that you have no problem with your use of alcohol, but you also report that when you drink, you become hostile and aggressive and have alienated a number of friends as a result. I wonder if your refusal to admit your problem with alcohol is also a refusal to see your responsibility in dissolving your friendships.

Self-Disclosure

Self-disclosure involves revealing one's own feelings and reactions to events and people as they occur. Within the counseling relationship, the counselor may choose to reveal the self to the client as a means of facilitating the client's openness. By sharing his or her reactions to the client or to the relationship openly in the here and now, the counselor is acting as a role model for the client's own self-disclosure. In addition, self-disclosure involves the counselor stating how he or she feels about what is going on in the counseling process, including expressions of frustration, anger, disappointment, and pleasure.

Self-disclosure may also include the counselor's relating experiences that may be similar to a client's own. This, however, needs to be minimized because it shifts the focus from the client to the counselor. In addition, relating one's own experience tends to equate it with the client's, and result in the client's becoming defensive and pointing out how his or her experience was different. Likewise, there is the danger that the counselor will imply that because he or she was able to overcome the experience, the client should have been able to do so too, thus resulting in the client feeling put down for his or her inability to cope.

Timing is very important in the success of self-disclosure, which needs to occur as soon as possible after the counselor experienced his or her feelings. At the same time, the self-disclosure must be brief so as not to take the focus off the client. By self-disclosing, the counselor acts as a real, genuine person and communicates that he or she trusts the client to handle the information that the counselor is providing. This communication of respect can be powerful in helping the client to feel better about the self.

Cognitive Restructuring

The basic concept within cognitive approaches to counseling is that the feelings that individuals are having result from a belief system that they have about situations and events in their lives. Thus, their thought patterns affect and often create their feelings and behaviors. In order to change, it may be necessary to modify the way the individual thinks about a particular situation. Ellis (1962) formulated the ABC principle of emotional disturbance, which emphasized the importance of cognitive control over emotional states. Ellis stated that one's perception of an event determined one's behavioral response to it. For Ellis, A is the existence of a fact or an event external to the person; B is generally the individual's attitude, beliefs, or interpretation of A; and C is the emotional consequence or reaction of the person. In his analysis, A is not the cause of C. Instead, B, the person's belief about A, causes C, the emotional response or reaction. For example, a counselor might explain to a client who is upset over feeling rejected by her boyfriend that it is not the rejection of her boyfriend (A) that is upsetting her, but her own *beliefs* (B) about being a failure and feeling as if no one could ever love her that are upsetting (C) her. Thus Ellis suggests that the individual is responsible for his or her own emotional reactions and disturbances.

While Ellis lists a number of irrational ideas that he believes are found in our society and invariably lead to self-defeat, his thinking on the irrational and the illogical can be summarized into three basic areas: (1) I must do well or be approved of by others at all times; (2) you have to treat me the way you are supposed to; and (3) the world must give me just what I want. These kinds of beliefs "color" an event that may be uncomfortable, disappointing, or frustrating, and intensify or exaggerate the emotional reaction that the person has to that event. While the person may be disappointed that he or she did not receive a job promotion, the belief that its absence indicates that others do not approve of the individual's work in the way he or she would like can make the disappointment become overwhelming and lead to inappropriate reactions to the event.

In working to change the cognitive structure the individual has provided for an event, the counselor must first help the client to recognize the irrational ideas that they have and the relationship of those ideas to the person's unhappiness and confusion. By doing so, clients become aware of the specific material to be dealt with in order to improve their emotional functioning. In addition, this insight tends to reduce feelings of powerlessness and despair by showing clients that they are not helpless victims of outside forces, but have control over themselves.

The second step is to help clients believe that thoughts can be challenged and changed. By exploring logically their ideas to determine those that are appropriate and those that are inappropriate, counselors can then dispute the inappropriate beliefs and move toward replacing them with appropriate ones.

The final step involves helping clients go beyond disputing irrational or inappropriate ideas by encouraging them to continue their efforts toward more reasonable thinking by rational reindoctrination. This includes dealing with the main, general irrational ideas, as well as developing a more rational philosophy of living, so that clients can avoid falling victim to other irrational ideas and beliefs. Thus, clients can work toward substituting rational attitudes and beliefs for irrational ones, leading to the elimination of negative, disturbing emotions, as well as self-defeating behaviors.

Behavior Contracts

The use of the behavior contract is one technique that has been widely adopted by counselors. The behavior contract is based on the idea that it is helpful to the client to specify, in advance, the kind of behavior desired and any reinforcement contingencies. Such an agreement enables individuals to anticipate changing their behavior on the basis of a promise or agreement that some positive consequence will be forthcoming.

Basically, a behavior contract is an agreement between two or more individuals in which those individuals attempt to change the behavior of at least one of the parties. Dustin and George (1977) suggest that such an approach helps to tell the client "what to do" without nagging. At the same time, the power of the individual's making a public commitment, in which he or she states to one or more other persons what will change in his or her life, becomes an important aspect of the behavior change itself. While the agreement may be oral or written, both parties must agree to the basic conditions. One aspect of the contract is the process of negotiating acceptable terms, which are characterized by (1) reality, (2) specificity, (3) freedom from threat, and (4) flexibility. Simply stated, this means that the client and the counselor choose realistic goals that they can meet. Such goals are specifically stated, leaving no question as to what is expected of each. In addition, the goals declare not only what is to be done, but a time frame in which it is to be done. An example of a simple contract goal might be that a client agrees to give his wife three hugs during her visit to the treatment program. Generally, the contract employs positive reinforcement for reaching goals, rather than punishment for undesirable behavior, thus eliminating threat. These goals often involve nothing more than the involvement and interest of the counselor in learning what results occurred when the client succeeded in completing the contract.

One example of how the contract can be used effectively involves the giving of some sort of pin or token or memento to an individual after treatment, but before any agreed upon aftercare program has been completed. A more appropriate use of a contract would be to provide positive feedback to the individual and agree that when he or she has completed the program, for instance three months of aftercare meetings, then the individual will receive the memento. In addition, counselors must be careful to avoid situations in which they inadvertently reinforce clients' relapse behavior as a result of some unwritten, unagreed upon contract that suggests that the counselor will be available to the client only when the client has relapsed.

Social Learning

Social learning refers to the process by which individuals learn through observing and imitating others. In general, this technique allows the counselor to foster desired behaviors in clients simply by demonstrating those behaviors. For example, when counselors model such appropriate communications skills as eye contact, open posture, listening, and responding with understanding, clients are likely to begin using the same skills.

In addition, counselors can cite other clients or patients as appropriate role models for specific behaviors. Individuals can demonstrate various social interaction skills, including assertion and saying "no" to peers who may be encouraging the client to use. However, social learning has many variations for presenting modeled behavior beyond live modeling of either the counselor or of other clients. The counselor can also use modeling by audio or video recordings (such as relaxation tapes or demonstrations of appropriate, effective ways of handling various situations); role playing, in which the individual has the opportunity to practice the use of a particular behavior style; and role taking, in which the individual may take the role of someone else to gain greater insight into the other person's behavior.

Assertion Training

A behavioral approach that has gained wide support, assertion training is particularly worthwhile for individuals who have difficulty asserting themselves in particular interpersonal situations. Although used primarily with individuals who are usually not assertive, assertion training can be appropriate for most people, since almost everyone has difficulty asserting themselves in certain situations. Corey (1977) points out that assertion training can be particularly helpful for the following people:

1. Those who cannot express anger or irritation.
2. Those who are overly polite and who allow others to take advantage of them.
3. Those who have difficulty saying "no."
4. Those who find it difficult to express affection and other positive responses.
5. Those who feel they don't have a right to have their own feelings or thoughts.

Assertion training is ordinarily practiced in a group setting. It emphasizes teaching clients to stand up for their own rights without violating the rights of others. Assertive behavior itself consists of expressing one's thoughts and feelings in direct, honest, and appropriate ways. It involves defending one's rights when one feels taken advantage of. It means expressing one's needs and wants to others without assuming whether or not the others will help meet those needs. Assertion training often involves individuals identifying the situations in which they would like to be more assertive, identifying the illogical beliefs that they have about the risks of being assertive, accepting the personal rights they have as individuals to act assertively, and then practicing assertive behavior in those situations. Individuals who have learned to be assertive usually feel good about themselves, recognizing that they have "stood up" for themselves without humiliating or criticizing others. Increased self-respect results.

Relaxation Training

Since most substance abusers have inadequate coping skills for dealing with anxiety, recovery can be greatly facilitated if those individuals can be taught to relax and reduce their anxiety. While it is important that counselors understand that anxiety is created by a number of social, emotional, and cognitive factors, relaxation can be used to deal with the outward aspects of anxiety so that the individual is more effective in dealing with the underlying situations.

Relaxation training is often based on the progressive relaxation training that Jacobsen (1938) developed to help individuals in relaxing muscles. Similar to the kind of relaxation that is taught to pregnant women, this technique directs the client's attention to relaxing a particular set of muscles, then working throughout the body in the same way. Relaxation is particularly important because it is incompatible with anxiety. Thus, as individuals learn to teach their bodies to relax, they learn how to reduce the anxiety they feel. Such relaxation can be used by those who are chemically dependent to deal with normal daily pressures, to reduce anxiety and tension related to highly charged emotional or social situations, to diminish the urges and cravings that often precede relapse, and to relax before sleeping.

In addition to providing progressive muscle relaxation opportunities during an individual or group session with patients, the counselor can have available a relaxation tape which the patient can listen to in private as a means of further working on his or her own relaxation techniques. Likewise, other forms of relaxation may be used, including transcendental meditation, soothing music, or various guided-fantasy techniques.

In addition, counselors can combine relaxation training with the verbal introduction of descriptions of anxiety-producing occasions to desensitize the client in those situations which previously caused anxiety.

Aversion Therapy

While aversion-therapy approaches have decreased in their impact in the field of chemical-dependency counseling, counselors may still wish to use the concept occasionally with a particular client. Aversion therapy is based on the idea that when a behavior or event is closely associated in time with an unpleasant stimulus, that behavior or event will become unpleasurable also. The use of medications to induce vomiting when a patient has taken a drink of alcohol is an example of how aversion therapy has been used. By creating an aversion to, or distaste for, alcohol, counselors are attempting to interrupt drug-use behavior. By tapping imagination, however, counselors can employ the same technique in a somewhat less dramatic fashion. By providing verbal stimuli which involve pairing the mood-altering substance with an aversive, imagined consequence (for instance, nausea and vomiting) aversion to that substance may be increased. Thus, no administration of physically aversive stimuli is needed and the patient may learn a negative reaction to situations that were formerly positive.

SUMMARY

Counselors who work with those who are chemically dependent use the same basic set of counseling techniques and strategies that they use in working with other clients. The difference lies primarily in understanding the characteristics of chemical dependency and adapting those interventions to the particular needs of the client. Action counseling was described and proposed as an appropriate model for this intervention strategy.

The focus of much of the counseling is the continuing need to challenge the individual to overcome denial and to accept the need to take responsibility for recovery. Thus, the counselor typically uses confrontation more frequently than with other clients. In addition, there is frequently a greater need for counselors to use such cognitive and behavioral techniques as cognitive restructuring, behavior contracts, and assertion training to help the client change the way he or she thinks and behaves.

Many clients have a battered self-concept and are eager to find some-one who understands their feelings of anger, guilt, and hopelessness. Thus, the ability to communicate empathic understanding is a necessary condition for helping those who are chemically dependent work toward recovery and personal growth.

6 ———

Using Group Counseling in Treatment

INTRODUCTION

Group counseling and therapy have become an increasingly popular form of treatment for those who are chemically dependent. Today, group approaches have become predominant in working with such individuals. Part of this emphasis results from Alcoholics Anonymous traditions dating back to 1935, which have highlighted the importance of self-help groups in the recovery of the alcoholic.

While the term *group counseling* has become very popular, and practices under this or related names have been a primary treatment modality, there is still variation in what it means to different individuals. Professionals in the field of chemical-dependency counseling have a variety of ideas about what a group is, beyond the definition that it consists of three or more members who influence each other and are influenced by others. Such a group of individuals who meet and interact with one another in a face-to-face setting are seen as belonging to a group for the purpose of achieving some objective or goal, whether clearly specified or understood. Certainly, most professionals would agree that in such a group setting individuals meet to satisfy personal needs and to develop an interdependence upon one another. Such individuals tend to establish roles and norms as a result of sharing common attitudes, feelings, and experiences. In addition, these groups go through stages that can be observed and described by those who study such group behavior.

Differences in how group counseling is seen can be highlighted by looking at various definitions that have been offered. Glanz (1962, 326) offered his definition of group counseling as "the establishment of a group of persons for the purposes of individual growth and development in the area of personal and emotional problem-solving."

Muro and Freeman (1968, 9) proposed that group counseling be used to refer to

> a form of small group activity in which the participants are psychologically healthy and engaging in mutually supportive and stimulating inquiry into the values and meanings which are becoming attached to their lives in the larger world outside the group.

Later, Forrest (1978, 93) offered a further developed definition of a group, especially applicable to working with alcoholics:

> Group psychotherapy is essentially an interpersonal transaction involving a group leader who, by virtue of a particular type of educational training and life experience, can potentially help facilitate behavioral growth and change on the part of other group members, who, in this particular context, share the same problem of alcohol addiction.

Finally, the definition of Weiner (1984, 2) is offered as a simple but important statement, suggesting that any group interaction can have a positive influence on the lives of those involved, and that, therefore, any group has the potential to be therapeutic for its members. Weiner defines group therapy as "a deliberate effort to alter the thinking, feelings, and behaviors of the group members." For the purpose of this chapter, group counseling is defined simply as the "use of group interaction to facilitate self-understanding as well as individual behavior change" (George & Dustin 1988, 5).

NEED FOR, AND VALUE OF, GROUP APPROACHES TO COUNSELING

Group counseling, whether it is inpatient or outpatient, offers a dimension not found in individual counseling of any theoretical modality. Group counseling provides for not only the insight and feedback of the therapist, but for the collective insight and feedback of the group itself. This dimension, accompanied by the increased psychological protection which most individuals experience within a group (as opposed to their experience in an individual setting), frequently results in individuals feeling less anxious and more willing to talk about the thoughts, feelings, and behaviors that have influenced their lives.

Although group-treatment methods had often been justified on the basis of economic advantages, since it is generally less expensive when the counselor is able to meet with a number of individuals simultaneously, the main reason for using a group approach is because it works, particularly with those who are chemically dependent. Some of the reasons result from human nature; other reasons grow out of the characteristics of those individuals who have become chemically dependent.

From the moment most people wake up in the morning until the time they go to bed at night, they find themselves part of a group. Being human means that we are involved with other people. We tend to identify with our family, our community, our school, our church, our organization. Most individuals work as part of a group, interact with social acquaintances as part of a group, and spend much of their leisure time as part of a group. It is in group experiences that we find a sense of belonging, a sense that we as individuals are okay or not okay; therefore, we are highly concerned with the nature of our relationships with family, friends, and colleagues. These relationships produce or reduce stress, feelings of loneliness, low self-esteem, a sense of failure, or a desire to improve our lives. As we interact, we find ourselves sharing our successes or hiding our supposed failures. Through the interaction of the group, we get positive reinforcement for the things we do well, and either encouragement or a reprimand when we fail. Kinney and Leaton (1987) point out that as politicians take opinion polls to see how they are doing with their constituents, each of us runs our own surveys to find out how we are doing in the relationships we have with people around us. For the chemical dependent, relationships with other people are typically very poor. Secretive, isolated, rejecting, and rejected—the chemically dependent individual is generally unaware of how his or her use of mood-altering chemicals has been creating problems in relationships. Recovering and staying sober in the real world will require reestablishing human relationships.

In a sense, the counseling group provides an opportunity for the individual to experience the world anew, since the group becomes a microcosm of the society the individual will experience daily. As such, the group reflects the world beyond and adds an element of realism to a setting and interaction which is often seen as artificial. Group counseling can provide such factors as peer-group pressure, social influence, and conformity that come into play as part of the therapeutic process, just as these factors influence and affect the individual's attitude and behavior change outside the group. At the same time, the group setting provides the opportunity for the individual to learn that other people can be a source of safety and strength to them in the struggle that lies ahead.

Since the group process provides the opportunity for individuals to experience the same kinds of struggles and conflicts within the group that they experience outside it, group members have the opportunity to explore their styles of relating with others and to learn more effective behaviors in those relationships. The group thus becomes an opportunity for individuals to learn who they are, what their capabilities are, and what their impact and importance to others is. By interacting honestly and openly, members receive the opportunity to adjust and correct their mental pictures of themselves, since the group setting allows them to receive feedback and support from others concerning their perceptions of how each is experienced in the group. Consequently, the group members often learn to take risks regarding new attitudes, such as trusting, caring, and helping. They have the opportunity to get to know others at a relatively intimate level, if they wish, as a result of experiencing one another in a highly safe environment. Thus, the view of themselves which chemically dependent individuals frequently have—seeing themselves in a very negative way and having an overwhelming sense of shame for their behavior—is subject to change as the individuals receive positive feedback from others and experience the positive gains from the emotionally intimate relationships they establish.

At the same time, the group setting provides a peer pressure that is often more powerful in pushing members to action both within and outside the group. Members of the group are urged toward the activity involved in facing and acting on the real issues and concerns in their lives. Likewise, the possibility of learning new behaviors is increased by the opportunity to observe other group members who may be seen as role models in terms of the specific behaviors which the individual wishes to change. This is particularly true when members of the group are at differing stages of recovery, since this provides the opportunity for those who are further along to provide hope and direction to those who have just begun. Dustin and George (1977) point out that group discussion can strengthen discriminatory learning about behavior, as members are able to compare effective behavior with behavior that does not achieve desired goals.

However, the most important element in this process is the development of a sense of belonging, and the kind of closeness that provides a caring, but challenging, environment for personal growth. Part of this, of course, results from individuals becoming aware of similarities between their problems and the problems of other group members, which leads to decreased feelings of isolation and peculiarity and a sense of commonality with others.

THERAPEUTIC ELEMENTS IN GROUP COUNSELING

Probably the most important question to be asked about group counseling is What elements or factors are important in making it effective in helping those individuals who participate? On the one hand, a group approach to counseling is a well-established mode of treatment, with substantial evidence in the literature that supports its effectiveness. On the other hand, the question of what it is about the group approach that makes group counseling effective is less clearly understood. One part of the difficulty results from the fact that any kind of therapeutic change in an individual is an enormously complex process and is the culmination of a multiple interplay of various experiences. Therefore, attempts to answer the question are faced with the immense difficulty of handling a complex set of therapeutic variables.

While such researchers as Frank (1971), Truax and Carkhuff (1967), and Carkhuff and Berenson (1967) have had great success in identifying and validating that certain elements are consistently related to effective individual counseling, only limited efforts have been made to discover those same kinds of consistent, basic elements in group counseling that are consistently related to effectiveness. If such elements were clearly identified, a more solid scientific footing for group counseling would be established and group therapy could become more effective.

Some therapeutic elements have been tentatively identified. They were originally proposed as the result of the subjective experiences that various individuals encountered in a group setting. In some cases, such elements are included because the observations made were done in a systematic, although not empirical, manner. (When empirical research is available to demonstrate the relationship of a particular therapeutic element to outcome, it will be summarized.) In addition, there is a difficulty in identifying therapeutic elements as a result of the tendency to use different language to describe the same phenomenon. Thus, in identifying those essential elements of the group process that result in a therapeutic value for the group members, it is necessary to understand the concept without becoming too engrossed with the specific term chosen to identify the process. With this in mind, a definition of *therapeutic element* can be proposed using that suggested by Bloch (1986, 679), who defines a therapeutic factor as "an element occurring in group therapy that contributes to improvement in a patient's condition and is a function of the actions of the group therapist, the patient, or fellow group members."

The first major effort to produce a unifying classification of therapeutic elements was made by Corsini and Rosenberg (1955). Other writers attempted to take the classification further, sometimes adding other therapeutic factors and sometimes integrating previously defined factors; they include Hill (1957), Berzon, Piovs, and Farson (1963), Ohlsen (1977), Yalom (1970), and Bloch, Reibstein, and Crouch (1979). For the purposes of this chapter, however, the therapeutic elements to be presented are those identified by George and Dustin (1988), who proposed a somewhat simpler model for identifying those therapeutic elements which they believed to be necessary and sufficient for effective group counseling. These elements include the following:

1. Instillation of hope.
2. Sense of safety and support.
3. Cohesiveness.
4. Universality.
5. Vicarious learning.
6. Interpersonal learning.

Instillation of Hope

Instillation of hope is a therapeutic element through which the group member gains a sense of optimism about his or her progress or potential for progress through actual counseling experience. This is particularly crucial in working with groups of chemically dependent individuals, who have often developed a sense of hopelessness as a consequence of numerous failures in attempting to control their use of mood-altering chemicals and the resulting problems which those failures have brought to their lives. The instillation of hope frequently occurs as the individual group member learns that other members of the group have often suffered from many of the same concerns. Such individuals provide hope for others that their own concerns and problems can be resolved. This, of course, is one of the great strengths of such support groups as Alcoholics Anonymous and Narcotics Anonymous, since in these groups the leaders almost always have suffered from the same disorders as the members. These leaders become living inspirations to the new members, who are able to believe that because the leader was able to overcome his or her problems they will also. In addition, a major part of these meetings is dedicated to testimonials from the group leader and from various members of the group. These testimonials are of major importance in increasing the sense of hope that the members attain.

Since hope is basically the belief that change is possible and that one is not a victim of the past, it is essential that the group leader believe in the efficacy of the group. The belief that the group leader is able to help each member who commits himself or herself to counseling and remains with the group for an appropriate period of time is important for the group leader and needs to be shared with each group member to increase that member's optimism about his or her group experience. At the same time, hope comes from a recognition that one has untapped reserves of spontaneity, creativity, courage, and strength, which members first recognize in the lives of other group members and then accept for themselves.

Although many chemically dependent individuals enter group counseling with little hope that their lives can change, it is important that the group leader work toward instilling such hope and then build on it by developing clear-cut expectations of what will be expected from each member of the group. The more members understand and adopt those expectations—to discuss their problems openly, to work toward specific behavior change, and, when necessary, to confront other group members to bring about new behaviors—the more those individuals will increase their feelings of power and optimism about reversing the direction of their lives (George & Dustin, 1988).

Sense of Safety and Support

The need to feel a sense of safety and support within the counseling group—where individuals can be themselves, give up their façades, discuss their problems openly, accept others' reactions to them, and express their own genuine feelings toward others—is a need that is clearly essential to a therapeutic experience within group counseling.

ACCEPTANCE

One factor which increases this sense of safety and security is that of feeling genuinely accepted by other group members. This not only enhances self-esteem, but provides solid support for various behavior changes which the individual wishes to attempt. Such acceptance ordinarily involves the communication of the individual's right to have his or her own feelings and values, and to express them. Acceptance also comes from demonstrated caring, when individuals believe that others are listening to them and are involved with their concerns. As a result, group members are more likely to risk the kinds of changes in their lives that will be therapeutic in the long run.

TRUST

This is another key factor in establishing a sense of safety and support within the group. When the individual feels a large level of trust in the group, it is likely that the person will express his or her thoughts, feelings, reactions, and ideas. In addition, when members trust the group, two particularly important behaviors or effects are likely to occur: self-disclosure and catharsis. A number of studies have indicated that successful group members disclose themselves. This is likely to be true because of two major factors: the person is able to receive understanding and acceptance from the other group members, building self-worth; and group members discover that other group members whom they may admire have problems as difficult as their own and that these individuals are not giving up. As a result, universality, which will be discussed later in the chapter, can begin to have an effect.

CATHARSIS

The release of strong feelings, bringing relief, can be therapeutic in that energy is expressed that has been previously tied up in repressing certain threatening feelings. The relief that results from the person's knowledge that other people now know about these intense feelings and the situations that brought them about is often a major step in an individual's self-acceptance. Of course, catharsis by itself has limited value; it is only when catharsis is complemented by the individual's subsequent cognitive growth that its potential is realized.

Cohesiveness

Cohesiveness results from an individual's feeling that he or she belongs, and is part of a particular therapeutic group. This sense of togetherness involves allegiance, agreement with the group's objectives, and attraction to the group leader and to the other group members, among other aspects (Frank 1957).

A number of research studies support the idea that cohesiveness is an important element within group counseling. Yalom (1985, 68) summarized a large segment of this research and concluded that the overall evidence indicates that the members of a cohesive group, in contrast to the members of a noncohesive group, will:

1. Try harder to influence other group members.
2. Be more open to influence by the other members.
3. Be more willing to listen to others and be more accepting of others.
4. Experience greater security and relief from tension in the group.
5. Participate more readily in meetings.
6. Reveal more of themselves.

7. Protect the group norms (for example, by exerting more pressure on individuals deviating from the norms).
8. Be less susceptible to disruption as a group when a member terminates membership.

INTIMACY AND EMPATHY

Two factors that contribute to the importance of cohesiveness as a therapeutic element are intimacy and empathy. As individuals experience closeness within the group, an intimacy develops, creating a stronger sense of trust in others. In consequence, individuals often become aware of the barriers in their lives that have prevented intimacy. At the same time, empathy—involving a deep understanding of the struggles of another individual—begins to have an impact on cohesiveness. As commonalities among the individuals emerge that unite them, a cohesive bond forms. The feeling that one is alone decreases with the realization that certain problems are common among the various members of the group.

ALTRUISM

Also included under this umbrella of cohesiveness is the concept of selflessness. In a cohesive group, the person is more likely to become part of the therapeutic process of offering help to other group members. As a result, the individual engages in those activities that will enable him or her to benefit from the realization that he or she has something of value to offer to other group members. This results in the realization that in the counseling group members receive through giving, not only reciprocally (the receiving sequence), but also from the act of giving itself. Such giving is particularly important, as it undermines the sense of being demoralized and of having nothing of value to offer others. Thus, for the chemically dependent individual, this act of giving is a refreshing, self-esteem-boosting experience, indicating that he or she can be of importance to others. At the same time, group members are enormously helpful to one another in the process itself. By offering support, reassurance, insight, and understanding, they provide spontaneous, genuine reactions and feedback, enabling other members to gain insight into how they relate to other people. Perhaps the major reason that altruism is powerful in the group setting is the one pointed out by Frankl (1969), when he suggested that it is only when we as individuals are able to transcend ourselves, when we have forgotten ourselves in an absorption in someone or something outside ourselves, that we obtain real self-actualization and meaning in life.

Universality

Another key element in the therapeutic process of group counseling is that of universality, the sense that one is not unique in one's problems. Since many chemically dependent individuals enter the group setting with some reluctance because they believe that their problems are unique to themselves, the positive impact that occurs whenever they learn that others do have concerns similar to their own is enormous. A sense of relief often results as these individuals hear the self-disclosure of other group members, and a growing insight into the nature of their own problems takes place. Yalom (1985) reports that individuals often indicate that they feel more in touch with the world and see this process of commonality with other group members as one of a "welcome to the human race" experience.

One exercise which has often been used to increase this sense of universality involves having each member of the group write on paper a secret that he or she would be highly unlikely to share with the rest of the group. The secrets are then collected and redistributed, with each member receiving a secret other than his or her own. The individual then reads someone else's secret and tries to describe the way he or she believes the other person feels with such a secret. One of the most positive outcomes has been that those who share their secrets discover that they were not devastating to the other group members, but were accepted. In addition, the pattern of those secrets seems to indicate that the kinds of issues which create the major problems for most of us have many common elements, among them feelings of basic inadequacy, guilt, and a sense of interpersonal alienation.

Thus, as members of the group learn that others share the kinds of feelings, thoughts, and concerns which have disturbed them, they begin to feel a sense of commonality with other people and to lose the sense that something is wrong with them.

Vicarious Learning

Although vicarious learning has been called different things by different theorists, from the very beginning it has been recognized as an important element of group counseling. Corsini and Rosenberg (1955) speak of "spectator therapy," which they describe as gaining from the observation and imitation of fellow patients. Yalom (1970) uses the term "imitative behavior" to describe the same basic factor. Finally, Bloch, Reibstein, and Crouch (1979, 681) employ the phrase "vicarious learning" to describe the factor of "learning about oneself through the observation of other group members, including the therapist."

George and Cristiani (1986) point out that while individuals in groups are focusing on resolving their own interpersonal or intrapersonal difficulties, they are also exposed to interpersonal relationship skills being modeled by the group leader and the other group members. A great deal of research has been done on the effects of imitative learning as part of the group process; it has led to the conclusion that modeling can be deliberately used in group-counseling sessions as a means of demonstrating desirable behavior before group members try out the new behavior, with the group providing feedback.

In many ways, vicarious learning brings into the group process other group members who may be experiencing similar concerns. In doing so, those individuals not only gain additional insight into what is occurring within them, but may also learn what does not fit their own experience. As Yalom (1985, 17) points out, "finding out what we are not is progress toward finding out what we are."

In a particularly important study of group counseling, Jeske (1973) had each member of the group press a button whenever that individual found himself or herself identifying with another group member. Those individuals who showed the greatest improvement recorded twice the number of such identifications as did those who did not improve at all. Jeske concluded that the group leader should promote such intermember identification to facilitate the therapeutic process.

Interpersonal Learning

There is little doubt that interpersonal learning plays a major role in the course of group counseling. Interpersonal learning includes comprehending the effect that the individual has on other persons, as well as the impact of other persons on the individual. Bloch (1986) points out that interpersonal learning has two components: input, chiefly through feedback; and output, an actual process whereby the group member attempts to develop more effective modes of relating to others. Certainly the attempt to relate constructively and effectively within the group is important to many chemically dependent individuals as they attempt to develop new ways of interacting in a more satisfying manner with those around them. As social beings, we are only able to develop self-esteem, a sense of personal satisfaction, and security from contacts with others. Thus, as the group develops, individuals within it begin to interact with one another in the same way they interact with others in their lives. Thus, the group becomes a type of laboratory, revealing maladaptive interpersonal behavior and atti-tudes—arrogance, grandiosity, nonassertiveness, sexualization, compliance. As individual members receive feedback from others, they learn the effect of their behavior. As a result, group members are able to understand clearly the impact they have on others and to learn how often they create the kinds of reactions that they receive from other individuals.

As group members gain greater awareness of the impact of their behav-ior upon the feelings of others, the opinions that others have of them, and the opinion they have of themselves, they also become increasingly aware of their own responsibility for what happens in their interpersonal worlds. Likewise, as each individual accepts personal responsibility for that interpersonal world, that person can begin to struggle with the resulting implication that he or she is the only one who is able to alter that world.

A major factor in facilitating the interpersonal-learning element of group counseling is that of emphasizing the present—the here and now—of the group interaction. By doing so, the group deemphasizes both the past and the current outside life of each of the members and focuses on the power and efficiency of the interpersonal interactions that are occurring at the moment. Such an experience involves both an affective and a cognitive component. That is, group members not only share important emotional experiences, but they also step outside it and examine, understand, and integrate the meaning of what they have just undergone. Thus, a rotating sequence of affect followed by cognition occurs.

Additional Elements

Other therapeutic issues that seem to be more process-oriented, rather than being elements of the group experience itself, are likewise important in facilitating the group experience.

IMPARTING OF INFORMATION

One of these is the element which Yalom (1985) called "imparting of information." This aspect of counseling can include information that is rather specific in nature. For instance, facts about various career issues that might be important to the chemically dependent person, the effects of mood-altering chemicals on sexuality, and the importance of such slogans as "No gain without pain" or "One day at a time" can be emphasized.

USE OF HUMOR

Another therapeutic factor that occurs across the various elements and is therefore not identified individually involves the use of humor in the group-counseling process. Although it can be a negative factor in group situations, especially when it consists of a pseudo-humor exercised at the expense of some person or some group, humor can become an important healing aspect of the group. There are some truly humorous dimensions to the human condition. When group leaders possess the ability to laugh at themselves and to see the humor in their own human frailties, the group becomes more likely to do so also. Humor does not include sarcasm, ridicule, or put-downs. Rather, spontaneous laughter with one or more members of the group can help establish an additional bond of genuine caring for each other and confidence in the helping nature of human rapport. On the whole, humor is an important aspect of a healthy group; for when group members learn to laugh at themselves and at each other, they are often able to carry this valuable skill into life outside the group. In many ways, the visible bubbling-up of joy, freedom, and well-being is an important sign that the group is truly therapeutic.

LEADERSHIP STYLES IN GROUP COUNSELING

Leadership style evolves in part from the leader's use of various counseling skills. No one leader will employ all the skills. Rather, the leader's familiarity with and acceptance of certain skills will make a difference in the type of leadership that he or she provides in the group, which is highly personal and individual, since some skills are not right for a particular group leader and may not feel comfortable.

In 1961, White and Lippitt described three leadership styles, based upon earlier research they had conducted with Curt Lewin. This description has become the classic conceptualization of leadership styles for counseling groups.

The original, authoritarian leadership style was characterized by a leader who made all policy decisions for the group. All techniques and activities were decided upon by the leader and communicated to the group members. In addition, authoritarian leaders tended to make personal remarks directed at individuals, remarks that included praise as well as confrontation. In addition, the authoritarian leader tended to remain aloof from the group. In such settings, in which the leader gave orders 45 percent of the time, group members tended to react aggressively and with more dependence upon the leader than did members exposed to the other leadership styles.

In the democratic leadership style, all policies tended to be discussed by the group. Such leadership included giving the group members overall goals, along with alternative steps and activities to accomplish those goals, and then working with them in deciding which alternatives to choose. Democratic leaders tended to make objective rather than personal remarks, and were more likely to participate in the group as a member. Giving orders only 3 percent of the time, the democratic leader tended to develop groups which were friendlier and more group minded.

The third leadership style identified in this classic study was "laissez faire," characterized by minimum participation from the leader. The leader tended to supply materials and to state that he or she would give information only when members asked specific questions. Although only 4 percent of the leadership-style statements gave orders, the members of such groups were less satisfied and seemed less organized than did those in groups involving the democratic style.

Although this description of the three classic leadership styles leaves the impression that the democratic leadership style is somehow far superior to the authoritarian leadership style and the laissez-faire leadership style, such a conclusion is not as helpful as a recognition that these styles exist. For one thing, no one leadership style will be effective with every group. The membership of the group, particularly in terms of how long members have been in a group, is an important factor in determining an appropriate leadership style with the chemical dependent. In groups where most members have little experience as such, the leader is looked to for direction and needs to provide some structure for the group experience. As the group becomes more familiar with the workings of the process, less structure is needed and the group leader can gradually adopt a more democratic leadership style. For experienced groups, the laissez-faire style may be appropriate.

Two additional leadership styles have been described as being highly therapeutic (Barlow, Hansen, Fuhriman, & Finley 1982). The speculative style includes a "here and now" focus by the leader, a tendency for the leader to speak for himself or herself, and a focus upon the meaning of individuals' behavior. Confrontive leadership involves a "here and now" focus, in which the leader reveals the impact that behaviors within the group have on the leader. This style includes a focus on documentation of statements from the present and from previous interactions between the leader and the group members. Confrontive leaders are generally seen as being more charismatic and less peer-oriented than speculative leaders.

A charismatic leadership style is particularly important in the area of chemical-dependency counseling, as members of the group often look at the leader through an irrational concept of the leader as an ideal. While it is an intoxicating temptation to be adored by a whole roomful of individuals (Rutan & Rice 1981), such a strategy has severe limitations, in that the leader may be seen in a highly unrealistic fashion. Such leaders face the danger of failing to move the group from the position where he or she has an early responsibility in decision making toward the position of less involvement by the leader in determining the direction of the group. By so doing, the group leader takes on greater responsibility, and thus diminishes the role of the individual group members in the accomplishments of the group. This reduces the impact of the group members, because they see any personal change as stemming from the group leader rather than from their own efforts and activities.

In identifying one's own leadership style, it is important to look at a combination of the strategies and skills which the leader incorporates in his or her group leadership. The means by which leaders communicate and the perceptions of them by the group are important aspects of that leadership style. Probably as important as any other issue is that of flexibility in leadership. Flexibility will include the ability to choose to focus on one individual, a pair of group members, or the whole group. It will also include the ability to emphasize the thinking, the affect, or the behavior involved in the group. Another aspect of flexibility is the degree to which the leader is the center of the group interaction, as opposed to when the interaction remains among the group members.

The extent to which the group leader speaks to the moment, or the "here and now"; asks other members to communicate in, and focuses remarks and interactions upon, the "here and now"; and, of course, structures the group so that "here and now" statements are held to be desirable goals is a final consideration of leadership style (George & Dustin 1988).

USING SPECIFIC TECHNIQUES IN A GROUP SETTING

Regardless of their typical leadership style, effective group leaders need to possess the ability to employ a variety of counseling techniques within the group setting. These techniques, which include the ones discussed in chapter 5, sometimes require specific attention to how they can best be used within the group setting. Some of the most important practices in the group experience are outlined in the following section.

Self-Disclosure

Self-disclosure has become a concept with divergent definitions within group counseling; basically, however, it is the experience in which the group leader expresses his or her own feelings, values, opinions, and beliefs to the group. Such self-disclosure includes, and is ordinarily limited to, what the group leader is feeling at the moment about the self, about the members of the group, or about the interaction that is occurring within the group. (An exception would be when the group leader recognizes that he or she had important cognitive or affective reactions to a previous group experience and believes that sharing those reactions is important to the group.)

Self-disclosure, then, does not ordinarily include information about the leader's age, marital status, or previous experiences. Rather, it involves revealing one's feelings and reactions to events and people as they occur to facilitate the growth of the group. When the group leader acts as a model of openness, group members learn to share their immediate feelings and reactions. In addition, such self-disclosure provides feedback to other group members about the impact of their behavior on the leader.

Perhaps the major effect of self-disclosure is to personalize the leader within the group. As the leader discloses his or her own thoughts and feelings, members of the group are more likely to see the leader as a human being, one whom they can imitate in their own lives. This can create greater hope of learning how to cope with the problems of daily living; furthermore, a sense of caring results from the leader's disclosure, since the leader is indicating trust toward the group members by sharing his or her own experiences. Occasionally, group members may ask personal questions about the leader: "How old are you?" "Why did you become a counselor?" "How long have you worked in this field?" In such instances, it is usually best just to give a direct, brief answer and then return the focus to the issue, concern, or problem with which the group is dealing. Continual questioning of this sort often indicates that group members feel anxious and are attempting to avoid it by turning the focus onto the counselor. When this happens, rather than disclosing facts about himself or herself, the group leader may wish to respond to the dynamic of the question that seems to be occurring: for instance, "I think you feel as if you've been under attack by the group long enough, and you are asking me questions as a way to turn the focus off yourself."

In addition, the impact of self-disclosure is greatly increased because group members are able to see the leader as being real or authentic or genuine. Most human beings fear that if others see them as they actually are, they will be rejected or put down or made fun of. As a result, many individuals begin the process of pretending to be other than they really are for self-protection. By presenting themselves in a genuine manner, group leaders act to undermine the fear of the members that such behavior is dangerous and that one needs to be perfect in order to be accepted.

Immediacy

Immediacy includes an awareness of one's emotional experiences in the here and now. Closely related to the skill of self-disclosure, it involves the individual's recognizing what he or she is experiencing with little or no distortion. Such an attitude usually includes the sharing of that experiencing, which involves a certain degree of risk taking.

To facilitate such immediacy often means that the group leader needs a set of techniques that will plunge the individual, and the group, into an intense awareness of what each is experiencing. The leader must be active and continually work toward the shifting of material from the outside to the inside, from the abstract to the specific, from the generic to the personal. This is often done through genuine self-disclosure on the part of the leader.

One means of promoting this process is by responding to all available data, verbal and nonverbal. By pointing out such simple issues as choice of seats, being on time, eye contact or the lack of it when talking, and socializing patterns within the group, the leader helps to turn the attention or focus of the group toward the current happenings within it. One risk of attention to nonverbal elements is that the leader will be tempted to interpret this data, rather than simply pointing out what has happened and encouraging the group to give it meaning. Of course, when an individual or the group seems to be unable to find meaning for the occurrence, the leader may wish to suggest a tentative meaning. For example, he or she might say, "Could it be that the reason you continue to kick your foot in such a fashion when I am asking you about your feelings toward your spouse is because you really want to kick somebody?"

Perhaps the most difficult, but the most likely to be productive, source of information about the group process comes from the leader's own feelings. If, for example, he or she feels impatient or discouraged or bored or frustrated, the leader must recognize this as important data about the working of the group and use it to the group's advantage.

Confrontation

Confrontation appears to be highly emphasized by professionals in the area of chemical-dependency counseling as a means of forcing individuals to overcome denial and to recognize how their chemical dependency has caused problems. Confrontation basically involves presenting information about an individual that he or she is unaware of. Such a statement typically has important meaning and high emotional investment for the persons involved. The information that is presented typically points out an incongruency on the part of a member or various members of the group. Such inconsistency might result from the person saying one thing verbally while contradicting it nonverbally ("You say you are angry, but I noticed that you're smiling as you're saying that. Is it possible to be angry and to smile at the same time?"); an incongruency between statements made on different occasions ("You said yesterday that your family was the most important thing to you in your life. Today, you indicate that your job is the most important thing to you."); and a gap between what a person says and does ("You keep saying that you want to learn to take risks in your relationships with other people. However, the last three times that you have been given assignments which involve the taking of such risks, you have neglected to fulfill what you were asked to do."). Notice that each of the examples gave no interpretation of the incongruence, but simply pointed it out to the individual. As a result, the group leader provides the opportunity for the member to gain the greatest good from the confrontation by having to struggle toward learning what the incongruence means to that member.

Certainly a major purpose of confrontation is to promote insight and growth in the group member. Whenever confrontation is used to hurt or to punish, the result is negative and the interaction is not therapeutic. Rather, effective confrontation comes from an attitude of caring, an attitude of willingness to increase one's involvement with the member, and an attitude of wanting to promote the growth and development of that person. Finally, leader confrontation can be used to model the technique for the entire group. As such, it can become an example of assertive behavior, which is an important part of recovery in chemical dependency.

Cognitive Restructuring

Cognitive restructuring is another process that is particularly useful in group approaches to counseling. When irrational, illogical attitudes and ideas are expressed by some members of the group, it is likely that other group members share them. The failure to challenge and to reformulate those ideas to logical, rational ones can result in their being reinforced in the minds of the other group members. On the other hand, challenging irrational ideas and helping the member replace them with more reasonable ones can have an effect on other members of the group who have shared similar beliefs.

One way of challenging such irrationality in the group setting is to use exaggeration and humor in showing the absurdity of the idea. For instance, if a group member were to indicate that he or she could not share a personal experience because other people might find it disgusting, the group leader could respond, "Wouldn't it be awful if you were to tell this whole group about what happened to you, and as you were talking part of the group fell asleep, part of the group got up and walked out, part of the group laughed at you, and others just simply vomited at how disgusting you are? Wouldn't it be awful if all of this occurred and you were so devastated by it that you had to crawl back to your room and get in bed and you would never be able to get out of bed because of your embarrassment and you would wither away and die because you told us what happened?" By exaggerating the potential effects of an irrational idea, the group leader helps the entire group to see how often we catastrophize or exaggerate the effects of our own behavior. As a result, members of the group are encouraged to look at situations more realistically.

Another way to challenge irrationality is through reason. For example, the leader might point out, "If you do share this experience with the group, it is possible that some members will find it disgusting. But it is also possible that other members of the group will be impressed by your courage in sharing something that was so important to you. But the only way you will know how they respond is if you take the risk to share. By not sharing, you reject yourself, without giving the opportunity for others to reject you. And besides, even if other people reject you, that will not mean that you are any less of a person."

Role Playing

Role playing is another technique which tends to have increased impact when done in a group setting. Group members can be encouraged to act out the roles that they assume in the relationships and situations which are most important to them. By doing so, they gain the opportunity to receive feedback from other members about how they might improve their interactions in those situations.

In addition, it is often useful for group members to practice new ways of relating to others. Through role playing, the group member is helped to bridge the gap between the safety and comfort of the group and the real world. By providing for experience of success, the group leader gives the member an opportunity to learn the comfortableness that comes from having engaged in a behavior previously. Sometimes the leader can use role playing to help group members understand the effects of alternative behaviors in troubling situations.

PHASES AND STAGES OF GROUP PROCESS

For group counseling to have its maximum effect, the group must develop through various stages. Although such stages are often seen as separate entities that occur in a logical sequence, stages in real counseling groups are different. There is considerable overlap between the stages, as groups move from one stage to the other in a somewhat jerky, hesitant manner. As a result, there may be some movement toward the next stage and then regression to a previous stage. In addition, continuing groups may have a frequent change in the membership, so that some individuals will have been in the group for a long time, while others may be attending their first or second session. In such cases, the stages of group development can be seen more clearly through the individual's particular growth and the stage of the group process in which he or she is currently functioning.

Orientation and Exploration

The initial stage of a group is a time of orientation and exploration—determining the nature and structure of the group, getting acquainted with the members, and becoming involved with the workings of the particular group. As the group develops, or as a new member begins to function within the group, the group leader needs to establish a balance of comfort and anxiety. Apprehension needs to be reduced to a point where individuals feel reasonably free to participate, to the degree that they are able to look more objectively at themselves and their interactions with others. Such a reduction in anxiety leads to the openness necessary for group work. At the same time, most professionals believe that a minimal level of anxiety is necessary to motivate individuals to make positive changes in their lives. Thus, modest levels of anxiety are associated with behavior change, while high levels of anxiety act to prevent any learning from taking place.

A major emphasis during this stage is that of increasing trust among the group members. Without it, group interaction is likely to be superficial, with little self-exploration and little constructive confrontation of one another. As a result, the group faces the risk of never moving beyond this stage. The leader establishes the expectation that group members can be trusted by being congruent, by being willing to do what he or she expects the members to do, and by using genuine, appropriate self-disclosure.

This early stage is also important in helping group members to identify the goals they have for their group experience. These include the more general priorities for the entire group, which relate to the group-process objectives. In addition, members are encouraged to establish their own individual goals. Since most have only a vague idea about what they want from a group experience, the leader needs to help in translating these vague ideas into specific and concrete goals with regard to the desired changes and to the efforts the individual is willing to make to bring about such changes.

Yalom (1985) maintains that one way these goals may be encouraged is by using the "agenda-go-round." He suggests that at the beginning of each session the leader go around the group asking each member to identify what he or she would like to achieve or gain from this particular session. Such individualization of goals permits the leader to work in a situation where individuals are at differing stages of their own development. In addition, this permits the newcomer to the group to learn about the kinds of goals which members may have for the sessions. Yalom also suggests that in identifying these goals, the individual be helped in stating the goal in such a way that it is achievable in a particular session. He goes on to point out that not all goals can be worked on in a given session, but that the process by which individuals identify them is an important part of therapeutic change.

Transition

Moving from the early stages of the group's experience to a point where cohesiveness and action occur requires a transitional period. This intermediate stage involves more open attitudes and feelings, with the resulting conflict, resistance, confrontation, and attempts to dominate. Although each person encounters unique difficulties in his or her transitional period, almost all individuals experience variations of these particular difficulties.

During the transition stage, group members test themselves, each other, and the leader. As people feel freer to criticize each other, conflicts develop as some assert their viewpoints in a judgmental or dogmatic manner. Some individuals will behave inconsistently, being aggressive at first and then very quiet. Others will be quiet and share only their "most acceptable" thoughts and feelings with the group. In addition, pressure to conform tends to intensify and creates further conflict as members attempt to maintain their individual identities, while seeking acceptance from other group members. Thus, norms and roles become solidified, and those with greater influence have a greater impact on the development of the guidelines for expected behavior.

Resistance is a major force during this transition stage. It may be directed at the subject matter, the group, or the leader, and may take the form of withdrawal, attacking others, or questioning the purpose of the group. This dynamic presents a critical opportunity for the leader to demonstrate and model the kind of openness to criticism that he or she expects from the members. By facing such attacks and challenges, without retaliation or withdrawal, the leader reinforces the members in sharing openly their thoughts and feelings about the workings of the group. If the leader can accept internally that such resistance is a sign that the individual is working through his or her attitude and becoming comfortable in the group, the leader is more likely to deal with such challenges directly and honestly, to share how he or she is affected by the confrontation, and to encourage continuing open communication.

Action

Stage 3—the action stage—occurs as conflict and competition decrease and the individual drops his or her preconceptions about the group and learns to accept and be accepted. This stage, in which individuals move toward doing something about changing the way they conduct their lives, is characterized by cohesiveness, productivity, and intimacy. At this point, the group member has learned to identify more closely with others and has lost the sense of isolation he or she may have experienced in earlier sessions. Interpersonal respect and trust develop as members learn that self-disclosure does not result in catastrophe. Greater closeness and cooperation result, bringing about greater intimacy among group members.

During stage 3, there is an increase of morale, mutual trust, and self-disclosure. Some members now feel free to reveal the "real-unreal" secrets that they have been hiding: sexual secrets, long-buried past transgressions, or other embarrassments. The cohesiveness that is developing results in greater self-disclosure as a consequence of others showing greater respect for their concerns and listening more carefully to their attitudes and feelings. As group members express greater understanding of situations, problems, and feelings, communication becomes less defensive, aggressive, or manipulative. As a result, group members become more genuine in what they say and more willing to reveal personally significant material. Thus a circular process occurs; as individuals reveal more, the group expresses greater understanding, and members become even more open.

Problems sometimes result in stage 3 when group members suppress all expression of negative affect and return to being too nice to each other. While such group behavior may be supportive and understanding, it does not allow for confrontation or open expression of negative feelings. By trying to facilitate growth with kindness alone, the group faces the danger of reverting to stage 1, in which little meaningful self-disclosure occurs. Thus, what is most important in stage 3 is for group members to challenge each other toward constructive behavioral change. By being able to have more give-and-take discussions, members feel freer to express feelings without fear of punishment. They are able to work through negative feelings toward each other, instead of avoiding those feelings. They face crises inside and outside the group experience by discussing them and working them through. Most important, they take on greater responsibility for their behavior and the consequences of it.

Completion

Ending the group experience is a critical and often difficult experience for all concerned. Thus stage 4—the completion stage—is in many ways as important as the very first session in the overall effect on the lives of those who participate. Individual members need to anticipate the ending of their experience and to work within sessions at a speed and intensity that will allow them to accomplish their goals in the allotted time. How individual members handle the end of the group often reflects the degree of growth that they have experienced. Sometimes, a person may be experiencing anxiety, overfunctioning without the group's support, and a resulting fear that his or her life will regress to their using behavior. They may also be disappointed about never seeing some of the group members again. There may even be anger toward members of the group or the leader.

However the group members deal with their feelings, the leader can help them face the reality of termination and reinforce their new attitudes about self-disclosure by encouraging them to bring their feelings and attitudes into the open. Thus, the emotional aspects of ending the group can be used to help group members make the transition to the outer world. By doing this, the leader is not denying the sense of loss and sadness that may accompany the members' leaving the group, but is instead allowing that mourning to become an enriching experience for the persons in the group.

A major concern during the completion stage is encouraging the individual to put into words what he or she has learned from the group experience and how the individual intends to apply the increased self-understanding and behavior change outside the group. Such an examination must be concrete and specific. This experience can be enhanced by employing the giving and receiving of feedback skills that members have learned as part of the group experience. Thus, after the individual has been asked to give a brief summary of how he or she has perceived himself or herself in the group, what conflicts have become more clear to them, what were the turning points in their lives, and what they expect to do with what they have learned, others in the group are asked to give feedback about how they have perceived that individual and their feelings about the person.

While feedback from other group members, as well as from the leader, need not be 100 percent positive, the trend should be in that direction. The leader often sets an example by focusing on individual progress and by giving the member ideas as to future work that needs to be done. By minimizing negative feedback, the leader helps to prevent member defensiveness that may lead to discounting the value of the whole experience.

SUMMARY

Group approaches have been an essential part of treating chemical dependency since the beginning of Alcoholics Anonymous. This emphasis recognizes the power of the group to force chemical dependents to face the problems drinking or using have caused in their lives and to provide the kind of emotional, psychological, and social support they need for recovery.

Elements of group counseling which enable the group process to be therapeutic include the instillation of hope, a sense of safety and support, cohesiveness, universality, vicarious learning, and interpersonal learning. Other important elements include the imparting of information and the use of humor.

While each group leader develops his or her own leadership style, certain styles have been identified. The authoritarian style is one in which the leader makes most, or all, of the policy decisions for the group. The democratic style features a leader who discusses all policies with the group members. The laissez-faire style entails minimal participation by the leader. Other styles include the speculative style and the confrontive style.

While various counseling techniques may be used differently in a group setting, the group experience always tends to develop through various stages. These include the initial stage of orientation and exploration, the transitional stage, the action stage, and the completion stage.

7

Issues in Recovery and Growth

INTRODUCTION

Perhaps the central issue in the recovery and growth of the individual who is chemically dependent is the need for a strong support system. For most individuals, Alcoholics Anonymous provides the foundation needed to maintain sobriety and to continue personal growth and development. Alcoholics Anonymous does this by providing a peer group which understands the particular dangers that the recovering individual faces and which is willing to confront when justified or to give encouragement when needed.

This chapter focuses on AA—its twelve steps, its twelve traditions, and its slogans. There is also a need for the counselor to understand the concept of spirituality, especially as it differs from religion.

Finally, the issue of relapse, as well as steps to be taken in preventing it, are discussed, with a look at an alternative approach to recovery—the cognitive/behavioral model of relapse prevention.

PROVIDING SUPPORT SYSTEMS

Alcoholics Anonymous

Because the first support group to deal with chemical dependency was Alcoholics Anonymous, and because most of the other effective support groups at a national level were developed on the basis of the AA model, it is the major support system that is important in the whole process of recovery. Many of the same ideas that are found in Alcoholics Anonymous are found in such other groups as Narcotics Anonymous (NA) and Cocaine Anonymous (CA). These organizations have borrowed heavily from the twelve steps, the slogans and traditions, and the overall theory behind Alcoholics Anonymous.

First of all, it is clear that some individuals who are alcoholic are able to maintain recovery without involvement in AA. Likewise, it is clear that some individuals who attend AA are unable to maintain sobriety. However, to use those two points as a basis for failing to use the power and help of AA in maintaining sobriety is failing to see the forest for the trees. Just as some individuals who have high blood pressure are able to avoid a stroke or a heart attack in spite of their failure to take an antihypertensive medication, and just as some individuals have a stroke or a heart attack in spite of taking such medications, the individual alcoholic who attempts to maintain sobriety without AA or an equivalent support system (and these are few and far between) is failing to take advantage of all the support and help needed to be sober.

Alcoholics Anonymous dates back officially to June 10, 1935 (Wilson 1957). Its real beginning, however, came in May 1935, when Bill Wilson was continuing his failing struggle to overcome the obsessive compulsiveness of his alcoholism. Wilson was a margin trader on Wall Street who had great dreams, but consistent failures, in his professional life. Thirty-nine years old at this time, he had gone through his fourth drying-out period in a Manhattan hospital after periods of panhandling on the streets, falling down stairs, lying in his own vomit, and stealing from his wife's purse (Robertson 1988). His marriage was on the rocks. Although he had managed to stay sober for the previous five months, he was having difficulty maintaining that sobriety. Most important, he felt a sense of aloneness, that no one was there to help him.

Wilson's struggle for sobriety had been aided by a spiritual experience while in treatment. He had also been helped by Dr. William Silkworth, a New York specialist in alcoholism, who had convinced him of the grave nature of alcoholism. In his frantic attempts to stay sober, Wilson had learned of the Oxford Group, a popular nondenominational movement which had sought to recapture the essence of first-century Christianity.

While in Akron, Ohio, on a business trip in May 1935, Wilson became discouraged after a deal had fallen through and felt the familiar urge to drink. Feeling panicky, he used a church directory to identify a minister and called to ask if the minister could help him get in touch with other alcoholics. After several phone calls, he made contact with another devout member of the Oxford Group, who invited Wilson to her home and arranged a meeting between Wilson and Dr. Bob Smith. Smith, too, was a chronic alcoholic, who had a failing surgical practice and who had lost most of his hope for reversing the direction of his life.

Years later, Dr. Smith wrote of his experience in meeting and talking to Bill Wilson: "Of far more importance was the fact that he was the first living human with whom I had ever talked, who knew what he was talking about in regard to alcoholism from actual experience" (Robertson 1988, 35). The emphasis on gaining support from someone who had experienced the same devastation in his or her life became a founding principle of AA.

From this seemingly chance meeting began the movement that was to develop into Alcoholics Anonymous. Convinced that permanent recovery from alcoholism was vitally dependent on one alcoholic working with another, the two men began working with other alcoholics who were admitted to the Akron City Hospital. Their very first case responded immediately, became AA member number three, and never had another drink. Their work at Akron continued through the summer of 1935, with many failures, but with some heartening successes as well. By the time Wilson returned to New York in the fall of 1935, the first AA group had actually been formed, though no one realized it at the time (Alcoholics Anonymous 1976).

With Wilson's return to New York, a second small group promptly developed. In addition, various alcoholics who had picked up their ideas in Akron or New York were working to develop similar groups in other cities. By 1939, the membership had reached about one hundred men and women and had begun to call itself Alcoholics Anonymous after the title of its own book.

With the publication of the first edition of *Alcoholics Anonymous*, a flurry of inquiries began coming into the New York office which had been established. By the end of 1939, it was estimated that more than eight hundred alcoholics had become involved in various AA groups. Today, millions of individuals have been influenced by the philosophy, the writings, and the fellowship of Alcoholics Anonymous.

In the "Big Book," as *Alcoholics Anonymous* is ordinarily called, the claim is made that of those alcoholics who came to AA and really tried, 50 percent got sober and remained that way, 25 percent got sober after some relapses, and, even among the remainder, those who continued participating in AA showed improvement. The "Big Book" acknowledges that other thousands who came to a few AA meetings decided they did not want the program and got no value from it. However, it is clear that a large number of individuals have maintained sobriety as a result of their participation in AA.

Perhaps more important than the claims of the "Big Book" are the data that support the idea that AA has been an effective force in achieving and maintaining sobriety. Leach and Norris (1977) have documented AA's effectiveness. They discuss various research studies which show that close to 60 percent of those who attend AA have been sober for more than a year. This is from a group of individuals whose alcoholism had become so threatening that they had lost hope of maintaining sobriety by themselves.

Perhaps the most important question for the counselor is "Why is AA effective?" Perhaps because it provides emotional arousal, hope, and dependence on others for relief. Meetings of AA typically involve a speaker who is enthusiastic, accepting, and humorous, and most of all whose story strikes a familiar chord in the listener. As opposed to many other approaches that had been used prior to the development of AA (and which still continue to be used to a lesser degree in our society), AA offers a nonjudgmental setting with no obligations. The alcoholic is not made to feel guilty, nor is he or she threatened with impending consequences. Self-esteem is reestablished, and a resulting relief occurs. The zeal and enthusiasm of the members of AA often result in new members being swept up in the excitement and hope of a sober life.

Another factor in helping AA be so effective has been the development of the twelve steps, the twelve traditions, and the various slogans which have become part of the AA experience. Beginning with the powerful effect of the very first of the twelve steps ("We admitted we were powerless over alcohol— that our lives had become unmanageable"), the strength of AA begins as the individual works to overcome denial. This initial admission that a person needs help is central to the whole experience of AA.

In addition, the elements that were identified and discussed in chapter 6 are central to the AA fellowship. For example, hope is provided by hearing the accounts of other alcoholics, who often have suffered even worse experiences and yet have been able to reach a point where they no longer drink. A sense of safety and support is provided, as individuals do not identify themselves in any way other than by their first names and the group members provide fellowship. In addition, the use of an AA sponsor acts as a means of encouraging persons to take advantage of the support that is available. The sense of solidarity and identity that develops over time becomes the essence of the cohesiveness that is needed for an effective group. The factor of universality is clearly apparent as AA newcomers listen to the various stories of members and recognize that they are no longer alone in their experiences. Vicarious learning takes place as individuals develop a sense of how other AA members have worked to overcome cravings and compulsive feelings in their own disease. Thus the AA group, while not a formal therapy community, usually provides the same kinds of therapeutic factors as an effective therapy group.

In addition, the Alcoholics Anonymous experience is such that it can become part of an overall therapeutic plan for the individual. Rather than seeing AA as a rival in treating particular individuals, psychiatrists, psychologists, and other mental-health professionals are recognizing that the AA approach and the psychotherapeutic approach can be combined for maximum effect. This, of course, is partially based on the counselor's sense of the value of AA, as well as on an understanding of how it operates. When the clinician develops an enthusiasm and acceptance for the power of Alcoholics Anonymous, it contributes to the psychotherapeutic experience and enables the therapist to use the support of AA in facilitating the overall therapeutic process.

The Twelve Steps

Probably no other aspect of any therapeutic approach has been more powerful than the use of the twelve steps in Alcoholics Anonymous. (They are presented in table 7.1.) On the surface they are simple and easy to understand. In practice, however, they represent some very difficult, sometimes complex, concepts for initiating and maintaining sobriety. To better understand the use of the twelve steps, several points are important. The first is that a person does not simply go through the twelve steps, one by one, never to return to an earlier step. Realistically, individuals do take the steps in their numerical order, but are often forced to return to an earlier step to reestablish its concept in their lives. Thus in AA meetings there is a continuing study and discussion of the twelve steps, one by one, and their application in the lives of each individual.

A second point that needs to be made about the twelve steps is that they require a sincere commitment to the *program*, the specific, practical plan of

Table 7.1 The Twelve Steps

---

1. We admitted we were powerless over alcohol—that our lives had become unmanageable.
2. Came to believe that a Power greater than ourselves could restore us to sanity.
3. Made a decision to turn our will and our lives over to the care of God as we understood Him.
4. Made a searching and fearless moral inventory of ourselves.
5. Admitted to God, to ourselves, and to another human being the exact nature of our wrongs.
6. Were entirely ready to have God remove all these defects of character.
7. Humbly asked Him to remove our shortcomings.
8. Made a list of all persons we had harmed, and became willing to make amends to them all.
9. Made direct amends to such people wherever possible, except when to do so would injure them or others.
10. Continued to take personal inventory and when we were wrong promptly admitted it.
11. Sought through prayer and meditation to improve our conscious contact with God as we understood Him, praying only for knowledge of His will for us and the power to carry that out.
12. Having had a spiritual awakening as the result of these Steps, we tried to carry this message to others, and to practice these principles in all our affairs.

---

growth and recovery which includes the combinations of principles and behaviors practiced by AA members in their daily lives. Members regularly exhort one another to "work the program." To do so, however, requires several factors, including honesty, openness, patience, and effort (Hegarty 1982). You will note that the first letters of these four requirements form the word *hope*. Since alcoholics have ordinarily developed a pattern of deceit and dishonesty as they have attempted to hide their alcoholism and its effects on their lives from others, recovery depends on individuals being totally honest about the realities of their lives. Putting delusion and denial aside, stopping the use of masks and allowing others to see them as they really are, and learning to become honest are the first and essential steps of the process toward recovery. Openness involves a willingness to look at new ideas and new concepts and to avoid quick judgments, so that persons are able to give an honest effort to approaches that may help their recovery. Patience is necessary, since the alcoholic has spent many years developing the thoughts, feelings, and behaviors that have become a pattern of his or her life. Thus, there is a desire to have immediate relief and immediate change, but patience with growth and recovery is necessary. Effort simply means to be willing to think new thoughts, to try new behaviors, to make an effort to do those things which are necessary in "working the program."

Step 1. *We admitted we were powerless over alcohol—that our lives had become unmanageable.* Step 1 becomes the very foundation of recovery. Admitting that one is powerless is one of the most difficult acts a human being can perform. Previous behavior has involved the sense that if every condition were right, persons could handle their own problems. For example, people often say, "My only problem is my family. If they did not criticize me all the time for how much drinking I do, I wouldn't drink so much. They just don't understand me." Some people blame the neighborhood, their jobs, or any other element of their lives to avoid recognizing that the problem is within themselves and that they are unable to do anything about it.

A reluctance to examine our powerlessness is as characteristic of the illness as are any withdrawal symptoms or physiological damage that may have been done. Part of this reluctance is based on a fear of what admitting that one has an illness will do to one's life. Just as the diabetic often denies the reality of his or her disease, the alcoholic is often unwilling to admit that he or she is unable to control drinking. To admit that one is powerless is a recognition that one must seek, and accept, the help that is necessary to deal with the illness. To admit that one is alcoholic means that the individual must begin the pathway of sobriety, including the commitment to drink no more.

The other side of admitting our powerlessness over alcoholism is a recognition that it is not a result of moral weakness, but an illness. Recognizing powerlessness and accepting illness allows the individual to eliminate the self-condemning behavior of remorse and guilt that have previously led to further use of alcohol. Thus, the emotional pain that accompanies one's admission of powerlessness becomes the emotional lift that results from the recognition that the person is alcoholic, not because he or she is a bad person, but because he or she is sick.

Unmanageability is, of course, related to being powerless. A person who had the power to control drinking and the results of that drinking would be able to manage his or her life. However, the unmanageability which results directly from the powerlessness has a strong impact on one's social and personal life.

Social unmanageability, which follows the act of drinking alcohol or taking some other mood-altering chemical, means that the individual's social behavior is unpredictable and cannot be controlled through the traditional methods used in our society. Arguments, fights, telling off-color stories, dancing seductively, or engaging in a variety of behaviors that are not ordinarily acceptable to the individual result from the person's inability to manage his or her social behavior. The individual develops relationships with persons whose value systems are much less strict than their own, partly out of a fear of rejection by previous friends and partly because of the need for acceptance of their new behavior. Thus emotions, behavior, and social values have become affected. On the job, increased absences, lost productivity, and shirked responsibilities result from the use of chemicals.

At a personal level, the use of mood-altering chemicals affects the individual's maturity. Using causes the person to respond to life in a self-defeating way. Immature behavior includes such issues as overreacting to various situations, making excuses for behavior, throwing temper tantrums, and developing a sense of grandiosity. These help to develop a lack of manageability in one's life and create a sense of chaos.

Probably more than any other of the twelve steps, step 1 requires that individuals continually reaffirm their sense of powerlessness and the un-manageability of their lives. One of the great dangers to recovery is that the person begins to feel too confident, too secure, and loses the sense of powerlessness. When this happens, the individual is at great risk for returning to the alcoholic life.

Step 2. *We came to believe that a Power greater than ourselves could restore us to sanity.* Step 3. *We made a decision to turn our will and our lives over to the care of God as we understood Him.* These two steps, which involve the recognition of a higher power and a submission of our lives to that higher power, are often difficult for many people to accept. This difficulty is often the result of the individual's believing that he or she must accept the Judeo-Christian concept of God that is most often found in our society. Such a belief creates problems for these individuals for a variety of reasons, including a sense that "God" is responsible for many of their problems. Such problems include the death or serious illness of family members, the loss of important jobs, or various physical handicaps. By blaming God, the individual has often closed the door to an acceptance that God can restore him or her to sanity.

The key to these steps, of course, involves two aspects: the recognition of the clear limitations of one's own power and the resulting need to acknowledge greater resources than one's own; and the flexibility of using one's own concept of God as "we understand him." Thus, accepting a power greater than oneself is simply an extension of step 1. If one acknowledges one's powerless-ness, then the future is bleak unless there is a parallel acceptance that there is a power greater than oneself who can provide resources to enable the individ-ual to bring about some degree of manageability in his or her life. At the same time, one must recognize that one's higher power may not be a person, but an idea or a concept. For instance, for many AA members, the AA group itself is the higher power that provides the resources and support the individual needs to maintain sobriety. For others, the higher power is the development and acceptance of a value system that brings hope and meaning to their lives.

Step 4. *We made a searching and fearless moral inventory of ourselves.* Al-though AA has sometimes been criticized for allowing the individual to avoid responsibility for his or her own behavior, step 4 makes it clear that one has moral obligations. The soul-searching it requires does not bring about perfec-tion, but allows people to look at where they are from a moral standpoint, so that they can develop a plan for where they want to go. The fear that often accompanies an initial commitment to recovery is the fear that the individual can never become a "better" person. As step 4 pushes the individual to look at his or her life, values, and the correspondence between them, this fear lessens. Individuals search out the truth about themselves so that they no longer have to hide or run from it. And as individuals, they come to know their own masked selves. They are able to see the big picture, which includes not only their flaws, but also their strengths. This self-inventory enables them to move toward the future by pinpointing the flaws that need to be eliminated and by highlighting the strengths that need to be emphasized.

Step 5. *We admitted to God, to ourselves, and to another human being the exact nature of our wrongs.* Step 5 continues the fourth step by sharing what one has learned in that process. In many ways, the first four steps are internal and require no involvement of others. Step 5, however, insists that the individual begin to open up his or her life. By admitting the exact nature of one's wrongs, one is beginning to check out his or her own self-honesty. By sharing, the individual is taking the risk of receiving feedback that he or she is not looking at himself or herself realistically. In addition, the commitment that results from such public sharing becomes a powerful tool in the process of recovery. Finally, such sharing becomes the first step the individual takes to begin to involve others in his or her life without the kind of mask that had been used in the past. It is a recognition that humans are social beings who need the warmth and caring of others. And in this sharing, we learn that both our failures and our successes are part of who we are and that neither is very important. What is important is that the individual is on the journey to a better life.

Step 6. *We were entirely ready to have God remove all these defects of character.* Step 7. *We humbly asked Him to remove our shortcomings.* Steps 6 and 7, then, become the next act of working toward personal change. As the person has progressed through steps 4 and 5, recognizing and admitting the nature of his or her wrongs, that individual has reached the point of understanding that those defects of character need to be eliminated. Such character flaws (e.g., insecurity, jealousy, grandiosity, and temper tantrums) may have become habits that are as familiar to the person as the kinds of food that he or she prefers. As such, simply recognizing that they exist does not get rid of them. By moving toward action to let these defects go, the person is accepting the idea that character flaws are hiding places and excuses for trouble and is willing to give them up because he or she no longer needs to hide behind them.

Probably the key word in steps 6 and 7 is *humbly*. For the alcoholic, the need to feel good about oneself and to feel a sense of self-esteem has been so undermined by the failures associated with alcoholism that the person has often compensated by overemphasizing the pride and satisfaction that he or she has in things done well. In many ways, humility and the acceptance of it in one's life is an extension of step 1. Humility is not self-abasement; rather, it is an acceptance of one's own limitations as a human being. By asking God to remove one's shortcomings, the individual is clearly committing himself or herself to the need for change in his or her life. By asking to have those shortcomings removed, the individual is taking the initial step to do what can be done to improve the quality of his or her life.

Step 8. *We made a list of all persons we had harmed, and became willing to make amends to them all.* The personal inventory conducted in step 4 becomes the foundation for the social inventory of step 8. Step 8 thus takes the personal moral inventory and extends it to the harm that one has done to others, recognizing that we are social beings who live, work, and play with other people. Likewise, it continues the sense of responsibility that we have as human beings and helps the individual to understand that while there is no personal responsibility for the illness of alcoholism, he or she is responsible for personal behavior.

The point of the eighth step is not to heap blame on oneself, but to face up to the truth. Although the emphasis appears to be on what one has done in the past, the real focus is on willingness to make amends today. By compiling a written list, one is acknowledging that he or she has actively or passively harmed others by using mood-altering chemicals. Becoming willing to make amends is a recognition of our personal responsibility and our willingness to clean up our past.

Step 9. *We made direct amends to such people whenever possible, except when to do so would injure them or others.* From my perspective, this is one of the most sensitive and powerful of the twelve steps. It is sensitive because it recognizes that to make direct amends in some situations would create further pain and harm to others. Being "open and honest" in all situations can sometimes be insensitive and create enormous pain for others. At the same time, step 9 is powerful because it requires that the person put together humility and courage, and as a result helps that individual to develop self-respect and peace of mind. By accepting personal responsibility for one's past in such a way as to make amends, one assumes responsibility for his or her contributions to the well-being of others. Since direct amends are not always possible, step 9 recognizes that indirect approaches may also be helpful. Simply writing a letter to an absent friend may help. At other times, one is expected to change one's attitude and behavior as a means of making amends.

Step 10. *We continued to take personal inventory and when we were wrong promptly admitted it.* Step 10 is a recognition of the importance of continually reviewing one's life. It indicates that a person does not become perfect simply by working the twelve-step program. Rather, it is based on a recognition that human beings continue to make mistakes and have recurring problem areas. This tenth step, then, acts much like an oil check in one's automobile, identifying areas of difficulty. By admitting those wrongs, we continue to admit our powerlessness and we continue to work on our humility. Practicing the tenth step helps to keep the individual honest and promotes emotional maturity.

Step 11. *We sought through prayer and meditation to improve our conscious contact with God as we understood Him, praying only for knowledge of His will for us and the power to carry that out.*

Step 11 reasserts the need for a commitment to one's higher power. By doing so, the individual continues to recognize the need for a power greater than the self to maintain sobriety. Seeking through prayer and meditation requires the person to withdraw from daily events long enough to open the mind to new ideas and to new insights. Praying for knowledge of God's will is a recognition that the individual's will for himself or herself has, in the past, caused little but grief. And although the person has made progress toward sobriety by working through the first ten steps, step 11 requires that the individual put aside any developing grandiosity—a sense that the sobriety is the result of his or her own power—and accept one's powerlessness with humility.

Step 12. *Having had a spiritual awakening as a result of these Steps, we tried to carry this message to others, and to practice these principles in all our affairs.* The twelfth step becomes an important part of the AA program. The individual acknowledges that accepting the gift of sobriety entails the responsibility of sharing that sobriety with other people. This is done by carrying the message to others. It does not involve having small groups go house to house in various communities to seek out those who may be suffering from alcoholism; it does require that the person do what he or she can—using his or her strengths—in helping others to initiate and maintain sobriety. This may involve becoming sponsors for new AA members, chairing meetings of AA, speaking to AA groups, or even setting up the chairs before the AA meeting starts.

In many ways, step 12 is a recognition that the twelve-step program is more than just the maintenance of sobriety, but also involves a way of life for the individual. It is a recognition that the person cannot be an AA member only in meetings, and then go home and be a tyrant. Rather, it requires that individuals take the spirit of Alcoholics Anonymous wherever they go. Learning to accept the world as it is, the individual learns to accept the self and to learn to love who he or she is becoming. Accepting the twelfth step is committing oneself to becoming all that a person is capable of becoming.

The Twelve Traditions

To accompany the twelve steps, which are like a map for the AA member to follow in maintaining sobriety, the twelve traditions establish some guidelines for the AA member in following the twelve steps (see table 7.2). Each of these twelve traditions represents major ideas that have been promoted by AA.

1. *Our common welfare should come first; personal recovery depends upon AA unity.* This tradition represents the emphasis of AA on the common

welfare of all its members. It does not represent a deemphasis on the importance of the individual, but simply stresses that AA is a large group of which each member is a small part.

2. *For our group purpose, there is but one ultimate authority—a loving God as He may express Himself in our group conscience. Our leaders are but trusted servants; they do not govern.* The second tradition emphasizes that there are no elected or appointed leaders in AA groups; rather, the group must continue to act as a whole, with leadership being provided by a "collective conscience" which results from the group's commitment to the importance of a higher power and the turning over of their lives to that higher power.

3. *The only requirement for AA membership is a desire to stop drinking.* AA is seen as a support group that is classless, open to anyone who suffers from the disease of alcoholism. In effect, whenever two or three alcoholics wish to commit themselves to sobriety and establish their own AA group, they are allowed to do so as long as it remains open to other individuals.

4. *Each group should be autonomous except in matters affecting other groups or AA as a whole.* Since there are no leaders, each AA group is responsible to no one but itself and its developing conscience, except for those plans or activities which may concern the welfare of other AA groups.

5. *Each group has but one primary purpose—to carry its message to the alcoholic who still suffers.*

Table 7.2 The Twelve Traditions

One—Our common welfare should come first; personal recovery depends upon AA unity.

Two—For our group purpose there is but one ultimate authority—a loving God as He may express Himself in our group conscience. Our leaders are but trusted servants; they do not govern.

Three—The only requirement for AA membership is a desire to stop drinking.

Four—Each group should be autonomous except in matters affecting other groups or AA as a whole.

Five—Each group has but one primary purpose—to carry its message to the alcoholic who still suffers.

Six—An AA group ought never endorse, finance, or lend the AA name to any related facility or outside enterprise, lest problems of money, property, and prestige divert us from our primary purpose.

Seven—Every AA group ought to be fully self-supporting, declining outside contributions.

Eight—Alcoholics Anonymous should remain forever nonprofessional, but our service centers may employ special workers.

Nine—AA, as such, ought never be organized; but we may create service boards or committees directly responsible to those they serve.

Ten—Alcoholics Anonymous has no opinion on outside issues; hence the AA name ought never be drawn into public controversy.

Eleven—Our public relations policy is based on attraction rather than promotion; we need always maintain personal anonymity at the level of press, radio, and films.

Twelve—Anonymity is the spiritual foundation of all our Traditions, ever reminding us to place principles before personalities.

---

6. *An AA group ought never endorse, finance, or lend the AA name to any related facility or outside enterprise, lest problems of money, property, and prestige divert us from our primary purpose.* The fifth and sixth traditions are perhaps the leading reason that AA has continued to be a powerful force for sobriety. By not going into business, AA keeps the focus on its primary purpose, "to carry its message to the alcoholic who still suffers."

7. *Every AA group ought to be fully self-supporting, declining outside contributions.* This emphasis on self-support continues to focus the AA group on sobriety, and helps to prevent futile disputes over the issues of property, money, and authority.

8. *Alcoholics Anonymous should remain forever nonprofessional, but our service centers may employ special workers.* Thus, while AA rejects the employment of professional counselors, it recognizes that certain services do require other kinds of workers and allows this to be done. However, by refraining from hiring individuals to provide counseling for alcoholics at a fee, AA continues its tradition of alcoholics working with alcoholics on a voluntary, supportive basis.

9. *AA, as such, ought never be organized; but we may create service boards or committees directly responsible to those they serve.* Although each AA group must have some degree of leadership in planning the focus of meetings, this tradition reminds the AA group that the least possible organization is the best organization for AA. A rotating leadership is recommended. Thus, while a few leadership positions may need to be filled, the emphasis continues to be on those who hold them simply carrying out the wishes of the group; individuals in such positions do not govern.

10. *Alcoholics Anonymous has no opinion on outside issues; hence, the AA name ought never be drawn into public controversy.* As we have seen, AA continually strives to focus on maintaining the sobriety of its members. While individuals involved in AA can, on their own, express opinions on such issues as politics, religion, or economics, they are not to present them as positions of Alcoholics Anonymous or while concurrently representing themselves as AA members.

11. *Our public relations policy is based on attraction rather than promotion; we need always maintain personal anonymity at the level of press, radio, and films.* AA attempts to avoid sensational advertising and personal recognition of its members; this prevents individuals from promoting themselves, rather than the goals and purposes of the group.

12. *Anonymity is the spiritual foundation of all our Traditions, ever reminding us to place principles before personalities.* By placing principles before personalities, AA members practice a genuine humility—that of recognizing that AA is more than an organization of individual members. Rather, it is a group of individuals whose lives are committed to a greater purpose, that of providing support for each other in an effort to maintain sobriety and to do so in a way

that recognizes the need for a higher power and a gratefulness to that higher power for the blessings provided.

AA Slogans

Before leaving the subject of Alcoholics Anonymous and its contributions to recovery, it is important to emphasize the value of the many slogans that have come out of the AA experience. Although many sound corny, their simplicity provides a kind of "easy handle" to emphasize and remind the alcoholic of significant issues in remaining sober. Perhaps the most important slogan is "One day at a time." Individuals in a variety of situations who face gigantic tasks often feel overwhelmed; alcoholics often feel the same way about the need to stay sober for the rest of their lives. By emphasizing that one can only take a step at a time, the plan for sobriety becomes manageable. To emphasize this point, AA members are often reminded that in difficult periods of their lives, they may have to emphasize sobriety for one hour at a time or even one minute at a time. By doing so, the focus is on responsibility at this moment for one's choice of whether or not to drink or use. Other important slogans have included "Easy does it," "Let go and let God," and "Live and let live."

Other Support Groups

After Alcoholics Anonymous was formed to provide support for the alcoholic who wanted to live a sober, productive life, a need to support family members who were also affected by alcoholism was recognized. Many of the wives of the early members of AA recognized that their own emotions, thinking processes, and behavior had been disturbed by their association with, and attempts to live with, alcoholics. They soon realized that in spite of their husbands' having stopped drinking there were still continuing problems. As a result, Al-Anon was formed to provide a structured program for family members who wanted to recognize and do something about their life patterns that had developed while living with an alcoholic. In addition, Al-Anon encouraged its members to develop an acceptable life style for themselves, independent of the actions of the alcoholic.

As a result, a twelve-step program patterned after the twelve steps of AA was developed; it emphasized the Al-Anon member's powerlessness over the alcohol use of others, rather than their own alcohol use. The support and hope brought about through Al-Anon has been a major factor in helping families and close friends deal with personal issues related to the alcoholism of someone they love. Many of these concerns were discussed in detail in chapter 3.

Another important support system that developed as an outgrowth of Al-Anon is Alateen, set up for teenagers who had problems with the alchohol use of others. Since the teenager is in a rather different power position than the spouse, a special group was needed to provide the adolescent with an opportunity to deal with his or her own feelings of shame and isolation. Like AA and Al-Anon, Alateen is a self-help group, not a professional program with trained therapists. In consequence, Alateen has allowed many teenagers to deal with their sense of stigma and to work toward healthy, productive lives.

THE IMPORTANCE OF SPIRITUALITY IN THE RECOVERY PROCESS

Perhaps no other issue has created greater argument and frustration than the issue of spirituality. This may be because of the Judeo-Christian tradition of the United States, which has resulted in many individuals believing that their spirituality is one aspect of their relationship with the higher power they call "God." Since Alcoholics Anonymous, and most professionals in the field, believe that the spiritual aspect of recovery is essential, the continuing concern exists that spirituality will be narrowly defined as a commitment to some particular religion. Thus, the issue often becomes one of articulating the idea that while religion can incorporate a healthy spirituality, spirituality is a much broader concept than any particular religion and does not require adherence to any set of religious beliefs.

For the vast majority of AA members, any reference to a higher power is a reference to the Judeo-Christian conception of God with its concomitant characteristics of creativity and sustaining power. However, the idea of spirituality in recovery emphasizes the need for a higher power, which may or may not be an omnipotent deity at all. Instead, this higher power is to be seen as a commitment to a higher principle than one's own impulsive, selfish pleasure. Thus, the higher power of spirituality can be a supreme deity, but it can also be an organization (such as Alcoholics Anonymous) or a set of moral principles to which the individual is committed.

Spirituality is, in a sense, a life force which provides the energy for growth that enables us to move beyond ourselves and to experience a passion for or a commitment to a cause greater than ourselves. As a result, spirituality involves our ability to experience enthusiasm, emptiness, euphoria, despair, and pleasure. In many ways, spirituality is the force that enables us to set out on, and continue, the journey of living, with its hazards and obstacles. Spirituality might be seen as having two aspects: a conceptual model or path which the individual is committed to follow to gain some progress toward a specific goal; and a set of guidelines which the individual follows in order to remain on the path chosen and to make progress toward a specific goal.

Another way of looking at spirituality is to recognize that it has to do with the relationship of the individual to whatever or whomever is most important in the individual's life. By determining what is most important to that person, he or she is beginning the process of learning how to use that commitment to make the most of his or her life.

Spirituality becomes such an important issue in recovery because the addiction to alcohol has ordinarily resulted in the person losing sight of what is really important in his or her life. The individual has pushed aside the previous commitment to a higher power, to a family, to a career, and to a value system in order to make excuses for and increase opportunities for the use of alcohol. By doing so, the person has increasingly built his or her life and actions on the individual will, a particular way of thinking and behaving. By emphasizing spirituality, the focus is placed on regaining the sense of commitment to those around us and to a life that is lived by a series of rules that are important to the individual. Since values are simply the rules that one lives by, the development of the value system becomes a major aspect of spirituality. Although the value system may reflect a commitment to a particular religious point of view, it is not limited to such. In effect, the value system—the rules one lives one's life by—can become the higher power by itself.

By moving from "I want what I want when I want it" self-indulgence, the alcoholic is admitting his or her hopelessness and committing the self to change and movement away from the familiar defenses that have been used to justify attitude and behavior. The alcoholic is moving away from isolation and withdrawal from emotional intimacy with others to a position where he or she recognizes the need for human contact.

Thus spirituality entails a surrender of one's attempt to manage life without help and a commitment to taking personal responsibility for the recovery process. This surrender involves a recognition that recovery is an option, a choice that the individual takes in admitting his or her powerlessness and in recognizing that only he or she can make choices that will eliminate effectively the old drinking patterns. In addition, spirituality involves the development of an attitude of grateful living, gratitude that the individual has been blessed with the opportunity to begin again and to move toward a productive life.

THE PROBLEM OF RELAPSE

Unfortunately, not everyone who makes a commitment to recovery is able to maintain it. The obsessive nature of addiction often results in the individual returning to controlled or uncontrolled using, often substituting a new drug for the old one, with the logic that only the previously preferred drug creates a problem in that individual's life. Relapse is most likely to occur within the first year of treatment, with estimates that 37 percent of users relapse within the first year and 70 percent relapse at some time. Denzin (1987) suggests that relapse is a complex social act with four phases. He describes the first phase as being highlighted by the individual lapsing into permissive thinking concerning his or her recovery program. This may involve going to places where he or she previously used or being with old friends who are users. This lapse in thinking may also involve attending fewer AA meetings, losing contact with one's sponsor, or returning to previous thinking processes, including the sense that one must be rewarded for recent successes of sobriety. The second phase of relapse is the actual using of a mood-altering chemical. Often this involves the individual's being in a situation where he or she feels a social obligation to use; for instance, having a glass of champagne at a wedding reception. At other times, it involves acting out the belief that because he or she has been able to maintain sobriety for some time social drinking is possible. In phase three, the individual gets high or drunk. When a chemically dependent person is using, little can be done. Rather, help must be withheld until the individual sobers up and recognizes the need for the fourth phase, in which he or she seeks help.

After a relapse, the counselor can do several things. He or she can ask the individual to analyze the initial using experience, both in terms of precipitating factors and of what happened to the person during that experience. By identifying precipitating factors and the kinds of internal and external pressures which led to using, the chemically dependent individual may recognize a pattern and employ it to avoid future use.

In addition, by analyzing the experience of using itself, the recovering person may not only identify what needs were being met by using, but may also help to discover those excuses for using that must be eliminated. Most important of all is that relapse not be reacted to by creating unnecessary guilt and hopelessness for the chemically dependent person.

Relapse, however, may be best dealt with by prevention, encouraging individuals to recognize the danger signs that precede the actual use of the mood-altering chemical. These danger signs, which may include those on the "relapse symptoms list" found in table 7.3, can be divided into four categories: behavior, feelings, thoughts or attitudes, and delusions of control. Behavior includes various acts of displaying one's own self-importance, in which the individual becomes conceited and pompous, with language highlighting that the person is attempting to portray that he or she "has it all together," with all the answers. The AA slogan that a person "must walk the talk" reemphasizes the need to put words into action and highlights the point that individuals who talk without acting are likely candidates for relapse.

Relapse is also often preceded by feelings of inadequacy, guilt, fear, and anger, but they are covered by self-centeredness and arrogance. Since the emotions are unavailable to the individual, he or she often feels nothing except a sense of discomfort or some degree of emotional pain. Since the individual has previously dealt with such issues by using, failure to resolve these feelings is likely to lead to further using in the future.

Table 7.3   Relapse Symptoms List

1. I start doubting my ability to stay sober.
2. I deny my fears.
3. I adamantly convince myself that "I'll never drink or use again."
4. I decide being abstinent is all I need.
5. I try to force sobriety upon others.
6. I become overconfident about my recovery.
7. I avoid talking about my problems and my recovery.
8. I behave compulsively (overwork or underwork, overtalk or withdraw, etc.).
9. I overreact to stressful situations.
10. I start isolating myself.
11. I become preoccupied with one area of my life.
12. I start having minor depressions.
13. I start unrealistic or haphazard planning.
14. I live in the "there and then."
15. I find my life plans beginning to fail.
16. I start idle daydreaming and wishful thinking.
17. I view my problems as unsolvable.
18. I long for happiness but don't know what it is.
19. I avoid having fun.
20. I overanalyze myself.
21. I become irritated with friends and family.
22. I experience periods of confusion.
23. I am easily angered.
24. I begin blaming people, places, things, and conditions for my problems.
25. I begin doubting my disease.
26. I eat irregularly (over- or undereating, snacking, etc.).
27. I have listless periods.
28. I sleep irregularly (over- or undersleeping).
29. I progressively lose my daily routine.
30. I experience periods of deep depression.
31. I sporadically attend AA and Aftercare meetings.
32. I develop an "I don't care" attitude.
33. I hoard money, sex, or power.
34. I openly reject help.
35. I develop aches and pains.
36. I rationalize that drinking or using can't make my life worse than it is now
37. I feel powerless and helpless.
38. I feel sorry for myself.
39. I have fantasies about social drinking or using.
40. I begin to lie consciously.
41. I increase my use of aspirin or nonprescription medications.
42. I completely lose confidence in myself.
43. I develop unreasonable resentments.
44. I stop attending AA or Aftercare.
45. I am overwhelmed with loneliness, frustration, anger, and tension.
46. I begin visiting drinking or using "friends" and places.

(continued)

Table 7.3   (*continued*)

---

47. I convince myself I'm cured.
48. I make or experience a major life change.
49. I start drinking or using a chemical that is not my drug or drink of choice.
50. I practice controlled drinking or using.
51. I lose control.

The thinking patterns of the person heading toward relapse are often subject to delusion and rigidity. The individual is often convinced that recovery is easily maintained and that he or she "has it made." Rigidity in dealings with others often results, with intolerance, faultfinding, judgmental attitudes, and perfectionistic thinking present. In a sense, these delusions and rigid attitudes simply reflect the individual's movement toward denying that he or she is powerless over drugs.

Finally, relapse is likely to occur when the user hits bottom, experiencing a sense of alienation and loneliness. The latter is likely to occur because the individual is either unwilling or unable to share genuine feelings and attitudes with friends. As a result, the person withdraws into the self, fearing both failure and discovery. And, like a pan of boiling water, they let out steam a little at a time, rather than risking the emotional pain that would come from removing the lid and "letting it all hang out."

Thus, to maintain recovery and to prevent relapse, individuals are encouraged most of all to stay honest with themselves and with others by refusing to let secrets build up in their lives—secrets which create the emotional turmoil that often precedes relapse. In addition, individuals are encouraged to identify symptoms that indicate relapse dangers and to assess regularly their avoidance of those symptoms. At the same time, recovery is greatly dependent on the individual's taking positive steps toward the prevention of relapse. Such steps include attendance at AA meetings, continuing contact with an AA sponsor, and other activities that have been particularly valuable in that individual's recovery.

More recent approaches to relapse prevention have developed from the cognitive-behavioral models of addiction. These approaches generally emphasize self-management programs which, while they may or may not include participation in a twelve-step program, are usually viewed with great skepticism by twelve-step-program advocates, since the idea of self-management tends to run counter to the admission of powerlessness central to the twelve-step programs. Others, however, argue that the use of a self-management program within the overall twelve-step recovery process increases the possibility of successful recovery.

The goal of self-management programs is to teach the individual how to anticipate and cope with the problem of relapse. With the focus on changing or modifying behavior, these approaches often combine such elements as behavioral skill training, cognitive interventions, and life style change procedures. Thus, the underlying concept is that while the individual who is chemically dependent had no responsibility or control over having become addicted, that individual is responsible and does have control over what he or she does in sustaining recovery. This can include using self-management principles to modify behavior that may be leading toward relapse.

The purists who support the use of cognitive-behavioral models for relapse prevention generally believe that chemical dependency is a "powerful habit pattern, an acquired vicious cycle of self-destructive behavior that is locked in by the collective effects of classical conditioning and operant reinforcement" (Marlatt 1985, 11). As "overlearned, maladaptive habit patterns," these behaviors often occur prior to or during stressful situations (including unpleasant feeling states) and thus represent maladaptive coping responses—maladaptive in the sense that they lead to negative, unpleasant consequences in the future through their effect on health, family, friends, job, and self-esteem.

This view is in conflict with the traditional disease model in that it proposes that the individual is capable of self-control; that the individual can choose moderation or abstinence as a goal; that there is a detachment of the self from the person's behavior; and that the individual needs to learn behavioral coping skills for recovery to be successful (Marlatt 1985).

In employing the cognitive-behavioral model, the counselor needs to assess high-risk situations for relapse and outline methods for teaching individuals to cope effectively in these situations. This would involve an analysis of the cognitive factors associated with the relapse process, including self-efficacy (perceived judgments or self-evaluations individuals make about their competency to handle effectively a specific situation), outcome expectancies (what will happen as a result of engaging in a particular behavior), attributions (inferred causes about *why* an individual behaves in a certain way), and decision making (the manner in which an individual makes a conscious choice). Marlatt and Gordon (1985) have edited an impressive volume that describes these concepts in detail.

Thus the counselor has the choice of using either the twelve-step program or a cognitive-behavioral model as the sole strategy for relapse prevention, or integrating the rather different approaches by using cognitive-behavioral strategies as an adjunct to a twelve-step program. This would permit the individual, while participating in a twelve-step program, to work concurrently on identifying high-risk situations for relapse and developing cognitive-behavioral strategies for modifying behavior and thus lessen the risk factor. Such an approach is also likely to reduce the tendency to turn a slip or lapse into a full-blown return to pretreatment drinking or using patterns, using the slip as a learning experience to prevent such behavior. Future focus on recovery is likely to involve such an integration of ideas and strategies.

SUMMARY

Since it is widely recognized that inpatient or outpatient treatment for chemical dependency is only the first step in a lifetime of recovery, it is essential that counselors adopt this view and attempt to maximize the probability of success in recovery. The major contribution to recovery has come from Alcoholics Anonymous (AA) and other twelve-step programs.

Alcoholics Anonymous has long provided an effective support system, furnishing hope and a program that has enabled millions to live successfully in recovery. The twelve steps, the twelve traditions, and the various slogans of AA are central and provide guidelines for recovery. In addition, AA groups can provide the therapeutic elements identified by group theorists as being responsible for personal growth and development.

Central to the AA program is spirituality, which involves a commitment to a higher power than one's own selfish pleasure. Such a commitment provides an energy for growth that enables individuals to move beyond themselves and to experience a cause greater than themselves. Spirituality usually involves a renewed commitment to a set of values by which individuals live their lives or the development of a new set of values to which commitment can occur.

Recovery unfortunately also includes the possibility of relapse and thus must provide for steps to prevent it. Since relapse is usually characterized by the individual gradually returning to old thinking and behavior patterns, AA provides one prevention program by engaging the person in regular examinations of that thinking and behavior. Newer approaches to relapse prevention have been developed by cognitive-behavioral theorists that focus on identifying high-risk situations and developing strategies for reducing the risks. While this approach is typically seen as being in conflict with the AA view, the postion taken here has been that cognitive-behavioral methods can be used effectively within the AA approach.

8 ———

Working with Special Populations

INTRODUCTION

While chemical dependency and its overall effects on individuals remain the same for members of all subgroups within a population, certain subgroups possess specific characteristics that may affect the process by which their members become dependent, as well as the specific effects dependency has on that group. To work effectively with such individuals requires the counselor to be familiar with the basic issues that are peculiar to that group.

Adolescents, with their concurrent problems of development and maturation; women, with the differential role expected of them by society; the elderly, who face the problem of aging and who are likely to be frequent users of prescription drugs; and the mentally ill, who may use various mood-altering chemicals to self-medicate—all of these groups need special consideration.

ADOLESCENT DRUG ABUSE

In the mid 1970s, a marked increase in the use of alcohol and other drugs occurred among adolescents, following the marked increase of consumption by college students and the general population that had begun a decade earlier. The increased use of various mood-altering chemicals in the 1960s appears to have lessened the negative attitudes toward drug use and enhanced its acceptability, without the stigma that had existed only a few years earlier. During this period, the myth that various drugs were not harmful to the individual had a dramatic effect on society. As this attitude filtered down to adolescents (who throughout recent history have tended to imitate the behavior of adults), a period began in which there was not only a greater number of individuals who used drugs, but also a greater amount of usage on the part of many individuals.

While in the 1960s university students placed much of their focus on marijuana, LSD, and other psychedelic drugs, during the 1970s the increase in drug use among adolescents was greatest in the areas of marijuana, stimulants, and cocaine. While the exact numbers of adolescents who were using, and possibly abusing, various mood-altering drugs is difficult to determine, various studies have suggested that by 1982 as many as 60 percent of all high-school seniors had already used marijuana, that 70 percent of high-school seniors had used alcohol in the past month, and that 16 percent of all high-school seniors had used cocaine (Johnston, Bachman, & O'Malley 1982).

More important, perhaps, has been the increased number of adolescents who have abused various drugs to the extent that it has had a profound effect on their lives. During the 1980s, there has been a tremendous increase in the number of treatment programs for adolescents whose lives have been virtually destroyed by drug abuse; and there is every reason to believe that these programs have treated only a small number of those who needed help. While the 1980s have seen an increased emphasis on educating youth about the dangers of the abuse of alcohol and other drugs, the use of mood-altering chemicals has shown only a small decline. At the same time there has been a big jump in the use of cocaine, especially crack, and in the blending of cocaine with other drugs—with marijuana, for instance, to make a smokable substance called "Primo," among other names.

Since the American Safety Council estimates that more than one-half of all accidental deaths in this country are related to alcohol or other drug abuse, we can safely assume that many of these deaths are those of young people who were involved in highway accidents related to alcohol or other drugs. Approximately 17 percent of the U.S. population are young drivers (age 16 to 24), yet this group was involved in 48 percent of accidents resulting in fatalities in 1981, with 23,690 deaths and 9,834 of the drivers themselves being killed (MacDonald 1984).

Likewise, homicides resulting from drug-related activities have shown a dramatic increase in the 1980s, and many related areas have been affected as well, among them family relationships, scholastic performance, and mental health. In addition, young people's military performance and overall quality of life have been diminished. Finally, it is well known that virtually all alcoholics and other drug addicts began their use as adolescents.

Developmental Issues in Adolescent Drug Abuse

What is obvious sometimes needs to be said. Adolescents do not suddenly appear out of the blue at age 13. They have already experienced a number of developmental stages. Their development, however, has been influenced by a variety of factors and, as a result, they may or may not have developed in a normal pattern. Some adolescents have been part of a sound family; others have drifted from one unstable situation to another. Many have lived in one- or two-parent families where the parent(s) have been inadequate in meeting the needs of the child. Some adolescents were given up for adoption at birth or at an early age; many were even abandoned. Some have had good health all their lives, while others were born with various kinds of health impairments. But for every adolescent, growth and development have been influenced by all of these factors, as well as by personal interactions and the family system in which they lived.

Adolescence is probably best understood as a transitional stage, very similar to other transitional stages. This process allows young people to adjust to growth, development, change, and the new demands of the roles that adolescents are expected to fill in society gradually, thus avoiding the potential crisis of sudden change. Transition, however, presents new challenges, as well as opportunities, and new stress situations are experienced.

As a result, the adolescent is particularly vulnerable to looking for alternative ways of coping with stress.

Offer (1986) suggests that there are three developmental routes which individuals follow in their pathways through normal adolescence: continuous growth, surgent growth, and tumultuous growth. Based on his sample population, Offer describes the continuous-growth group as being favored by circumstances, with excellent genetic and environmental backgrounds. They had stable family environments, in which the family tended to function in a relatively effective manner. As a result, such individuals had strong egos, were able to cope well with both internal and external stress, and had generally mastered previous developmental stages without serious complications. These adolescents accepted general cultural and societal norms, feeling comfortable within this context, and showed only minimal rebellion against living by these norms.

Persons in the surgent-growth group differed from the continuous-growth adolescents only in that they were more likely to come from families where there were some minimal genetic and environmental difficulties. However, they likewise tended to accept the general cultural and societal norms and also showed little rebelliousness against them. Offer estimates that the continuous-growth group and the surgent-growth group comprise about 80 percent of the adolescent population.

On the other hand, the tumultuous-growth group was the one from which most problems with adolescence came. This group is composed of individuals with far less favorable backgrounds. There was a much greater history of mental illness in their families; the parents had greater difficulties in their marital relationships; and there was a greater overall familial instability. As a result, the moods of these adolescents were far less stable, and they were more likely to be prone to mood swings and mood lability. In general, they were described as experiencing a great deal of adolescent turmoil and had significantly more overall psychiatric difficulties than other teenagers. As we will see, adolescents who are more prone to various psychiatric difficulties are also at greater risk for abusing various mood-altering substances.

DEVELOPMENTAL TASKS

Generally, the tasks of adolescence have included the acquisition of the attributes of young adulthood. These general developmental tasks are particularly important at this stage of the individual's life. The first requirement is to come to grips with the physical and emotional changes that are part of this stage of development. Kinney and Leaton (1983) have identified four tasks which relate to these physical and emotional changes and which need to be mastered.

The first involves understanding and accepting the biological changes that are occurring within the individual. Such changes mean that the person is becoming extremely sensitive about his or her own body. Individuals are extremely conscious of the reactions of other people to the size of their body and to the development of its various parts, particularly those that are associated with sexual behavior, including pubic hair, breast size, and penis size. With these changes in physiology come other changes that affect the individual's emotional stability, and the mood swings that accompany this developmental stage are often difficult for other family members to handle. Thus, the resulting turmoil can have a profound impact on the adolescent's sense of self and on the development of his or her degree of comfort with the body and with the emotional self that is developing.

The next task is defined as a struggle to become comfortable with the individual's sexuality, particularly the emerging sexual preference. While in the preadolescent period boys have tended to be far more comfortable being with other boys and girls more comfortable being with other girls, during adolescence this comfort becomes disturbed by the increasing desire to be with the opposite sex. In concert with the physiological changes that have occurred, the adolescent experiences high levels of insecurity and self-consciousness when with individuals of the opposite sex. Thus a great deal of intrigue and confusion, accompanied by experimentation, occurs as the individual works toward a sense of comfort about his or her own sexuality. This whole process, of course, can be greatly intensified if the teenager is experiencing any degree of uncertainty about his or her own sexual preference, since at this age, even more than during adulthood, homosexuality is highly stigmatized.

The third task is that of choosing an occupational identity. During adolescence, the person begins to focus on what he or she wants to do in life. Increasing pressure is put on the individual to decide whether or not to go to college, what classes to take in school, and what kind of job to prepare for. Often adolescents get part-time jobs, either because they want or need the money, or because they wish to become independent of their families. These work experiences, which may be related to later careers, are often seen as a bridge between childhood and adulthood. The adolescent tries out various roles and job experiences and begins to discover which are most fulfilling. And by succeeding in a work experience, the individual's self-confidence and self-esteem are likely to be developed and enhanced.

The final task for the adolescent results from the developmental struggle toward autonomy and independence. The whole idea of a transition between childhood and adulthood rests, to some degree, on teenagers' sense of moving from a position of being dependent on others for their well-being to a position of being able to care for themselves alone. In this struggle toward independence, however, there is a great deal of vacillation between "I'd rather do it myself" and the need for support and encouragement from others. As a result, the developmental period is often characterized by a type of rebellion, one ordinarily rooted in the adolescent's frustration and recognition of this fluctuation of mood and behavior. While these behaviors are typical and can be recognized as alternating unpredictably between adult and childlike responses, the struggle is further complicated when the significant adults in the individual's life use this vacillation as an excuse to put down the individual and to make the adolescent feel like he or she is developing poorly. This rebellion takes many forms and is often seen in a variety of behaviors. Manner of dress, musical interests, employment of slang, and the use of alcohol and other drugs result in increased amounts of arguing with parents, teachers, and other people in authority.

In addition to the four tasks identified by Kinney and Leaton, a fifth task, which is related to the other four, is that of developing a sense of personal identity. As a child, the individual is more closely identified with the family, and the parents in particular. As the person moves toward adulthood, more of his or her identity is related to the individual's own characteristics and developing personality style, and becomes less and less related to the family identity itself. This developing identity is highly related to the growth of the individual's self-image. As the teenager seeks identity, trying to determine who he or she is, what he or she would like to do, what he or she can do, and developing the will to nourish the self-confidence to do these things, a major change is occurring in the individual. This task becomes important as the adolescent is successful or not successful in his or her own eyes in establishing the kind of identity that is desired.

These five tasks are influenced in their development by the cognitive changes which the individual is undergoing simultaneously. According to Piaget, cognitive development during adolescence is characterized by the ability to formulate and to execute abstract plans of action based on hypothetical events, and to consider at the same time the effects of a variety of variables in a problem situation. As the person moves away from only being able to engage in concrete thinking and takes steps toward abstract thinking, he or she begins to develop the ability to reflect and to recognize his or her own thoughts and opinions.

At this cognitive level of developmental change, the individual begins to question previously accepted values, both moral and religious, and moves toward an independence in thinking that may—and often does—bring about a change in others' expectations of that person. These changes may also result in greater turmoil and conflict with the family, as the adolescent no longer accepts those values which the family has provided in the past. One result of this pressure is often that of the adolescent turning to his or her peers for support, and sometimes guidance, in developing and redefining the values that the adolescent wishes to adopt.

DEVELOPMENTAL AREAS

Another way of looking at the task of adolescent development is to identify its five areas as being values, thoughts, feelings, physicalness, and behavior. The formation of values is an extremely important part of the whole task of adolescent development. Values, which can be defined as the rules one uses for running one's life, give meaning to the experience that the individual has. By developing and learning how to use these values, the adolescent is able to apply meaning to a situation in a more flexible and realistic manner than was done in the past, when the child simply had to live by the rules that the family had established. One of the contributing causes of the increase in adolescent drug abuse may be the inadequate development of values that has occurred for many adolescents during the past decade. As parents have attempted to deal with such issues as situation ethics and personal freedom, they have sometimes failed to understand the importance of children developing a set of values by which to evaluate the experiences and behavior within their lives.

The development of thinking, in which the individual learns to analyze the thoughts that occur to him or her and to provide a logical pattern for decision making, is often pushed to the background as feelings are overemphasized for the adolescent. In many ways, the excessive worrying that the teenager does is simply the result of his or her emotions kicking the whole thought process into gear. The ability to think and to make decisions in a logical manner is largely dependent upon experience in making decisions and in living with their consequences. In adolescent development, the sudden opportunity to make decisions can be overwhelming and can result in some rather illogical kinds of behavior. A more effective way of developing this thinking process in the adolescent actually begins very early in life when the small child is given opportunities to make minor decisions, sometimes no more important than whether to take his or her nap on the bed or on the couch. This ability to analyze thoughts and to reach logical decisions is frequently missing in the adolescent who regularly abuses various drugs.

The third area of development is that of feelings. It is difficult for many individuals to remember that feelings are basically automatic responses to situations. They are shaped by the way an individual thinks about a situation, including the value that he or she places on it, but the feelings themselves are automatic indicators of what this situation or event means to the individual, what interpretation the person gives to it. Seen in this light, emotions are simply indicators of what is being experienced by the individual and are not experiences to be avoided.

In the ideal situation, the event triggers a set of emotions, which triggers thinking patterns, which trigger values, which lead to action. In the adolescent substance abuser, the development of these first three areas—values, thinking, and feeling—does not occur in an appropriate manner. As a result, impulse control does not develop either, and the individual becomes more likely to develop an "if it feels good, do it" attitude toward behavior.

The fourth area of development is physicalness, which includes all the physical transformations which occur during adolescence. When the physical aspects of development are combined with the development of values, thinking, and feeling, the four crystallize and culminate in the development of behavior; this is basically all society sees, and it becomes the focus of most of the frustration and attention of the family and others in the individual's life. Thus, for appropriate behavior to develop in the adolescent, he or she must first undergo similar growth in the ability to form and use values, in the ability to think and make decisions, in the ability to identify and accept the feelings being experienced, and in the normal physical changes that will occur. Chemical dependency results in a lack of development in these tasks; at the same time, this absence of growth often leads to substance abuse and possible chemical dependency on the part of the adolescent.

DEVELOPMENT OF SELF-ESTEEM

One other area that requires attention is development of self-esteem. Low self-esteem promotes drug use, and drug use promotes low self-esteem. Almost every major study of dangerous drug use patterns among adolescents has identified preexisting poor self-esteem as a major factor. Individuals with a poor self-image are more susceptible to experimenting with other avenues of feeling good about themselves and are also more prone to give in to peer pressure of various sorts. Being a teenager is very tough. Although one of the myths that our society has often placed upon young people is that "being a teenager is the time of the best years of your life," adolescence often involves greater emotional difficulty and social conflict than any other period in the individual's life. Thus, just being a teenager is tough enough if all is going fairly well. However, if there are added pressures on the individual—such as those resulting from parental divorce, a serious illness in the family, the death of a significant other, or various stress-inducing situations—then the person's ability to cope is greatly undermined.

Self-esteem results from a multiple series of events within the individual's life. First, and most important, is the sense of acceptance and respect that the child receives from the significant people in his or her life. In the early years, these are generally within the nuclear family; but roughly by the time the child reaches age 11, the need for acceptance shifts to the peers that he or she associates with during the major part of the day. Such acceptance includes warmth, interest, and liking for the individual as he or she is, without conditions or demands for change. When rejection and severe punishment occur in these relationships, children are rarely able to develop positive self-feelings.

A second factor in the growth of self-esteem is a history of achievement. While success is interpreted differently by different individuals, it can be measured in the individual's sense that he or she has some approval from family and friends. Thus, appropriate rewards for good behavior will result in the child feeling good about himself or herself and will lead to further success. A third factor in the development of self-esteem is the pattern by which the individual learns to deal with error, defeat, and frustration. The child of overindulgent parents is apt to have problems, as is the child of neglectful parents. Pampered children will be poorly prepared for dealing with failure because they have never had to experience it; underindulged children will be poorly prepared for dealing with failure because it will have been a constant in their lives. By attempting to protect the child from boredom, loneliness, and the normal experiences of frustration, the parent is failing to allow the child to develop his or her own pattern and ability for dealing with difficulties.

Stages of Adolescent Drug Use

While studies show that a great number of adolescents have used drugs at one time or another, they also show that most do not move beyond social use and some never go beyond simple experimentation. In order to understand the problem of drug abuse among adolescents, it may be helpful to examine the stages through which they typically move in their use of mood-altering chemicals.

EXPERIMENTAL USE

The beginning stage can best be identified as experimental use. Junior-high-school age students, especially boys, are great experimenters in a number of activities and are especially prone to experiment with various types of mood-altering substances, whether they be the fumes from glue, the alcohol left over from the previous night's party, or the joint which is passed around after school. Certainly some of these individuals will decide that chemical use is not for them, although a majority will continue to explore and become regular users. During this experimental stage, the attitude seems to be that it is okay to try out new things, since adolescence itself seems to be a period of trying out new behaviors and of coming to grips with new thinking and feeling patterns. This normal turmoil of adolescents, which is baffling to both young people and their parents, means that if the experimental use of drugs pays off in the sense of the adolescent believing that it has helped him or her to cope with the demands of life, then that use is reinforced and the individual is likely to continue using. On the other hand, if experimentation does not provide a payoff or results in greater negative consequences, then the adolescent is less likely to try again.

SOCIAL USE

The second stage of use for the adolescent is social use, in which the individual begins to use drugs in social situations. At this stage it's not only just okay to try out drugs, but has become okay to do drugs when the situation is appropriate. Thus, the social user tends to develop rules for when drug use is appropriate and ordinarily sticks with them. The difficulty here is not so much quantity or frequency, but when drugs are being used and what kinds of behavioral changes result. In addition, the risk factor of how well the adolescent is doing in making and following rules comes into play. The 20 percent or so of adolescents who have had difficulty in establishing a value system become particularly at risk for drug abuse. These individuals, who see life as a situation of chaos, are prone to begin to see the use of alcohol and other drugs and the effect of those drugs on their lives as being *the best thing going for them.*

PREOCCUPATION

As a result, these individuals are likely to enter the preoccupation stage of drug use, in which they have moved from using drugs only in social situations to using drugs as a major part of their lives. At this point, more and more of the adolescent's time, energy, and money are spent on thinking about being high and ensuring that a steady supply of drugs is available. Now mood-altering chemicals are the best thing in the person's life, not friends, sports, family, or other activities. The focus becomes "how or when I can next get high." For such individuals, few daily activities will not include drug use, and the person will accept this as being normal. While problems with parents, school, or the police may result in the adolescent deciding to cut down or to quit using drugs entirely, the effort rarely succeeds for more than a few weeks. However, these periods of abstinence do add to the delusion that the person could quit if he or she really wanted to and that there is no problem. In many ways, the transition from social use to preoccupation involves a changing of the rules. The new rules center around drugs and their use. As the effects of these drugs become more and more predictable to adolescents, their behavior changes and the resulting reactions of their friends and family lead them to believe that their friends and family are not predictable. Thus, stability in their lives comes to seem more related to drug use than to their relationships with others.

DEPENDENCY

The fourth stage is dependency, or addiction, in which the *only* thing that matters is using. By this time, negative personal feelings have been building steadily, and the individual requires daily, sometimes hourly, relief from them. As a result, the adolescent is unable to distinguish ordinary from drug-related behavior; he or she finds being high normal, and this delusion cannot be undermined through any rational or moral argument, persisting even in the face of overwhelming evidence that the adolescent's abuse is out of control and is creating major problems in his or her life. The teenager will continue to insist that there is no problem, that he or she can quit at will, and that his or her life has not been affected in a negative way by the use of mood-altering chemicals. In a sense, dependency has resulted in a tunnel vision, blinding the person to the ramifications of drug use.

By now, major changes have taken place. The individual's performance at school has greatly deteriorated, and he or she will rarely go to school for a full day. Low self-image, and self-hate, have developed. Casual sexual involvement and the tendency to have a different type of friend is common. Parents frequently have given up. Desperate attempts to find money to purchase drugs have brought about the likelihood of various illegal behaviors, including selling drugs, theft, and prostitution. Even for the adolescent, by this stage there may be an effect on the physical condition. A loss of weight, an increase in various illnesses, memory problems, and some depression are frequent. For the teenager, the dependency stage brings about a loss of control over use.

CHEMICALLY DEPENDENT WOMEN

> Nice women don't drink! You know, this is a hangover from Victorian times. I think there's definitely a double standard of behavior that's applied to women. A woman alcoholic is branded, zap. Tramp, loose woman, whore, you name it. (Weiner 1976, 61)

This statement was made by a nurse who was a recovering alcoholic and who continued to work with other recovering alcoholics. In many ways, she pinpoints a major difficulty in dealing with the problem of chemical dependency among women. The double standard, the stigma, the sense of being a failure—all contribute to a greater reluctance for a woman to admit that she has a problem and to seek help.

Many professionals in the field of alcoholism treatment are convinced that even the most conservative estimates of the number of women in the United States who have multiple problems in their lives resulting from their abuse of alcohol and other mood-altering chemicals is still low. While estimates of the number of women alcoholics in the United States have ranged from 1.3 million to 5 million, with a much smaller total being seen as addicted to other mood-altering drugs, there is evidence that the number of women who are chemically dependent is much closer, and may be equal to, the number of chemically dependent men.

It is likely that the seemingly smaller number of women who have experienced problems as a result of their drug use stems from a variety of societal factors which treat women differently than men. In the past, a smaller percentage of women worked outside the home than did men. In consequence, fewer women were at risk of being discovered abusing drugs in the workplace. Because women's primary function at that time was in the home, the only persons who were likely to become aware of their drug abuse were members of the family, who often, either out of shame or well-intended enabling, protected them from the rest of society. With the rapidly changing role of women in the United States, which has led to their filling the dual role of homemaker and career woman, a larger number of drug-abusing women have been put at risk of being discovered by their employers. With this has come a rapid increase in the number of women seeking help for drug addiction. However, even within the workplace, there appears to be a greater sympathy for women and a greater reluctance to label them as having an alcohol or other drug problem.

In addition, women have been in the past (and probably will continue to be in the future) less likely to be the primary vehicular driver in the family. In the two-parent family, this role has traditionally fallen to the male. As a result, men have typically driven far more miles on the average than women. This has left women less vulnerable to being stopped by law-enforcement officers for driving problems, or accidents, resulting from their drug use. Again, the increasing number of women working outside the home, combined with the increasing number of single adult women, has brought about an increase in the number of women who have been stopped for drug-related driving offenses. However, the evidence suggests that women are less likely to be actually arrested and more likely to be sent home with some sort of warning, thus enabling them to avoid the consequences of their behavior.

Finally, because of the stigma that is often attached to women who abuse alcohol and other drugs, families are less likely to seek help for that person. This is partially the result of the family being less willing to admit that the woman has a problem, since women, as part of the feminine life style, are not expected to abuse alcohol and other drugs, much as men's use of alcohol and other drugs is often seen as masculine. In consequence, it is very likely that women continue to be the hidden drug abusers in American society.

One other point demands special attention. Because traditionally women have been more willing to seek medical help for their problems, they have also been more likely to become victims of a different kind of drug abuse—that of prescription drugs. Prescriptions for various minor tranquilizers have been overwhelmingly written for women. Whether this reflects sexual bias on the part of the prescribing physician, or is simply the result of women being more willing to talk to physicians about the stresses in their lives, is still a matter of dispute.

Either way, however, the facts are clear. Women are much more likely to abuse prescription drugs than are men. Reports suggest that more than 60 percent of all individuals who are treated in an emergency room or who die as a result of their use of minor tranquilizers are women (Hughes & Brewin 1979). This group of drug abusers is even less likely to receive treatment, since their families can more easily justify doing nothing about the drug abuse, either through ignorance concerning drug abuse or through denial of the disease. Their justification that the woman is simply responding to the medications provided by her treatment physician gives a rationale to their lack of involvement in seeking treatment for the drug abuse.

Issues of Gender

As important as any other in understanding the incidents of, and reaction to, women who abuse alcohol and other drugs are the issues related to what is acceptable and not acceptable behavior for each sex. Just as people often accept a male drunk and even think him funny at times, they ordinarily will not accept a drunken woman's behavior, and many consider it inexcusable (Wegner 1983). This double standard frequently goes to an even greater extreme and results in people seeing the drunken woman, as was pointed out in the quotation that opens this section, as whore-like. Events that undermine a woman's self-image—particularly as they relate to her self-image as a female—seem to invite substance abuse. A miscarriage, infertility, menopause, mastectomy, the birth of a handicapped child, a hysterectomy, infidelity by her husband, separation, divorce, and desertion are all crises that have been frequently identified as precipitating escalation from social use to problem use (Lindbeck 1975). This becomes particularly relevant when it is recognized that while men are more likely to relate their use of alcohol and other drugs to job stress women are more likely to cite family stress.

Various studies have shown that there are significant differences between men and women who seek help for the treatment of alcoholism and drug addiction. Rimmer, Pitts, Reich, and Winokur (1971) found that male alcoholics, when compared with female alcoholics, had the following characteristics:

1. An earlier onset of alcohol problems.
2. A younger age at first drink.
3. More daily and morning drinking.
4. More frequent binges of drinking.
5. More histories of delirium tremens.
6. More blackouts.
7. More frequent loss of job and friends because of drinking.
8. More histories of school problems.

9. More alcohol-related arrests.
10. Fewer suicide attempts.

Horn and Wanberg (1973), in a similar study, reported the following differences between men and women as significant:

1. Women begin to drink later and experience first intoxication later.
2. Women drink more often at home, either alone or with their spouse.
3. Women have shorter drinking binges.
4. Women more often use alcohol in an attempt to improve job performance.
5. Men lose jobs more frequently because of drinking.
6. Men are more often gregarious drinkers, while women are more often solitary drinkers.
7. Women more often perceive their alcoholism as becoming worse.

Possible Physiological Factors

A variety of physiological factors have been predicted as being important in the number of women who become alcoholic. Some findings indicate a variability in the blood-alcohol level (given the same amount of alcohol) at different points in the menstrual cycle. While the role of hormonal status and its interaction with alcohol is still underexplored, it does suggest a direct connection between the hormonal status and the development of addiction to alcohol. Evidence also exists to suggest that other things being equal, women develop cirrhotic problems and complications more readily than do men. In addition, other findings suggest that the metabolic rate of women, taking body weight into account, leads to a quicker reaction to the introduction of alcohol into the body. Thus, while it seems likely that women and men have differing physiological reactions to various mood-altering chemicals, until these factors have been explored thoroughly there remains uncertainty as to just how such reactions are different.

Role of Women in Contemporary Society

While the problems that substance abuse produces for men and for women have many similarities, there are also differences. Obviously, both groups experience some degree of social disapproval and some medical consequences. At the same time, however, there are differences in how these consequences manifest themselves. Male alcoholics, who are more publicly visible, meet with consequences which are institutional, involving, for example, the workplace, hospitals, or the court system. For women substance abusers, who are less publicly visible, consequences appear to fall more within the primary groups to which they belong—family, intimate friends, and acquaintances. Partially because of the differences in the way society perceives the female alcoholic, women are treated differently when they abuse alcohol and other drugs. It seems likely that society would be more compassionate toward a woman who is depressed, phobic, or schizophrenic than it would toward a woman who is alcoholic.

Hafen and Brog (1983) have cited some specific stresses women face that are related to their drug abuse:

1. Home Stresses: Many women have given up a career and career goals to be at home with the family.
2. Work Stresses: Career women often have to work in a world with a male orientation which imposes pressure and loneliness on them.
3. The Overburdened Woman: Many women maintain the dual roles of homemaker and career woman, leading to additional stresses.
4. The Empty Nest Stage of Life: While research differs on this, the evidence is strong that the period after children grow up and leave home is particularly stressful and often results in a sense of emptiness, which may be filled by drug abuse.
5. The Loneliness of the Single Life: For even the well-adjusted single woman, such times as holidays, weekends, and the after-work hours may become particularly lonely and lead to a sense of emptiness.
6. Menopausal Crises and Post-Partum Depression: These periods often present women with additional stress, depression, and an accompanying sense of emptiness.

Since it has already been noted that women are more likely to point to specific stressors in their lives as precipitating their abuse of alcohol and other drugs, it is important to emphasize that most of these stressors, as well as the factors which have been earlier identified, tend to cluster around the concept of loneliness, or isolation. Whether this concept fully explains increased use or whether it is the result of increased use is still unprovable. However, a substantial percentage of women who are treated for chemical dependency have histories that suggest that they do not easily trust others, have difficulty making intimate relationships work, find it hard to control impulses, and are resentful and angry. Thus, the inevitable experiences of frustration that result from marriage, work, and childbearing often lead to feelings of resentment, loneliness, and failure that may be dealt with in a variety of ways. For many women the magical quality of alcohol, tranquilizers, and other drugs serves as an escape from their loneliness, isolation, and sense of failure.

Treatment Issues for Chemically Dependent Women

To begin with, professionals in the field of chemical-dependency counseling must fully consider the need to treat women in separate units. While traditionally the idea is that chemically dependent persons are the same, regardless of sex or other variables, some professionals are beginning to believe that there are social and psychological differences between male and female dependents. Lemay (1980) identified a variety of issues which need to be looked at in developing a treatment program for women. These include:

1. The need for women to understand the difference in male and female sex roles.
2. The need for women to look at their own conflicts with expected sex-role behaviors.
3. The need for women to learn to take responsibility for defining those roles themselves.
4. The need for counselors to help women sort out their sexual conflicts and to identify what they want from sexual relationships.
5. The need for women to learn to express anger or to be assertive, and to reduce or eliminate an unrealistic need for approval from others to validate their self-concept.
6. The need for women to examine the belief that all they need for happiness and well-being is the "perfect relationship."
7. The need for women to become aware of information about their basic personal rights (legal, financial, etc.) and to develop skills in living effectively.

While there has not been a major movement in the United States toward the development of separate treatment programs for women, the Betty Ford Center does have an all-women's building for treatment. The average woman who comes to this program is 44 years old, married, and has children and a job. She does better in therapy when her group is all female. This may be because in coed groups women tend to remain in the nurturing role of mother or wife and hang back while urging the men to do all the talking (Ford 1987).

In addition to some of the difficulties of treating men and women dependents together, many counselors face specific problems in treating female addicts. Lemay (1980) suggests that many counselors have their own prejudices about women who are addicted and, as a result, may treat women differently without a valid reason for doing so. Counselors may avoid sexual issues, they may not always recognize as many behavior options for women as for men, and they may lack familiarity with basic women's health issues. In addition, in treatment, few programs have provisions for women, and there are fewer supportive environments such as halfway houses. Even in programs where women and men are treated together, many have not recognized the need for special women's groups.

While the traditional approach has been to treat men and women together and to have some kind of special groups in which the men and women meet separately (although many programs do not have the men's groups at all), a more logical approach, based on the evidence that we now have about treatment, would be to have separate treatment programs for men and women combined with special groups in which they meet together. This would not only reduce some of the sexual tension and sexual harassment that occurs in most groups, but would also increase the likelihood that each treatment program could focus more accurately on the issues of the people being treated.

Kirkpatrick (1977) has strongly urged the development of programs designed especially for women, both outpatient and inpatient. As a founder of the Women for Sobriety program, Kirkpatrick indicates that female alcoholics need something more than AA or an alternative to it. She believes that alcoholic women have a greater sense of failure—as wives, as mothers, as daughters, as women. The Women for Sobriety program lists thirteen statements of acceptance which are to be used in addition to the twelve steps of AA. Table 8.1 lists these thirteen statements.

DRUG ABUSE AMONG THE ELDERLY

While the use and abuse of alcohol and other drugs generally decline in old age, the patterns of use vary from one drug class to another. Many new cases of drug abuse begin in later life. Alcohol remains a major problem for the elderly. Their vulnerability to the effects of alcohol justifies the need for an emphasis on alcoholism among older drinkers. Men continue to drink through their sixties at a rate that differs little from the prior decade of life, but there is a sharp drop after their mid seventies. And, as in earlier ages, the prevalence of heavy drinking, problem drinking, and alcoholism continues to be recognized in men to a greater degree than in women, with the percentage of women having problems dropping when they hit their fifties and sixties. Five percent to 12 percent of men, and 1 percent to 2 percent of women, in their

Table 8.1   Affirmations

---

1. I have a drinking problem that once had me.
2. Negative emotions destroy only myself.
3. Happiness is a habit I will develop.
4. Problems bother me only to the degree I permit them to.
5. I am what I think.
6. Life can be ordinary or it can be great.
7. Love can change the course of my world.
8. The fundamental object of life is emotional and spiritual growth.
9. The past is gone forever.
10. All love given returns two-fold.
11. Enthusiasm is only daily exercise.
12. I am a competent woman and have much to give others.
13. I am responsible for myself and my sisters.

From *Turnabout, Help for a New Life* by Jean Kirkpatrick, 1977, p. 161. New York: Doubleday.

sixties are problem drinkers (Atkinson 1984). Although most elderly alcoholics first used the drug during young adulthood, many did not initiate heavy drinking or develop alcohol-related problems until middle age or later.

There is less information available about the scope of drug problems in the elderly, although the data available do suggest that the prevalence is lower for alcohol than it is for other drugs, with the ratio of diagnosed cases being perhaps 1:4 or 1:5 (Reifler, Raskind, & Kethley 1982) However, with the elderly the greatest proportion of abused drugs other than alcohol continues to involve over-the-counter drugs, nicotine, and caffeine. Elderly women appear to be at greater risk than elderly men for abusing prescription drugs. However, with illicit drugs, the percentage of the elderly who abuse them continues to be rather low.

Several factors may explain the reduced prevalence of substance use and abuse in later life, particularly as it relates to the various illicit drugs. For one thing, biological sensitivity to the effects of alcohol and most psychoactive drugs increases with age. This increased tendency for drugs to induce cognitive impairment, a dysphoric affect, or physical symptoms may cause many people to limit their drug use in later life. At the same time, reduced income during old age may limit the availability of drugs. Generational differences in attitudes and practices regarding alcohol and other drug use may also be relevant, in that the older adult may have developed attitudes that result in lesser abuse.

However, the major factors believed to be relevant to decreased substance abuse among the elderly include early mortality, spontaneous recovery, and underdiagnosis. Early mortality is a factor simply because many alcoholics and drug addicts die before reaching old age, which results in a bias in the percentage of individuals who are drug abusers at that age. Spontaneous recovery helps to explain that many problem drinkers and users eventually become abstinent, often without treatment. These numbers, though small, may add to the bias reflected in the percentages of substance abusers among the elderly. Underdiagnosis, which is often a factor in all age groups, seems to be more important in old age because elderly abusers are more likely to be middle class and to conform even less to the socially deviant stereotypes of society. The substance-abusing older adult may be seen as an individual who is simply stressed out and who is suffering from various kinds of mental illnesses, such as dementia or depression. The elderly are more apt to be isolated from others who might recognize and report their problems.

Stresses for the Elderly

Older adults share a number of severe fears that result from aging and society's response to it. Physical changes often cause older adults to feel "left out," as they miss more of the interactions that occur. Their hearing often deteriorates. Their physical movements may become limited by stiffening in the joints. This slower pace may then be intensified by slower reaction time, so that the elderly become slower in responding to a stimulus, which makes the timing of the response a little late and thus, sometimes, inappropriate. These physical changes that result from aging often cause a feeling of being handicapped or different, and lead to a greater sense of loneliness. At the same time, the aged often believe that because of their slower pace and difficulties in communication, others consider them a burden or an obligation. In response, the older adult may withdraw, thus incurring greater loneliness.

Changes in social roles resulting from job retirement and an accompanying "retirement" from active roles in churches and other social organizations often have an immense impact on the older adult's self-concept. This role change seems to have a more serious impact on men, who no longer are breadwinners and who feel they have nothing to contribute. Women, on the other hand, frequently experience a similar change when their children grow up and leave home. However, retirement itself usually does not have quite as great an impact on women, since their traditional roles are not altered as much. Houses still must be cleaned, meals must be cooked, and laundry must be done. If the grandchildren live close enough for occasional baby-sitting, the woman's retirement role may be perceived as meaningful. At the same time, the role of the older adult—for both men and women—is changing, and these changes often concern the individual's feeling of diminished importance, of having less and less to offer.

Accompanying these physical and social role changes are great losses for the elderly. Their hopes and aspirations for success, for leaving legacies to society, and perhaps for leaving a comfortable inheritance to their families may no longer be realistic. At the same time, their diminished income may intensify the fear that their savings will not last long enough and cause them to be a burden to their families. These factors, along with loss of meaning and purpose in their lives, generally have much less impact than the loss caused by the deaths of spouses, siblings, and close friends. The grief generated by such personal bereavements is often intensified by other emotional responses, such as anger, guilt, and fear.

As older adults face these increasingly difficult situations, they often lose the emotional support they need: death isolates them. In their desire to be independent and to avoid being a burden on their families, older adults may discourage their families from too much contact, leading to greater isolation and loneliness. They may also react to their situation by complaining, thus pushing the family away. Emotional problems of the elderly can become greater because they lack someone with whom to talk. As this sense of loneliness, isolation, and anxiety increases, those older adults who have some history of drug abuse are likely to turn more and more to mood-altering drugs as a means of escape.

DRUG ABUSE AND THE MENTALLY ILL

The traditional view in chemical-dependency counseling has been to suggest that individuals who are chemically dependent shared an experience—that they had developed an addiction to a mood-altering drug. At times, there have been attempts to identify character traits of such individuals, resulting in the identification of a character pattern marked by excessive dependency needs, manipulativeness, impulsivity, and the inability to tolerate frustration. Consistent with this view, and largely dependent on the tradition of Alcoholics Anonymous, treatment approaches increasingly emphasized confrontation, limit setting, and the development of coping skills necessary for a life of sobriety.

In the last decade, increasing attention has been given to a recognition that a substantial number of individuals who are chemically dependent may also have a dual diagnosis that includes some other mental disorder. This has resulted in a growing awareness that in the evaluation of the chemically dependent it is important to separate those character traits and behaviors which preceded the major abuse of mood-altering drugs from those which evolved in response to the need to survive as a drug abuser. At the same time, many psychiatric clinicians have become aware of the need to distinguish between those symptoms produced by drug intoxication or withdrawal and those symptoms which may stem from an underlying mental disorder. As a result, a number of studies have found that many patients are concurrently suffering from other psychiatric disorders which, in some instances, have played a role in the increased abuse of mood-altering drugs. In other instances, the observed psychopathology has developed as a result of the drug use itself. Thus, it has become necessary to determine whether the abuse of drugs has resulted from the individual's need to find a way to cope with an underlying psychiatric problem.

Practitioners in the field of mental health, particularly those having frequent contact with young, chronically mentally ill patients, are becoming increasingly aware of the frequency with which this population couples their psychiatric illness with drug abuse. The issue regarding the relationship between mental illness and substance abuse, however, has also raised a number of questions about the relationship between drug abuse and mental illness. Can it cause mental illness in a healthy person? Can it precipitate mental illness in a person with a predisposition to the illness? Can it precipitate the relapse of a person who has already become mentally ill? On the other hand, individuals working in the field of chemical dependency more frequently ask if substance abuse has led to symptoms which will disappear once the person is clean and dry.

Numerous studies have established a relationship between alcohol abuse and such affective disorders as depression. Populations of alcoholics have been found to have higher than normal rates of affective disorders, and populations of individuals with affective disorders have been found to have higher rates of alcoholism than normal populations. Do alcoholics have greater problems with affective disorders because of their use of alcohol, or do individuals who are depressed have a greater tendency to abuse alcohol as a means of coping with their depression? Furthermore, a high incidence of alcoholism has been found in families of depressed patients, with a correspondingly high incidence of depression among families of alcoholics. Mayfield (1985) even suggests that alcoholism and depression are manifestations of the same disease. He also points out that alcoholism does not seem to be correlated to bipolar disorders, nor is the abuse of drugs other than alcohol related to depression. He summarizes the research in terms of paradoxical conclusions:

> If you feel very bad, alcohol will make you feel a lot better. But if you drink a lot of alcohol, it will make you feel very bad. Feeling very bad from drinking a lot does not seem to encourage people to stop drinking. Feeling a lot better from drinking does not seem to encourage people to continue drinking. (Mayfield 1985, 97)

Thus, depressed alcoholics may be classified into four subgroups: those exhibiting a depressive syndrome, which disappears after detoxification; those exhibiting reactive depression because of drinking-related problems; those with endogenous depression, operating independently of alcohol dependency; and those suffering from an episode of affective disorder. Mayfield cautions against the use of antidepressant medication for any but the fourth group and stresses the importance of accurate diagnosis through careful observation following detoxification.

Drug abuse has been noted to be a significant problem among young, chronically mentally ill patients who have been diagnosed as schizophrenic. Damron and Simpson (1985) found that among 100 schizophrenic patients in a Veterans' Administration medical center, there was a mean age of 37, and the records of 54% of the patients showed recent drug-abuse problems. Alcohol was the most commonly abused drug (47%), followed by marijuana (25%), amphetamines (9%), cocaine (6%), and opiates (5%). Excluding alcohol, 19% of the patients abused one drug, 7% abused two drugs, and at least 5% abused three or more drugs. Damron and Simpson's study included the reasons cited by these individuals for their use of mood-altering chemicals; the reasons given, in large part, directly related to trying to cope with the symptoms of their illness and trying to fit in with peers in an effort to reduce the social isolation so common among mentally ill.

Nace, Saxon, and Shore (1983) noted that 13 percent of alcoholic patients on a large inpatient unit met the diagnostic criterion for borderline personality disorder. In addition, Loberg (1981) found that while there were various subgroups of alcoholics that could be identified by their Minnesota Multiphasic Personality Inventory profiles, there did appear to be one subgroup of alcoholics who were sociopathic.

However, the data at this stage suggest that while there does seem to be a relationship between the severity of psychosocial distress and drug abuse, the distribution of psychopathology in the alcoholic population may simply mirror its distribution in the rest of the population (Skinner 1982). As a result, professionals in the field of chemical-dependency counseling must recognize that a significant number of individuals in treatment for chemical dependency also have a concurrent mental illness. Ideally, any assessment for a psychiatric disorder should be held off until the individual has been abstinent from mood-altering chemicals for at least four weeks, to allow for a return to normal neuropsychological functioning (Rounsaville & Kranzler 1989). However, in many treatment settings, the time period for treatment necessitates that a psychiatric diagnosis be attempted after a brief period of abstinence (3–10 days). These individuals need to be identified so that appropriate steps can be taken to develop treatment programs that will focus on their chemical dependency and on their specific mental illness.

Such treatment is very difficult. It requires a long-term approach, using the best information about the treatment of chemical dependency, including the need for such support groups as Alcoholics Anonymous as part of the recovery process, as well as the need to assess whether the individual is likely to respond to psychotherapeutic approaches or has a need for psychotropic medications. Such a patient population is undesirable in many ways—difficult to work with, having a poor prognosis for recovery, and lacking in the political and financial power so frequently needed in order to receive the necessary treatment. However, such a population must be recognized if an overall effective treatment program is to be developed for them.

SUMMARY

This chapter has reviewed some of the specific issues involved in working with subgroups within the general population: adolescents, women, the elderly, and the mentally ill. Each subgroup has distinct characteristics that result in particular dynamics and require some alteration in treatment strategy.

At the same time, chemical-dependency issues are the same and the overall treatment process is relevant. The counselor simply must be aware of the specific isssues related to the subgroup and incorporate this information into the development of the individual treatment plan.

9 ——

Professional Issues

INTRODUCTION

Professionals in the field of chemical dependency come from a wide variety of backgrounds, being one of the few truly multidisciplinary groups that provide counseling to individuals. That same variety of background, however, results in potential professional problems, as individuals with a number of previous experiences and academic backgrounds attempt to provide help. Part of the difficulty stems from the recent origin of chemical-dependency counseling; it is a new field, based on a tradition that often involves a tension between counselors whose primary credentials include being in recovery from their own chemical dependency and counselors whose primary credentials are academic, with professional degrees in counseling, social work, and psychology. As the field of chemical-dependency counseling matures and progresses, it is likely that this tension will increase for a while and then subside as professionals recognize the need for varied inputs into the whole treatment process.

Unlike other fields that involve advising, chemical-dependency counseling entails more than facilitative skills and attitudes. Counselors must respond to a number of complex legal and ethical considerations that have a direct impact on both the delivery of the counseling services and the attitude of the public (including those who are responsible for making referral) toward those services. Public acceptance of counseling as a valued service and of chemical-dependency counselors as respected professionals depends in large measure on the adherence of those professionals to a high level of ethical and professional behavior. Such acceptance sometimes depends on the profession's demanding respected credentials of its counselors. In addition, professional behavior calls for continual monitoring of the services being provided, to protect the public from inappropriate behavior on the part of counselors and to improve those services.

In this chapter, the personal characteristics of the counselor, training and credentialing issues, professional ethics, and his or her continuing development will be reviewed as they apply to chemical-dependency counselors.

PERSONAL CHARACTERISTICS OF EFFECTIVE COUNSELORS

Combs and Soper (1969) suggested that the primary "technique" of counseling was the "self-as-instrument." This idea was based on their research, which suggested that the counselor's self, or person, was the major facilitator of positive growth for clients. In addition, they found that effective counselors perceived other people as *able*, rather than unable, to solve their own problems and to manage their own lives. Effective counselors also perceived people as *dependable, friendly,* and *worthy.* Effective counselors were likely to identify with *people* rather than things, to see people as having an adequate *capacity to cope* with problems, and to be more *self-revealing* than self-concealing.

These studies have become a primary factor in emphasizing the importance of the personal characteristics that counselors have in determining how effective they can be in working with others. The field of chemical-dependency counseling, while it does require specific information and an emphasis on different techniques and skills than may be required in other fields of counseling, is consistent in its emphasis on counselors possessing facilitative personal characteristics.

One place to start is by analyzing the reasons why an individual chooses to become a chemical-dependency counselor. Certainly it is not a field with excellent financial rewards, nor is it one where stress and tension are minimal. Rather, such persons often learn that their professional lives seem to move from one crisis to another, since the very nature of chemical dependency results in individuals being inconsistent, irritable, and chaotic. As a result, professionals who enter this field usually do so because of a genuine commitment to helping others. Such individuals have a realistic and mature understanding of the pressures and demands of the job, and possess the insight to see the world and their own selves objectively. This includes a thorough probing of why they wish to enter the field.

The most commonly expressed motivation has to do with the need to help other addicts overcome dependency, and grows out of the professionals' having experienced the devastating effects of chemical dependency in their own lives. This may be because they themselves have been chemically dependent or because they have been affected by the disease of codependency, in which they have been closely associated with one or more individuals whose lives had been destroyed or nearly destroyed by addiction. This kind of motivation can be very positive.

However, the need or desire to help someone who is experiencing a problem similar to one's own may not always manifest itself in a constructive way. Some people may do so out of a subconscious need to work out their own lingering, unresolved personal problems. In addition, such individuals face the continuing problem of believing that everyone who is chemically dependent experiences the same difficulties in attitude, emotions, and behaviors as they did, rather than accepting the uniqueness of each individual's experience. Thus, while their own chemical dependency may have given these professionals extraordinary insight into the experiences of their patients, a problem results when counselors either assume that their patients have similar problems or insist that their patients must feel and think and behave the way the counselors did when they were actively dependent.

On the other hand, persons may enter the field of chemical-dependency counseling because they were favorably impressed by their counselors while in treatment for their own addiction. This kind of transference reaction rarely is positive, since the work itself is often very different from that which the individual expected, and the mystique of what the individual is doing wears off as the drudgery, repetitiveness, and frustration of the job increases. Others may enter the field because they view it as a means of having power and control over other individuals. Such persons are frequently guilty of using heavy-handed tactics and manipulative games as means of control, thus building their own egos. Their concern is more for their own prestige and power than for the well-being of their clients (Lawson et al. 1984). Guilt is another common, but undesirable, motivator. For individuals who are feeling bad about their own past, destructive behavior may enter the field as a means of feeling better about themselves, rather than as a means of helping others with similar problems. While well-intentioned, such counselors tend to be ineffective, because the guilt that they endure does not go away so easily and they become bitter and hardened by the process.

In a sense, any analysis of those personal characteristics which are related to effective *counselors* must begin with an analysis of those characteristics related to effective *persons*. A number of models of human effectiveness have been presented over the years, with many of them in the 1962 yearbook of the Association for Supervision and Curriculum Development, *Perceiving, Behaving, Becoming*. Rogers (1962) listed three characteristics of the "fully functioning" person, presenting them as trends and goals toward which the individual strives. He suggested that the fully functioning person: has an increasing openness to experience, as opposed to having defensive reactions to experiences perceived as being inconsistent with his or her self-image; is continually moving toward being a process, fully living each moment in the "here and now"; and has an increasing trust in himself or herself.

Combs (1962) provided his description of "adequate, self-actualizing" persons in the same yearbook, viewing them as persons who saw themselves as being liked, wanted, acceptable, and able; as possessing a capacity for identification with others; and as having perceptual fields that are maximally open to experience. George and Cristiani (1986, 15) presented a composite model of human effectiveness that includes the following personal characteristics:

1. Effective counselors are open to, and accepting of, their own experiences.
2. Effective counselors are aware of their own values and beliefs.
3. Effective counselors are able to develop warm and deep relationships with others.
4. Effective counselors are able to allow themselves to be seen by others as they actually are.

5. Effective counselors accept personal responsibility for their own behaviors.
6. Effective counselors have developed realistic levels of aspiration.

However, since the major mode of therapy within the area of chemical-dependency counseling is through group process, the literature related to personal characteristics of effective group leaders may be even more important. Corey and Corey (1982) identify some characteristics that they consider to be important elements of the group leader's personhood. Their list includes: courage, a willingness to be a model, a sense of presence, goodwill and caring, a belief in group process, openness, an ability to cope with attacks, personal power, stamina, a willingness to seek new experiences, self-awareness, a sense of humor, and inventiveness. Such a description seems almost overwhelming and requires a virtual superhero to meet.

At the same time, there is general agreement about the characteristics of an effective leader. Certainly honesty and openness are important, in that they imply a willingness to accept feedback and a willingness for the leader to examine his or her needs and values to determine their impact. Such a leader can be nonjudgmental and accepting, can value personal associations, and can have positive relationships. Without narrow or rigid behavior patterns, the effective counselor takes risks, is flexible and spontaneous, and has a healthy, realistic degree of self-confidence and enthusiasm. However, a more thorough look at these qualities is important, so that chemical-dependency counselors can evaluate their own personal characteristics in terms of effective and ineffective counseling.

Self-Awareness

One of the most important traits of effective group leaders is self-awareness. The ability to be open to, and accepting of, their own experiences can be very difficult to achieve. It involves individuals not trying to control their emotional reactions, but being able to accept their feelings as they are. This quality of openness to one's own emotional reactions and emotional state enables the counselor to separate his or her own feelings from what the patient or patients may be experiencing.

Self-awareness is often difficult to achieve because so many of our previous experiences have taught us to deny our feelings. Well-intentioned others pressure us to not feel depressed or angry or frustrated. Effective counselors can accept within themselves sadness, anger, frustration, resentment, and other feelings ordinarily considered negative. By accepting them as they are, without denying or distorting them, counselors have greater control of their behavior. Such awareness allows counselors to choose how they wish to react to and change their emotional states, rather than permitting their unconscious feelings to affect their behavior.

Certainly chemical-dependency counselors are touched by the pains, struggles, and joys of those with whom they work. Some patients may elicit anger in the counselor; others may evoke pain, sadness, guilt, frustration, or even happiness. When the counselor is afraid of the kinds of emotional reactions that he or she may have while working with chemical-dependency patients, two things are likely to result. One is that the counselor may detach emotionally from the experiencing of his or her patients in an attempt to prevent undesirable reactions. However, effective counselors recognize that by being aware of their own emotions, they can allow themselves to share those feelings, even for just a few moments. By fully experiencing their own emotions, counselors regain the ability to be compassionate and empathic with their patients, while remaining separate persons with their own experiencing. A second problem that may result from the counselor being afraid of the kinds of emotional reactions he or she is having is that patients often pick up on the counselor's struggle to deal with his or her own emotions, with the effect that the patient loses the opportunity to learn from the counselor how to deal with feelings that are not particularly satisfying.

Genuineness

No other personal quality is more important to counselors than that of genuineness! The counselor who is authentic, real, congruent, and honest is able to establish a special relationship with his or her patients, who recognize that the counselor is not playing a role or hiding behind a façade. Such counselors do not live by pretenses, but are willing to disclose the self and share feelings and reactions to what is going on in the group in an appropriate manner. Individuals who are genuine are willing to express, in their own words and in their own behavior, the various feelings and attitudes they hold. They have less need to present the appearance of one attitude while holding another. They do not pretend to know the answers when they do not. They do not act like loving persons at moments when they are feeling hostile. They do not act as though they are confident and full of assurance when they are actually feeling frightened and unsure. On a simpler level, they do not act as though they feel well when they actually feel ill.

Such genuineness does not mean that the individual counselor must disclose all feelings and attitudes to his or her patients. Rather, being genuine means that the individual has the choice of whether or not to share with others, but does continue to act verbally and nonverbally in a way that is consistent with the internal feelings being experienced. This occurs because genuine individuals are comfortable with themselves in their interactions. They have little need to change when they are with different people, but are able to continue in the same role, regardless of the individual with whom they are interacting.

Part of the difficulty for many individuals is that energy spent on playing a role or presenting a façade prevents them from using that energy for accomplishing tasks and solving problems. In addition, effective individuals, by simply being themselves when they are with others, are more able to develop cooperative relationships, because they have less need to puff up their own importance. Not only are they able to share the limelight, but they often create the situation where other persons can relax and use their own abilities to the maximum, since they feel less of a need to be perfect and can allow themselves to be genuine also.

Ability to Form Warm, Caring Relationships

Effective counselors are able to develop warm, caring relationships with people because they value them—their feelings, their opinions, their persons. Such a feeling is a caring that is nonpossessive, with little evaluation or judgment; the other person is accepted with few conditions. However, many people experience a certain amount of fear about allowing themselves to care for others, a fear based on the idea that one is taking a risk by experiencing such positive feelings. This risk is frequently seen as one of the individual becoming trapped or vulnerable to hurt. Other persons may take advantage; they may make demands that are difficult to reject; they may attempt to manipulate the counselor for their own personal gain; they may reject feelings by failing to reciprocate. As a result, some individuals keep their distance from others, rarely permitting themselves to get close to someone.

Effective counselors are less vulnerable to such fears, because they recognize that the risk involved with closeness is worth the value to be gained. They respond to others more freely, developing a close, warm relationship with those who share their interests and values. They have a wide freedom of choice in developing such relationships, because of their ability to care and their relative lack of fear about the risk that may come from caring. They are less concerned with *how many* close friends they have than with the warmth and value of those relationships.

This ability to form warm, caring relationships is related both to trustworthy types of behavior on the part of the counselor and to the basic trust the counselor has in other individuals. Certainly counselors cannot expect patients to have a basic trust in them unless patients perceive that the counselor also has a trusting attitude toward them. In a sense, such trust means that the counselor will not put some type of invisible barrier between himself or herself and the patients, keeping them at arm's length so that they will be unable to get a clear view of the counselor's personal weaknesses and failures. At the same time, patients must believe that the counselor is there to promote their well-being, rather than to promote the counselor. They must believe that the counselor will maintain appropriate, ethical behavior and that the patients will not be used or taken advantage of in some way. Without a mutually trusting relationship, little can be achieved in counseling.

Sensitivity and Understanding

Sensitivity is a major factor in counselor effectiveness. Being sensitive relates to an emotional as well as a cognitive response to each individual and makes possible a deeper and more spontaneous response to needs, feelings, conflicts, and doubts. It involves the ability to step outside one's own experiencing in order to sense and understand what the other individual is feeling or thinking at a particular moment. This sensitivity, which is frequently called *empathy*, is so important that most experts consider it a necessary and sufficient condition for effective helping. During the process of treatment of individuals who are chemically dependent, a wide range of feeling and thinking patterns results. When the counselor is able to more fully sense and understand these emotional and cognitive states, he or she is able to determine how to intervene in a helping manner.

As suggested, sensitivity is similar to *empathy*, as Rogers (1957) characterized it. His description involved sensing the other person's private world as if it were one's own, but never losing the "as if" quality. He suggested that to be able to sense the other's anger, fear, or confusion *as if it were one's own*, yet without one's own anger, fear, or confusion getting bound up in it, was a necessary condition for therapeutic effectiveness. This same kind of sensitivity has been a common goal for many centuries and is seen, for instance, in the statement "Grant that I may not criticize my neighbor until I have walked a mile in his moccasins." By doing so, two critical conditions can be met. The counselor is able to experience the patient's feelings as the patient is experiencing them, in the same way and with the same degree of effect and personal meaning. In addition, the counselor is able to maintain an individual identity and remains sensitively aware of the differences between him or herself and the patient.

This empathic understanding can be seen as a skill enabling the counselor to communicate that he or she understands, but it is important to recognize that the *attitude* of the counselor—seeking to see the world through the other person's eyes—is an essential factor in the interaction the counselor has with various patients. Thus empathy is more than simply a specific response pattern to a verbal or nonverbal communication by the patient; rather, empathy becomes an attitude that seeks to understand. As a result, the counselor is able to decide what kind of intervention he or she wishes to employ at a given moment with a particular individual by being sensitive to the particular dynamics that are occurring in that individual or group.

Sense of Humor

While counseling individuals who are chemically dependent is serious business, since victims of the disease face a bleak future without help, it still has some humorous dimensions. The ability to laugh at oneself and to see the humor in one's own human weaknesses can be extremely useful to the counselor. There are times when appropriately used humor can be as helpful as many other types of counselor behaviors, if not more so. At times, counselors take themselves so seriously that they miss an opportunity to put the importance of their problems into perspective. Occasionally, individuals and groups exhibit a real need for laughter and joking, simply to release tension. Such relief is not always an escape, but it can be an important part of the healing process. The counselor who can enjoy humor and use it effectively has an invaluable contribution to make.

Humor, as a therapeutic attitude of the counselor, does not involve sarcasm, ridicule, or cynicism. Rather, therapeutic humor stems from empathic listening and reflects a positive outlook on life. Such humor is spontaneous and natural, not artificial or contrived. Sometimes it consists of no more than a smile, a gesture, even a facial expression. When this occurs therapeutically, it brings the counselor and the patient, or the various patients, closer together by establishing an additional bond, a genuine caring for each other, a confidence in the helping nature of human rapport.

The ability to laugh is not only a valuable skill to be carried into life outside our professional responsibilities, but is also good in and of itself. The visible bubbling up of joy, of freedom, of well-being, is often the first sign that the relationship between the counselor and the patient(s) is truly therapeutic. By expressing the joy and satisfaction of connecting with and caring about others through humor, the counselor once again is using one of the basic conditions of social living in a therapeutic way.

Realistic Levels of Aspiration

Perhaps nothing can undermine the effectiveness of the counselor more quickly than to develop unrealistic expectations of his or her own effectiveness as evidenced by improvement of the patients with whom the counselor works. This may result from an extreme sense of caring and the desire to bring about immediate relief from the pain that the patient is feeling. The desire to see quick, observable change in patients is thus very natural and common among counselors.

However, persons ordinarily raise their goals slightly as a result of success and lower their goals after failure. In this way, they protect themselves both from too easy achievement and continued failure. Sometimes this self-protective mechanism is thrown out of balance, and individuals either set their goals too high, expecting results too quickly, which leads to inevitable failure, or too low, which robs them of a sense of achievement, no matter what they do.

Effective counselors, on the other hand, are able to set obtainable goals and to take failure in stride. Because they are aware of their own skills and abilities, and knowledgeable about realistic expectations of change in the patients with whom they work, they can accurately estimate what to expect from themselves and from others. Their acceptance of their experiences—both positive and negative—enables them to evaluate previous goals realistically and to use this evaluation to establish future goals.

EDUCATION AND TRAINING OF CHEMICAL-DEPENDENCY COUNSELORS

The ongoing question of whether one is adequately trained to be a chemical-dependency counselor is a source of difficulty in the field. Unfortunately, those who currently work as chemical-dependency counselors have tended to adopt one of two extreme positions: that chemical dependency counselors must be recovering addicts (or, at the very least, have a recovery program as codependents), or that chemical-dependency counselors must have a minimum of a master's degree in such related fields as counseling, social work, or psychology. Unfortunately, this polarization often results in unnecessary conflict among counselors and a lack of respect and appreciation for what each group offers to the treatment process.

Rather than emphasize the necessity of chemical-dependency counselors either being in recovery or having minimal academic training, a more reasonable approach is to demand that chemical-dependency counselors possess the minimal skills and knowledge that will enable them to have a therapeutic effect on the individuals with whom they work. This, of course, suggests some type of system for determining whether chemical-dependency counselors meet certain standards that allow them to work in the field. Such a suggestion meets with resistance, in part because there is evidence that individuals who cannot *pass* a written exam related to facts about chemical dependency or skills related to counseling have, nevertheless, demonstrated that they are effective in working with addicts. However, these are exceptions to the rule and should not cloud the issue of counselor competence.

Professionals within the area of chemical dependency need to have a working knowledge of chemical dependency, including the psychodynamics of denial and dependence, as well as the relationship between chemical dependency and value systems, life styles, and dysfunctional behavior. They need to have a knowledge of the values, attitudes, and consumption patterns related to our alcohol-drinking society. They need to have a knowledge of the ramifications of chemical dependency on the family, on the job, on the school, and on society, as well as their implications in the recovery process. They need to have an understanding of the basics of human growth and development, the basics of family dynamics and dysfunction, and other psychosocial and sociocultural implications of chemical dependency.

In addition, counselors in the field of chemical dependency must have a working knowledge of the effects of the use of mood-altering chemicals on the systems of the human body. Such knowledge includes the physiological components of withdrawal, the physiological mechanisms of addiction, and the complications resulting from the use of various mood-altering chemicals in combination with one another. Counselors must also have a working knowledge of the chemical-related problems (psychological, physiological, and medical) that result from the use of mood-altering chemicals and recognize the signs and symptoms indicating a need for other assessment of psychological, medical, or social intervention. Chemical-dependency counselors must also have an understanding of the criteria for evaluation of chemical dependency, including the different developmental stages, signs, and symptoms, as well as the behavior patterns of the addict during the progression through treatment and rehabilitation.

Finally, the counselor in the field of chemical dependency must have a working knowledge of a variety of counseling approaches, including their philosophies, methods, and objectives. At the same time, he or she must understand the practical relationship between the approaches and their use with actual patients. The counselor must understand the implications of various counseling approaches for individuals from various ethnic, cultural, social, and economic strata of society. All of this knowledge of counseling theory must be related to the philosophy and practice of Alcoholics Anonymous and other appropriate voluntary, self-help groups.

The issue of education and training of chemical-dependency counselors suggests that individuals with academic backgrounds (e.g., those with graduate degrees in a helping profession) also need to possess a thorough grounding in information related to chemical dependency. This would include information about the disease and its impact on individuals, families, and other groups. At the same time, counselors whose primary credential is that of being in recovery need to develop a knowledge of counseling approaches so that they will possess a repertoire of counseling behaviors that will enable them to make maximum use of their own experience in helping others deal with the disease of chemical dependency.

Certainly, individuals who become chemical-dependency counselors need to have a supervised experience working in the field. Although the hourly requirements may vary, the need for such an experience seems obvious. Working as a counselor based solely upon having had treatment oneself does not provide the opportunity for the individual to understand the other side of the coin, to understand the responsibilities and the roles that the counselor has to take. At the same time, to work as a counselor in the field without some hands-on experience of working with individuals who are chemically dependent is also a major deficit.

Perhaps it is most important to recognize the need for further education and training. In order to develop and maintain a high level of competence, chemical-dependency counselors need to engage in various activities to learn new skills, as well as to improve current ones. Such activities might include attending professional conferences and workshops designed for in-service training, taking advanced courses in related areas at colleges and universities, and working with colleagues to share knowledge and experience formally and informally. In addition, counselors need to continue their own study by reading books and professional literature related to the areas of chemical dependency and counseling. Periodic experiences that combine didactic and experiential learning are also desirable.

ETHICAL ISSUES IN CHEMICAL-DEPENDENCY COUNSELING

Chemical-dependency counselors, like all professionals, have ethical responsibilities and obligations. Although the literature contains numerous references to ethics and the legal status of the counselor, chemical-dependency counselors soon learn that the task of developing and maintaining a sense of professional and ethical responsibility never ends. For one thing, ethical problems pose particularly difficult situations for individuals in the various helping professions, but especially in the area of chemical-dependency counseling. First, clear-cut, specific ethical codes that contain adequate guidelines for ethical behavior in every possible situation that can be encountered in counseling relationships have yet to be developed. Second, counselors are likely to encounter situations where their ethical obligations may overlap or be in conflict. Often the counselor is working simultaneously with several individuals who are involved in their own close interpersonal relationships, whether in the family, the school, the job, or other institutions. In such situations ethical obligations become exceedingly complex.

Third, the increased use of group settings for working with individuals who are chemically dependent means that there are more people who listen to one another and over whom the counselor does not have total control with regard to such issues as confidentiality. In particular, the counselor has little influence on what other group members may say outside a session, even in slips of the tongue.

The principal rule supporting ethical obligations is that the counselor must act with full recognition of the importance of the rights of each patient, the ethics of the profession, and the relationship of moral standards and values, individual or cultural, to the life of the patient. In other words, the ethical responsibility of the counselor, whether dealing with an individual or a group, is to promote the welfare of those individuals who have entrusted their lives to him or her. Thus, any behavior on the part of the counselor that has a negative impact on the overall welfare of an individual or a group of individuals who seek the services of that counselor must be considered unethical.

The Nature of Ethical Obligations

Basically, ethics are suggested standards of conduct based on a set of values that are accepted by the profession. Thus, they represent an attempt on the part of an aspiring professional group to translate commonly accepted values into a set of standards that can serve to structure expectations for the behavior of its members in their relationships with the public and with each other. Such standards provide an outline for the implementation of the counselor's responsibility to his or her clients, and they inform those clients of what may be expected from the professional who is offering the service. These guidelines help place specific practices within the framework of the general objectives and goals of the profession, and perhaps limit activities that are contrary to these goals. In addition, such ethical standards offer some protection for the professional by clearly stating the limits of professional practice in particular areas.

Ethical Standards

While the field of chemical-dependency counseling has only recently recognized the need to develop a specific set of ethical standards, the professional areas from which counselors often come do have long-established, although recently revised, codes of ethics. While the National Association of Alcoholism and Drug Abuse Counselors only recently (1987) developed a code of ethics, the ethical standards for the American Association for Counseling Development (1988), the American Psychological Association (1981), and the National Association of Social Workers (1980) have all been revised.

In each case, members of the organizations reviewed and examined a wide range of ethical behavior and problems of professional practice that were of concern to a broadly based membership. Each code stresses adherence to rigorous professional standards and to exemplary behavior, integrity, and objectivity toward clients.

The fundamental rule is that the individual must be respected and protected at all times. Unethical behavior occurs when the counselor communicates a set of expectations while behaving in a way that is inconsistent with them. For example, the counselor structures group settings, verbally or nonverbally, to imply mutual trust, concern, and confidentiality. He or she upsets these expectations by assigning greater value to another societal role—for example, reporting to the patient's employer that the patient has been guilty of inappropriate behavior on the job that might lead to dismissal.

Confidentiality

The greatest ethical dilemma in counseling results from questions of confidentiality. The basic principle is that private information divulged by patients in the course of treatment is not to be used or repeated in any way that can be identified with the patient. While this allows for research and for generalized statements, it does not permit the counselor to divulge information about the patient without his or her knowledge and authorization, unless it is in the client's interest to do so. No information, even that a particular person is a patient in a treatment facility, can be revealed without first obtaining written consent while the individual is rational and drug free. Otherwise, one may not share private information, not even with a trusted colleague or spouse.

In addition, confidentiality is particularly difficult with regard to the experiences that occur in group counseling. It is extremely important that confidentiality be reviewed periodically with patients, stressing its importance in the group experience. One approach is to have the group members discuss what will happen if a member of the group breaks a confidence. This might be done by involving group members in role playing in a hypothetical situation in which a confidence has been broken, so that they may understand the kind of personal, emotional impact of such an experience. *Privileged communication* is a legal term referring to the right of such professionals as physicians, members of the clergy, psychologists, and nurses not to have to testify in court about information they have gained as part of their professional practice. Chemical-dependency counselors, unless they belong to a professional group named in their state's statutes, usually must testify when summoned to appear in court. In addition to this exception, chemical-dependency counselors also are obligated to violate confidentiality when there is clear and imminent danger of serious harm by the patient to him- or herself or to another. In such cases, professional consultation may be necessary to determine the severity of the danger involved. Many states also require chemical-dependency counselors to report incidents of child abuse, regardless of any privileged-communication statutes that may exist.

As a result of these exceptions, the chemical-dependency counselor has the ethical obligation to inform his or her patients about the limitations of confidentiality. In a sense the whole question must be seen in terms of distinct levels of confidentiality that can be established in counseling. The first level involves the professional *use* of information. Every counselor has the obligation to handle information about clients or potential clients only in professional ways. Such knowledge, no matter how it is acquired or how trivial it may seem, must never be used loosely in social conversation or in nonprofessional settings. This includes not only information obtained in counseling interviews, but also the fact of the patient *being a patient*. All facts should be handled in ways that ensure that they do not fall into the hands of persons who might treat them nonprofessionally.

The second level of confidentiality relates to information that arises out of a counseling relationship. In all such situations, clients have a right to expect that facts will only be used for their welfare. The very nature of the counseling relationship implies this, whether or not the counselor verbally communicates it. This sharing of information can pose a particularly difficult ethical dilemma when the counselor wishes to communicate the information to others—counselors, nurses, psychiatrists, the family, or an employer, for example—who may have a primary concern for the patient's welfare. Blocher (1966) points out that the ideal solution to the problem is to communicate clearly to the patient the intended level of confidentiality before confidences are accepted. If patients understand in advance that the counselor will use information only for professional purposes and only in the patient's best interest, then many of the resulting decisions will be professional judgments, rather than ethical choices.

A third level of confidentiality occurs when it is obvious that the patient will not communicate in complete confidence except in cases of clear and immediate danger to human life. In such situations, the counselor may provide the client with an opportunity for sharing some disturbing and shocking confidences in order to establish a helping, confidential relationship. The key to the whole matter rests in the counselor's ability to structure in advance the level of confidentiality at which he or she operates. Keeping that confidence once it is accepted at a particular level is an ethical matter. The counselor who does not keep such confidences will soon have none to keep.

Certainly issues of confidentiality are much more complicated than this brief summary suggests. Counselors in the field of chemical dependency need to be familiar with the appropriate codes of ethics, as well as the literature regarding their responsibilities. Corey et al. (1984) provide an excellent overview of this issue.

However, one area of ethical behavior that requires special attention is that of social contacts with patients and former patients. The extremes are fairly easy to recognize. Should a counselor enter into a dating or sexual relationship with a patient in treatment? The ethical codes of all helping professions forbid this. Is such a relationship permissible two weeks after treatment has ended? After six months? A year? Two years? Ever? While this situation is one most chemical-dependency counselors are acutely aware of, it is surprising how many violate this taboo. Apparently most fail to remember, not only that this behavior contravenes ethical codes, but that the relationship began in an unequal power relationship, placing the patient at a strong disadvantage. Dating a former patient, no matter how long after the treatment relationship ended, is not as clouded as it seems if the original inequality of the relationship is borne in mind. Therefore, post-treatment dating has many of the same problems that exist in dating a patient who is actively in treatment.

A more general relationship between the counselor and a former patient presents greater problems. While most counselors have little temptation to make social contact with their more seriously ill present and former patients, they do find many of their former patients well, happy, productive, and attractive in many ways. However relationships, even of a social nature, that result from the same unequal power relationship found in treatment are also unlikely to be as fulfilling as would be hoped.

The world of Alcoholics Anonymous presents its own difficulties. Even in large cities, counselors may find themselves sharing an AA group with former or present patients and will have to decide how self-disclosing they wish to be in such a situation. Since those counselors may attend AA meetings in order to facilitate their own recovery, the presence of the patients may cause problems. Thus the counselor needs to insist on what is necessary to ensure his or her own sobriety, which may mean being quite firm with patients who innocently feel not only that the patterns of the treatment setting are to be continued in AA, but who may also deliberately seek out AA groups that the counselor attends. In small towns, it may be impossible for staff and patients to find separate groups. Thus, there are no easy answers to this difficulty. However, an awareness of the dangers, accompanied by a desire on the part of the counselor to maintain his or her own sobriety, can enable the counselor to find a workable solution.

THE IMPORTANCE OF EVALUATION

Perhaps the newness of the field of chemical-dependency counseling explains why few chemical-dependency counselors tend to emphasize objective, systematic attempts to evaluate the results of their services. While those professional fields—counseling, social work, psychology—that have contributed individuals who work in chemical-dependency counseling have greatly emphasized the need and importance for evaluation, little has been done in the area of chemical-dependency counseling. Until recently, health-care providers in general were rarely asked to justify treatment costs or to demonstrate their effectiveness. However, there are now increasing demands to prove that the treatment of individuals suffering from chemical dependency pays off in results and dollars. Employee-assistance programs are constantly asked to point out savings in absenteeism, tardiness, accidents, and property damage when chemical-dependency treatment is sought.

To many chemical-dependency counselors, evaluation feels too technical, too mechanical, too dehumanizing. The need for precise objectives and goals, the statistical analyses, the need for a defensible research design, and the difficulties involved in gathering data where so many variables are difficult to control—all contribute to the lack of enthusiasm for evaluation. Add to this the lack of time the chemical-dependency counselor has for conducting such evaluation and it is clear that evaluation will have little priority in the counselor's schedule.

There is an even greater problem for many counselors—the concern that the evaluation results will indicate that the counselor is ineffective. Certainly, to face the possibility of not being effective is to risk anxiety and to have feelings of uselessness. Yet, counselors do have an ethical responsibility to their patients to know the impact and limits of the tools and techniques they use. Thus, evaluation efforts are necessary to determine the effects that counselors have on patients in one-to-one sessions and during group sessions, to assess the individual needs of the patient group, and to provide information that may be important in meeting accountability requirements desired by employers and agencies.

Chemical-dependency counselors need both process and outcome evaluation of what happens to their patients. This distinction between process and outcome is similar to that between formative and summative evaluation. *Formative evaluation*, like process evaluation, focuses on what is happening as the patient's treatment program occurs, so that future treatment planning can be altered to meet the needs of that patient more closely. Thus, it requires *ongoing* collection of information regarding the impact of the treatment program. Such information is not an attempt to evaluate the ultimate worth of the treatment experience, but rather focuses on the specific needs that have not yet been met. Although formative evaluation relies heavily on subjective judgments, it can still be very important in the planning of treatment for the individual.

Summative evaluation is the same as outcome evaluation, its aim being to judge the ultimate results of the group experience. It raises a number of difficult questions. How does one determine the success of a treatment program? Is the treatment program a success if the individual remains in sobriety for three months? For three weeks? For one year? Or is a treatment program effective, in spite of the individual having one or more relapses, if he or she is able to respond to the relapse by appropriate recovery behavior? While no attempts to answer such questions can be made in this book, it is important that chemical-dependency counselors and specific treatment programs work toward defining effectiveness in their particular treatment. What needs to be insisted on is strict accountability, honest self-appraisal, and accurate reporting of treatment goals and results. The sad part is not that different approaches exist, but that there has been so little effort to establish objective, long-term evaluation of treatment.

SURVIVING AS A CHEMICAL-DEPENDENCY COUNSELOR

One of the disturbing aspects of chemical-dependency counseling is the high turnover of treatment staff. This results from counselors choosing to find other work, as well as from a great deal of switching from one treatment program to another. Such a turnover is generally the result of individuals becoming frustrated and unhappy in their current job. Frustration is most likely the response of *burnout* that occurs with many helping professionals, but is particularly found among chemical-dependency counselors.

A primary reason that burnout is so prevalent among chemical-dependency counselors is that the field is psychologically fatiguing and stressful. Professionals have described themselves as feeling "drained or exhausted," "helpless, incompetent, overwhelmed," and "angry, depressed, and anxious." The environment in which chemical-dependency counseling ordinarily occurs is one of continuing chaos, as patients in various stages of recovery are both lashing out in anger over the changes in their lives that must be made for recovery and the psychological effects of withdrawal itself. This chaos results in individuals attempting to find and use mood-altering chemicals while in treatment. When this happens, counselors often feel betrayed and rejected, as if what they had done had little, if any, effect.

A study by Sarata (1982) identified some phrases used by alcoholism counselors to describe indicators of burnout among co-workers. These counselors described their colleagues as withdrawn, isolated, complaining, spaced-out, work-avoiding, critical of others, depressed, and often emotionally flat. If these descriptions are accurate, they suggest that individuals who have been excellent, effective counselors can show extreme deterioration as a result of not maintaining themselves on the job. While they may be also affected by their personal lives, often counselors will indicate that they feel better and more relaxed away from work, while reporting headaches, anger, and frustration at the workplace.

In order to prevent burnout, it is important that chemical-dependency counselors take steps to maintain themselves at peak work performance and to avoid some of the traps that may lead to job dissatisfaction. A major issue is that of establishing a separate life away from the professional setting in which the counselor works. Perhaps the nature of chemical-dependency counseling and the individuals who choose the field is such that they often feel a need to be totally committed to their work. However, maintaining relationships with family and friends away from the job provides the counselors with the opportunity for a "time out" from the emotional stress and problems that accompany their work. In the short run, of course, failure to allow for respites has little effect, but counselors run grave risks if they maintain a nearly total involvement over a long period of time. It is essential that chemical-dependency counselors learn to develop opportunities for interaction with friends, where one is not talking shop constantly and focusing the discussion on such a narrow topic.

Developing and maintaining an independent personal life away from the job is also a professional issue in that it models for patients the need to develop and maintain a balanced existence. Such a well-adjusted balance of professional and personal living provides a healthy model for patients to emulate. If nothing else, it helps to prevent individuals from becoming workaholics, instead of chemical dependents.

Another issue important in preventing burnout is maintaining an appropriate workload. Because chemical-dependency counselors are typically highly dedicated and committed individuals, they are vulnerable to being taken advantage of. They are often persuaded to spend extra hours at the job and to volunteer for the many extra services needed within the community to further their work. In addition, the rising incidence of individuals seeking treatment for chemical dependency has often resulted in caseloads becoming greater than what is reasonable for a counselor to maintain. The heavy caseload not only creates longer hours of work, but increases direct contact with patients and the probability of overintense involvement with them. For this reason, counselors within the field need to develop an understanding of the maximum number of patients that they can work with effectively at any given time. This number, of course, depends on a variety of factors, including other responsibilities that the counselor may have for marketing, administrative, and supervisory duties, as well as the overall responsibility that the counselor has for treatment. If, for instance, the counselor is expected to maintain frequent contact with the patient's family, employer or school, or other concerned individuals, then the number of patients the counselor can work with effectively is reduced. Likewise, if the time the counselor is required to use in group-education activities detracts from the time that he or she can spend in treatment planning, the number of patients must be reduced. For example, while three counselors may be able to work fairly effectively with twenty-five patients, one counselor working with eight patients will have a much greater demand on his or her time, since the counselor will be responsible for the whole group all the time. In addition, time needs to be developed for the treatment team to be able to sit down together and discuss treatment alternatives for patients outside any regularly scheduled staff meetings.

While there is a professional obligation for counselors to take steps toward increasing their knowledge and skills in the area of chemical dependency, such training also provides an opportunity for counselors to step outside their particular situation and become involved in new and different ways of thinking about their jobs. Attending workshops and other outside training experiences helps to insulate against burnout by providing some new stimulation for the work the counselors are doing. One indirect benefit of having counselors involved in outside training experiences is the informal sharing of ideas, as well as the sharing of frustrations, among the various participants. Counselors in chemical-dependency programs need at least one day per quarter for such professional rejuvenation.

Unfortunately, individuals who attempt to deal with burnout by switching jobs often find that relief is only temporary. The personal characteristics that have caused counselors to feel a great deal of stress, fatigue, frustration, and depression in a previous job ordinarily lead to the same results in a new job. Such individuals frequently move from one setting to another without ever settling down.

Perhaps all full-time chemical-dependency counselors should become active members of Al-Anon. Working with individuals who are chemically dependent on a continuing basis is likely to raise many of the same issues for the professional as were raised for the family. Such issues need to be discussed and analyzed in a caring, supportive environment. If nothing else, counselors need to learn that while they can provide knowledge about chemical dependency and tools that help to facilitate recovery, they cannot make anyone else sober. Continuing reminders that the counselor is also powerless to maintain someone else's sobriety may help to reduce the sense of frustration and anger the counselor may feel over the relapse of previous patients.

SUMMARY

Issues that are highly important to professionals in the field of chemical-dependency counseling include those personal characteristics that are related to effective counseling, the education and training of counselors, the ethical issues involved in the delivery of counseling services, the importance of evaluation, and the maintenance of the counselor's own emotional and psychological well-being.

Effective counselors possess six personal characteristics: self-awareness; genuineness; the ability to form warm, caring relationships; sensitivity and understanding; a sense of humor; and realistic levels of aspiration.

Ethical obligations are stated in the standards developed by the National Association of Alcoholism and Drug Abuse Counselors and the American Association for Counseling and Development. Both codes stress adherence to rigorous professional standards and to exemplary behavior and integrity toward clients. One ethical obligation is to evaluate the counseling provided and the effects it has on clients.

Chemical-dependency counselors have a high turnover because of the unique pressures and frustrations of their job. As a result, specific suggestions are made to help counselors avoid burnout and survive in the field.

References

CHAPTER 1

Berry, R., Boland, J., Smart, C., & Kanak, J. (1977). *The Economic Costs of Alcohol Abuse and Alcoholism, 1975*. Report prepared for National Institute on Alcohol Abuse and Alcoholism.

Fein, R. (1984). *Alcohol in America: The price we pay*. Newport Beach, CA: Care Institute.

Gold, M. S. (1984). *800–Cocaine*. New York: Bantam Books.

Kinney, J., & Leaton, G. (1983). *Loosening the grip* (2nd ed.). St. Louis, MO: C.V. Mosby.

Ohlms, D. L. (1988). *The disease of alcoholism*. Belleville, IL: Gary Whitaker Corporation.

Sexias, J. S., & Youcha, G. (1985). *Children of Alcoholism: A survivor's manual*. New York: Harper & Row.

Spalding, S. K. (1988). *Children of alcoholics*. Unpublished manuscript. Carbondale, IL: Southern Illinois University.

Spitz, H. I., & Rosecan, J. S. (1987). *Cocaine abuse*. New York: Brunner/Magel.

Wallace, A. F. C. (1969). The trip. In R. E. Hicks & P. J. Fink (Eds), *Psychedelic drugs*. New York: Grune & Stratton.

CHAPTER 2

Bandura, A. (1969). *Principles of behavior modification*. New York: Holt, Rinehart & Winston.

Brickman, P., Rabinowitz, V. C., Karuza, J., Coates, D., Cohn, E., & Kidder, L. (1982). Models of helping and coping. *American Psychologist, 37*, 368–84.

Cappell, H., & Greeley, J. (1987). Alcohol and tension reduction: An update on research and theory. In H. T. Blane & K. E. Leonard (Eds.), *Psychological theories of drinking and alcoholism*. New York: Guilford Press.

Clifford, C. A., Fulken, D. W., Gurling, H. M. D., & Murray, R. M. (1981). Preliminary findings from a twin study of alcohol use. In L. Gedda, P. Parisi & W. E. Nance (Eds.), *Twin Research 3*. New York: Alan Liss.

Clonninger, C. R., Bohman, M., & Sigvordsson, S. (1981). Inheritance of alcohol abuse: Cross-fostering analysis of adopted men. *Archives of General Psychiatry, 38,* 861–68.

Denzin, N. K. (1987). *The alcoholic self.* Newbury Park, CA: Sage Publications.

Donovan, D. M., & Marlatt, G. A. (1980). Assessment of expectancies and behaviors associated with alcohol consumption: A cognitive-behavioral approach. *Journal in the Studies of Alcohol, 41,* 1153–85.

Fingarette, H. (1988). *Heavy drinking: The myth of alcoholism as a disease.* Berkeley: University of California Press.

George, R. L., & Cristiani, T. S. (1990). *Counseling: Theory and practice* (3rd ed.). Englewood Cliffs, NJ: Prentice Hall.

Goodwin, D. W. (1985). Genetic determinants of alcoholism. In J. H. Mendelson & N. K. Mello (Eds.), *The diagnosis and treatment of alcoholism.* New York: McGraw-Hill.

Goodwin, D. W., & Guze, S. B. (1974). Heredity and alcoholism. In B. Kissin, & H. Begleiter, (Eds.), *Biology of alcoholism.* New York: Plenum Press.

Goodwin, D. W., Schulsinger, F., Hermensen, L., Guze, S. B., & Winokur, G. (1973). Alcohol problems in adoptees raised apart from alcoholic biological parents. *Archives of General Psychiatry, 28,* 238–43.

Hrubek, Z., & Omenn, G. S. (1981). Evidence of genetic predisposition to alcoholic cirrhosis and psychosis: Twin concordance for alcoholism and its biological endpoints by zygosity among male veterans. *Alcoholism: Clinical and Experimental Research, 5,* 207–15.

Isbell, H. (1955). Craving for alcohol. *Quarterly Journal of Studies on Alcohol, 16,* 38–42.

Jellinek, E. M. (1960). *The disease concept of alcoholism.* New Haven, CT: Hillhouse Press.

Jellinek, E. M. (1952). The phases of alcohol addiction. *Quarterly Journal of Studies on Alcohol, 13,* 673–84.

Lieber, C. S. (1976). The metabolism of alcohol. *Scientific American, 43,* 25–33.

Loehlin, J. C., & Nichols, R. C. (1976). *Heredity, environment, and personality.* Austin: University of Texas Press.

Marlatt, G. A., & Gordon, J. R. (Eds.). *Relapse prevention.* New York: Guilford Press.

Mathew, R. W., Claghorn, J. L., & Largen, J. (1979). Craving for alcohol in sober alcoholics. *American Journal of Psychiatry, 136,* 603–6.

Mello, N. K. (1983). A behavioral analysis of the reinforcing properites of alcohol and other drugs in man. In B. Kissin & H. Begleiter (Eds.), *The biology of alcoholism* (Vol. 7). New York: Plenum Press.

Mello, N. K. (1972). Behavioral studies of alcoholism. In B. Kissin & H. Begleiter (Eds.), *The biology of alcoholism* (Vol. 2). New York. Plenum Press.

Meyer, R. E. (1989). Alcoholism. In A. Tassman, R. E. Hales & A. J. Frances (Eds.), *Review of Psychiatry* (Vol. 8). Washington, DC: American Psychiatric Press.

Nace, E. P. (1987). *The treatment of alcoholism.* New York: Brunner/Magel.

Nathan, P. E. (1984). Contributions of learning theory to the diagnosis and treatment of alcoholism. In L. Grinspoon (Ed.), *Psychiatry Update* (Vol. 3). Washington, DC: American Psychiatric Press.

Nathan, P. E., & Lisman, S. A. (1976). Behavioral and motivational patterns of chronic alcoholics. In R. E. Tater & A. A. Sugerman (Eds.), *Alcoholism: Interdisciplinary approaches to an enduring problem.* Reading, MA: Addison-Wesley.

Pendery, M. L., Maltzman, I. M., & West, L. J. (1982). Controlled drinking by alcoholics: New findings and a reevaluation of a major affirmative study. *Science, 217,* 169–75.

Schuckit, M. A. (1984). *Drugs and alcohol abuse.* New York: Plenum Press.

Schuckit, M. A. (1982). A prospective study of genetic markers in alcoholism. In I. Hanin & E. Usden (Eds.), *Biological markers in psychiatry and neurology.* Oxford: Pergamon Press.

Schuckit, M. A., & Duby, J. (1983). Alcoholism in women. In B. Kissin & H. Begleiter (Eds.). *The biology of alcoholism* (Vol. 3). New York: Plenum Press.

Schuckit, M. A., & Rayses, V. (1979). Ethanol ingestion: Differences in blood acetaldehyde concentrations in relatives of alcoholics and controls. *Science, 203* 54–55.

Searles, J. S. (1988). The role of genetics in the pathogenesis of alcoholism. *Journal of Abnormal Psychology, 97,* 153–76.

Sher, K. J. (1987). Stress response dampening. In H. T. Blane & K. E. Leonard (Eds.), *Psychological theories of drinking and alcoholism.* New York: Guilford Press.

Sobell, M. B., & Sobell, L. C. (1978). *Behavioral treatment of alcohol problems: Individualized therapy and controlled drinking.* New York: Plenum Press.

Vaillant, G. E. (1971). Theoretical hierarchy of adaptive ego mechanisms. *Archives of General Psychiatry, 24,* 107–18.

Wise, R. A. (1988). The neurobiology of craving: Implications for the understanding and treatment of addiction. *Journal of Abnormal Psychology, 97,* 118–32.

CHAPTER 3

Ackerman, R. J. (1983). *Children of alcoholics: A guide for parents, educators, and therapists* (2nd ed.). New York: Simon & Schuster.

Ackerman, R. J. (1987). *Same house, different homes.* Pompano Beach, FL: Health Communications Press.

Balis, S. (1986). Illusion and reality: Issues in the treatment of adult children of alcoholics. *Alcoholism Treatment Quarterly, 3,* 67–91.

Baruth, G., & Huber, C. H. (1984). *An introduction to marital theory and therapy.* Monterey, CA: Brooks/Cole.

Becvar, R. J., & Becvar, D. S. (1982). *Systems theory and family therapy: A primer.* Lanham, MD: University Press of America.

Black, C. (1980). Innocent by-standers at risk: The children of alcoholics. *Alcoholism,* Jan.–Feb.

Black, C. (1981). *It will never happen to me!* Denver, CO: M.A.C.

Bowen, M. (1985). *Family therapy in clinical practice.* New York: Jason Aronson.

Brown, S. (1988). *Treating adult children of alcoholics: A developmental perspective.* New York: John Wiley.

Clair, D., & Genest, M. (1987). Variables associated with the adjustment of offspring of alcoholic fathers. *Journal of Studies on Alcohol, 48,* 345–55.

Cook, B. L. & Winokur, G. (1985). A family study of familial positive vs. familial negative alcoholics. *Journal of Nervous and Mental Disorders, 173,* 175–78.

Fossum, M. A., & Mason, M. J. (1986). *Facing shame: Families in recovery.* New York: W.W. Norton.

Friedman, A. S., Utada, A., & Morrissey, M. R. (1987). Families of adolescent drug abusers are rigid: Are these families either "disengaged" or "enmeshed" or both? *Family Process, 26,* 131–48.

Goldenberg, I., & Goldenberg, H. (1985). *Family therapy: An overview* (2nd ed.). Monterey, CA: Brooks/Cole.

Goodwin, D. (1976). *Is alcoholism hereditary?* New York: Oxford University Press.

Haley, J. (1980). *Leaving home: The therapy of disturbed young people.* New York: McGraw-Hill.

Haley, J. (1976). *Problem-solving therapy.* New York: Harper & Row.

Haley, J. (1973). *Uncommon therapy.* New York: W.W. Norton.

Hansen, J. C., & Liddle, H. A. (1983). *Clinical implications of the family life cycle.* Rockville, MD: Aspen.

Jurich, A. P., Polson, C. J., Jurich, J. A., & Bates, R. A. (1985). Family factors in the lives of drug users and abusers. *Adolescence, 20,* 143–59.

Kaufman, E., & Borders, L. (1984). Adolescent substance abuse in Anglo-American families. *Journal of Drug Issues, 2,* 365–77.

Kinney, J., & Leaton, G. (1987). *Loosening the grip: A handbook of alcohol information* (3rd ed.). St. Louis, MO: Times Mirror/Mosby College Publishing.

Minuchin, S. (1974). *Families and family therapy.* Cambridge, MA: Harvard University Press.

Okun, B. F., & Rappaport, L. J. (1980). *Working with families.* Belmont, CA: Brooks/Cole.

Reilly, D. M. (1984). Family therapy with adolescent drug abusers and their families: Defying gravity and achieving escape velocity. *Journal of Drug Issues, 2,* 381–91.

Rothberg, N. M. (1986). The alcoholic spouse and the dynamics of codependency. *Alcoholism Treatment Quarterly, 3,* 73–85.

Scarf, M. (1987). *Intimate partners: Patterns in love and marriage.* New York: Random House.

Smith, A. (1988). *Grandchildren of alcoholics.* Pompano Beach, FL: Health Communications Press.

Stabeneau, J. R. (1985). Basic research on heredity and alcohol: Implications for clinical application. *Social Biology, 32,* 297–321.

Steinglass, P., Bennett, L. A., Wolin, S. J., & Reiss, D. (1987). *The alcoholic family.* New York: Basic Books.

Steinglass, P., Tislenko, L., & Reiss, D. (1985). Stability/instability in the alcoholic marriage: The interrelationship between course of alcoholism, family process, and marital outcome. *Family Process, 24,* 365–76.

Symmonds, J. (1984). All grown up: The children of alcoholics. Unpublished manuscript. St. Louis: University of Missouri–St. Louis.

Wegscheider, S. (1981). *Another chance.* Palo Alto, CA: Science and Behavior Books.

Weiss, L., & Weiss, J. B. (1989). *Recovery from Codependency.* Deerfield Beach, FL: Health Communications.

Woititz, J. G. (1983). *Adult children of alcoholics.* Pompano Beach, FL: Health Communications.

Yalom, I. D. (1975). *The theory and practice of group psychotherapy.* New York: Basic Books.

CHAPTER 4

American Psychiatric Association. (1987). *Diagnostic and statistical manual of mental disorders* (3rd ed., revised). Washington, DC: Author.

Dahlstrom, W. G., & Welsh, G. S. (1960). *An MMPI handbook.* Minneapolis: University of Minnesota Press.

Forrest, G. G. (1978). *The diagnosis and treatment of alcoholism* (2nd ed., revised). Springfield, IL: Thomas.

Forrest, G. G. (1984). *Intensive Psychotherapy of Alcoholism.* Springfield, IL: Thomas.

Gold, M. S. (1984). *800–Cocaine.* New York: Bantam Books.

Horn, J. L., Wanberg, K., & Foster, F. M. (1974). *The alcohol-use inventory—AUI.* Denver, CO: Center for Alcohol-Abuse Research and Evaluation.

Lawson, G. W., Ellis, D. C., & Rivers, P. C. (1984). *Essentials of chemical dependency counseling.* Rockville, MD: Aspen.

MacAndrew, C. (1965). The differentiation of male alcoholic outpatients from nonalcoholic psychiatric patients by means of the MMPI. *Quarterly Journal of the Studies of Alcohol, 26,* 238–46.

McLellan, A. T., Luborsky, L., & O'Brien, C. P. (1980). Improved evaluation instrument for substance abuse patients. *Journal of Nervous and Mental Disease, 168,* 26–33.

Mayer, J., & Filstead, W. J. (1979). The adolescent alcohol involvement scale: An instrument for measuring adolescents' use and misuse of alcohol. *Journal for Studies in Alcoholism, 40,* 291–300.

Miller, W. R., & Marlatt, G. A. (1984). *Manual for the comprehensive drinker profile.* Odessa, FL: Psychological Assessment Resources.

Selzer, M. L. (1971). The Michigan Alcoholism Screening Test: The quest for a new diagnostic instrument. *American Journal of Psychiatry, 127,* 1653–58.

Vaillant, G. E. (1983). *The natural history of alcoholism.* Cambridge, MA: Harvard University Press.

Wanberg, K., & Horn, J. L. (1987). The assessment of multiple conditions in persons with alcohol problems. In W. M. Cox (Ed.), *Treatment and prevention of alcohol problems.* New York: Academic Press.

CHAPTER 5

Corey, G. (1977). *Theory and practice of counseling and psychotherapy.* Monterey, CA: Brooks/Cole.

Dustin, R., & George, R. L. (1977). *Action counseling for behavior change* (2nd ed.). Cranston, RI: Carroll Press.

Egan, G. (1986). *The skilled helper: A model for systematic helping and interpersonal relating* (2nd ed.). Monterey, CA: Brooks/Cole.

Ellis, A. (1962). *Reason and emotion in psychotherapy.* New York: Lyle Stuart.

Jacobsen, E. (1938). *Progressive relaxation.* Chicago: University of Chicago Press.

CHAPTER 6

Barlow, S., Hansen, W. D., Fhuriman, A. J., & Finley, R. (1982). Leader communication style: Effects on members of small groups. *Small Group Behavior, 13,* 518–31.

Berzon, B., Piovs, C., & Farson, R. (1963). The therapeutic event in group psychotherapy: A study of subjective reports by group members. *Journal of Individual Psychology, 19,* 204–12.

Bloch, S. (1986). Therapeutic factors in group psychotherapy. In A. J. Frances & R. E. Hales (Eds.), *Annual review* (Vol. 5, pp. 678–98). Washington, DC: American Psychiatric Press.

Bloch, S., Reibstein, J., & Crouch, E. (1979). A method for the study of therapeutic factors in group psychotherapy. *British Journal of Psychiatry, 134,* 257–63.

Carkhuff, R. R., & Berenson, B. G. (1967). *Beyond counseling and therapy.* New York: Holt, Rinehart & Winston.

Corsini, R., & Rosenberg, B. (1955). Mechanisms of group psychotherapy: Processes and dynamics. *Journal of Abnormal and Social Psychology, 51*, 406–11.

Dustin, R., & George, R. L. (1977). *Action counseling for behavior change* (2nd ed.). Cranston, RI: Carroll Press.

Forrest, G. G. (1978). *The diagnosis and treatment of alcoholism* (2nd ed.). Springfield, IL: Thomas.

Frank, J. D. (1957). Some determinants, manifestations and effects of cohesiveness in therapy groups. *International Journal of Group Psychotherapy, 7*, 53–63.

Frank, J. D. (1971). Therapeutic factors in psychotherapy. *American Journal of Psychotherapy, 25*, 350–61.

Frankl, V. (1969). *The will to meaning*. Cleveland: World Publishing Press.

George, R. L., & Dustin, D. (1988). *Group counseling: Theory and practice*. Englewood Cliffs, NJ: Prentice-Hall.

Glanz, E. C. (1962). *Groups in guidance*. Boston: Allyn & Bacon.

Hill, W. F. (1957). Analysis of interviews of group therapists' papers. *Provo Papers, 1*, 1.

Jeske, J. O. (1973). Identification and therapeutic effectiveness in group therapy. *Journal of Counseling Psychology, 20*, 528–30.

Kinney, J., & Leaton, G. (1987). *Loosening the grip* (3rd ed.). St. Louis, MO: C.V. Mosby.

Muro, J. J., & Freeman, S. L. (1968). *Reading in group counseling*. Scranton, PA: Intext.

Ohlsen, M. M. (1977). *Group counseling* (2nd ed.). New York: Holt, Rinehart & Winston.

Rutan, J. S., & Rice, C. A. (1981). The charismatic leader: Asset or liability? *Psychotherapy: Theory, Research and Practice, 18*, 487–92.

Truax, C. B., & Carkhuff, R. R. (1967). *Toward effective counseling and psychotherapy*. Chicago: Aldine.

Weiner, M. F. (1984). *Techniques of group psychotherapy*. Washington, DC: American Psychiatric Press.

White, R., & Lippitt, R. (1961). Leader behavior and member reaction in three "social climates." In D. Cartwright & A. Zander (Eds.), *Group dynamics: Research and theory*. New York: Row, Peterson, 527–53.

Yalom, I. D. (1970). *The theory and practice of group psychotherapy*. New York: Basic Books.

Yalom, I. D. (1985). *The theory and practice of group psychotherapy* (3rd ed.). New York: Basic Books.

CHAPTER 7

Alcoholics Anonymous (3rd ed.). (1976). New York: Alcoholics Anonymous World Services.

Denzin, N. K. (1987). *The recovering alcoholic*. Newbury Park, CA: Sage Publications.

Hegarty, C. (1982). *The winner's way*. Minneapolis, MN: CompCare.

Leach, B., & Norris, J. L. (1977). Factors in the development of Alcoholics Anonymous (AA). In B. Kissin & H. Begleiter (Eds.), *The biology of alcoholism* (Vol. 5): *Treatment and rehabilitation of the chronic alcoholic*. New York: Plenum Press.

Marlatt, G. A. (1985). Relapse prevention: Theoretical rationale and overview of the model. In G. A. Marlatt & J. R. Gordon (Eds.), *Relapse prevention*. New York: Guilford Press.

Marlatt, G. A., & Gordon, J. R. (Eds.) (1985). *Relapse prevention*. New York: Guilford Press.

Robertson, N. (1988). *Getting better.* New York: William Morrow and Company.

Wilson, W. G. (1957). *Alcoholics Anonymous comes of age: A brief history of AA.* New York: AA Publishing.

CHAPTER 8

Atkinson, R. M. (1984). Substance use and abuse in late life. In R. M. Atkinson (Ed.), *Alcohol and drug abuse in old age.* Washington, DC: American Psychiatric Association.

Damron, S. W., & Simpson, W. R. (1985). Substance abuse and schizophrenia: A health maintenance perspective. Presented at the 1985 American Psychological Association Convention.

Ford, B. (1987). *Betty: A glad awakening.* New York: Doubleday.

George, R. L., & Cristiani, T. S. (1990). *Counseling: Theory and practice* (3rd ed.). Englewood Cliffs, NJ: Prentice Hall.

Hafen, B. Q., & Brog, M. J. (1983). *Alcohol* (2nd ed.). St. Paul, MN: West.

Horn, J. L., & Wanberg, K. W. (1973). Females are different: On the diagnosis of alcoholism in women. *Proceedings of the First Annual Alcoholism Conference of the National Institute on Alcohol Abuse and Alcoholism.* Washington, DC: U.S. Government Printing Office.

Hughes, R., & Brewin, R. (1979). *The tranquilizing of America.* New York: Harcourt Brace Jovanovich.

Johnston, L. D., Bachman, J. G., & O'Malley, P. M. (1982). *Student drug use, attitudes, and beliefs: National trends, 1975–1982.* Rockvale, MD: National Institute on Drug Abuse.

Kinney, J., & Leaton, G. (1983). *Loosening the grip.* St. Louis, MO: C. V. Mosby.

Kirkpatrick, J. (1977). *Turnabout: Help for a new life.* New York: Doubleday.

Lemay, D. (1980). The need for and awareness of specialized issues in counseling alcoholic women. *Personnel and Guidance Journal, 59,* 103–15.

Lindbeck, V. (1975). *The woman alcoholic. Public Affairs pamphlet #529.* Washington, DC: U.S. Government Printing Office.

Loberg, T. (1981). MMPI-based personality subtypes of alcoholics. *Journal in the Studies of Alcohol, 42,* 766–82.

MacDonald, D. I. (1984). *Drugs, drinking, and adolescents.* Chicago: Yearbook Medical Publishers.

Mayfield, D. (1985). Substance abuse in the affective disorders. In A. I. Alterman (Ed.), *Substance abuse and psychopathology.* New York: Plenum Press.

Nace, E. P., Saxon, J. J., & Shore, N. A. (1983). A comparison of borderline and nonborderline alcoholic patients. *Archives of General Psychiatry, 40,* 54–56.

Offer, D. (1986). Adolescent development: A normative perspective. In A. J. Frances & R. E. Hales (Eds.), *Annual Review* (Vol. 5). Washington, DC: American Psychiatric Press.

Reifler, B., Raskind, M., & Kethley, A. (1982). Psychiatric diagnoses among geriatric patients seen in an outreach program. *Journal of the American Geriatric Society, 30,* 530–33.

Rimmer, J., Pitts, F. N., Reich, T., & Winokur, G. (1971). Alcoholism. II. Sex, socioeconomic status and race in two hospitalized samples. *Quarterly Journal of Studies in Alcoholism, 32,* 942.

Rounsaville, B. J., & Kranzler, H. R. (1989). The DSM-III-R diagnosis of alcoholism. In A. Tasman, R. E. Hales, & A. J. Frances, (Eds.), *Review of psychiatry* (Vol. 8). Washington DC: American Psychiatric Press.

Skinner, H. (1982). Statistical approaches to the classification of alcohol and drug addiction. *British Journal of Addictions, 77*, 259–73.

Wegner, M. (1983). *Surviving sobriety: The women.* Minneapolis, MN: Hazelton.

Weiner, J. (1976). *Drinking.* New York: W.W. Norton.

CHAPTER 9

American Association for Counseling and Development. (1988). *Ethical standards.* Washington, DC: Author.

American Psychological Association. (1981). *Ethical standards of psychologists.* Washington, DC: Author.

Blocher, D. H. (1966). *Developmental counseling.* New York: Ronald Press.

Combs, A. (1962). A perceptual view of the adequate personality. In A. Combs (Ed.), *Perceiving, Behaving, Becoming.* Washington, DC: Yearbook Association for Supervision and Curriculum Development.

Combs, A., & Soper, D. (1969). The perceptual organization of effective counselors. *Journal of Counseling Psychology, 10*, 222–26.

Corey, G., & Corey, M. S. (1982). *Groups: Process and practice* (2nd ed.). Monterey, CA: Brooks/Cole.

Corey, G., Corey, M. S., & Callahan, P. (1984). *Issues and ethics in the helping professions* (2nd ed.). Monterey, CA: Brooks/Cole.

George, R. L., & Cristiani, T. S. (1990). *Counseling: Theory and practice* (3rd ed.). Englewood Cliffs, NJ: Prentice Hall.

Lawson, G. W., Ellis, D. C., & Rivers, P. C. (1984). *Essentials of chemical dependency counseling.* Rockville, MD: Aspen.

National Association of Alcoholism and Drug Abuse Counselors. (1987). Code of ethics. *The Counselor, 5*, 21–24.

National Association of Social Workers. (1980). *Code of ethics, NASW.* Washington, DC: Author.

Rogers, C. R. (1957). The necessary and sufficient conditions of therapeutic personality change. *Journal of Consulting Psychology, 22*, 95–103.

Rogers, C. R. (1962). Toward becoming a fully functioning person. In A. Combs (Ed.), *Perceiving, Behaving, Becoming.* Washington, DC: Yearbook Association for Supervision and Curriculum Development.

Sarata, B. P. V. (1982). Burnout workshops for alcoholism counselors. Unpublished paper. Lincoln, NE: University of Nebraska.

Author Index

Subject Index